Skinny White Kids

A memoir

Mark Huband

GRUSKHAM BOOKS

First Published in 2020
By Gruskham Books

Illustrations by Anna Steinberg

For my brother Michael

Skinny White Kids

Prologue

There must be another time when my memories began, but today the earliest memory is of a departure – of that day when Gruskham House became the world to which we imagined we would one day return.

Even as we left, it became the place we froze in time. It is where our souls will lie forever, on a landscape that lingers behind everything that has followed, while we crammed our bodies into the Ford Popular, waved goodbye through the steam on the car windows, and drove away in silence towards a new home where my memories became my own.

Perhaps it was dry and cold as our car chugged through the era that was our journey, three slight young bodies on the back seat, Mum and Dad peering out ahead.

The England we passed through in 1967, when we left Yorkshire and moved south, has left its monuments. But they were not our monuments. I was a 'Sixties child', but I didn't know it, and nobody ever told me so, nor what it might mean. As we drove along in the slow lane of the vast and furious motorway, I was of no time. The monuments gathered, and I looked out at the passing of a land that was supposed to be me. We were the new world, my brothers and I. We were proof that the world had survived the war, and that new lives and a new generation had emerged from the wreckage, to be carried along motorways ending among buildings of concrete and glass which caught the sun that was setting as we arrived in Harlow, the Essex new town which became our home that year.

We stopped on waste-ground beside the cinema. I know that because Mum told me so, one summer day many years later. Where we stopped was of the times, because it was where people stopped when they had appointments at the office where the keys for the council houses were handed out. We sat in the back of the car, while an official gave Mum or perhaps Dad the key to our new home.

'I will take you there,' I say to my daughter, and I turn our car onto the circular road that loops through the world of that first day of sunlight, or was it pouring with rain? And my daughter stands where I once fell, on the square outside our house in Primrose Field. I tell her the stories I am carrying and she stares at me, confused, sensing her distance from my past, troubled that she cannot be there.

I turn and turn around the bushes of the square, which never lose their tiny leaves and the bright red berries which smell of piss when it rains. I turn and turn on my bicycle, with its red frame and white mudguards, when speed and balance at last carry me across and across the alternate blocks of concrete paving and tarmac that lead from our front door to the kerbstone that marks the end of the space from where I can see my home.

That was as far as I dared to go, and as far as I imagined I was allowed. Across the road was unknown.

Where the street curved to infinity there were flats, and inside was a man with long grey-black hair and long side-burns. He wore a pale brown leather jacket and a vest over his fat belly. In his hand he gripped a long chain pulled tight around the neck of an Alsation dog – the 'Station Dog', we called it – that had the same grey-black hair as the man. We ran when we saw them, my brother Paul and I. The man never smiled, nor did anything to frighten us. But we ran from the square when we saw him. We ran into our house, slammed the door, climbed half way up the stairs and peered down from a barely open window as they passed.

Once – a long time after we had moved there – we went into a neighbour's house with my mum and my dad to watch the first astronauts land on the Moon. Then, the world in which we had arrived in Harlow seemed like a part of the silver space ship and maybe even like a part of that other place where there was always sunshine – America – where people had fantasy cars and lots of money and from where rockets went to the Moon. I don't know why I knew about America. But people talked, and I imagined that America was the place in which everybody in the world would eventually manage to live, if they were lucky. I imagined everybody was fixed on the idea of a journey there, and maybe on staying there forever.

But before going to America I wanted to be invited into peoples' homes on our square, and to be a part of the lives of the people we passed on the long slope where on Saturday mornings the cold wind hurled stones at our faces as we cycled up to the towers of our town. I fought against the wind to get there, Mum and Dad cycling along beside us, encouraging one more turn of the pedals, then another, until the summit was reached and the path sloped down and we coasted through the puddles and into the damp echo of the last underpass whose tunnel rose up beside the stern blue light of the police station.

At the other end of the underpass, on the paved esplanade, strolling down the concrete slopes that had been warmed by the sun, chatting as they wheeled prams filled with babies, we could see the people who were the moment our town captured in a history that only some people knew we were living.

People looked out from the windows of the library. Everywhere there were windows. The glass gleamed, reflecting the big clouds. It was a stage. A family sat – mum, dad, child on a knee, the town's symbol carved from stone by Henry Moore – looking out across the empty space, across the stage we hurried to leave for fear that we would be asked which part it was we were playing.

Nearby, the fountains and lily ponds of the Water Gardens were an exotic place that mimicked the imagination that had designed them. They seemed of another world which I dreamed I might one day reach, as I locked-up my bicycle outside the library, pushed open the hard-sprung aluminium door that scraped the rubber matting, and followed Mum and Dad into the big open building that smelled of new carpets and varnish, and went straight to the shelf where I knew I would find the book I always took out.

It was a story of two families who lived in windmills. One family was happy and loud and painted their windmill in bright colours and hung flags from the rooftop. The other family was gloomy, and let the paint peel on their windmill. The happy family planted poplar trees around their windmill, to protect it if there was a storm. The gloomy family said this was a waste of money and stopped talking to the happy family.

I would always read the first few pages of the book in the library. Then I would take it to the counter to have it stamped and to have my ticket taken away by the lady whose spectacles hung round her neck on a chain.

I always had my reason ready in case she asked me why I was again taking out the same book. I imagined she had a list on which my name appeared hundreds of times alongside this one book, and could hear her telling me: 'You can't take out it again. Somebody else might want it. I watched you reading it over there. It is not fair that you should keep taking this book out. Think of yourself as a little bit bad, because you might be depriving somebody else.'

But I always had my explanation ready, and sometimes began to admit that it was me again, when I sensed she was about to ask me why and to tell me I could not have it. Even though she never asked, I always imagined she was about to, but was then distracted at the last minute. Then I would quickly take the book and walk away before she had a chance to remember that I always took this one. I always assumed she remembered me, and that her eyes were boring into my back, as I stepped away with it under my arm and hid among my brothers as we went back out into the sunlight of the paved esplanade where new, young trees grew, and where I knew I could pretend the woman's voice could not reach if she ordered me to stop.

We pushed our bicycles in a line, past the big shops.

Then, for a while, we were a part of the scenery, a young family pushing bicycles along the new street past Harlow's department stores, where people carried plastic bags filled with new things, or pondered the displays in the windows.

But there is no point in pretending that I knew what I was in those times. I had no point of view. I can't pretend to remember the beehive haircuts or the Teddy Boys or the prams with two large and two small wheels, or the Ford Anglia cars or the feeling that the Swinging Sixties were all around us. That only happened in photographs, during revivals years later. Life was too real to be grasped while it was happening. I just pushed my bike, with its red frame and white mudguards and fat tyres, holding my book under my arm until we reached the market square where fruit-sellers yelled their prices and I was scared that the crowds might split me up from my family, as we all glanced back and forth to make sure that nobody had come between us.

On the other side of the market square, after we had left the crowds behind, we sucked on the sweet fumes that poured out of grilles in the wall of the Gilbey's gin factory, and sped beneath old trees to Mum and Dad's friend Joan's house in the Town Park, where a white Mini that was parked in the driveway seemed fashionable and modern and we wondered if she was drifting away from us because we didn't have a car like hers, and heard her talking about her plans to go and live in Portugal with the man who was there, who sat in a corner learning Portuguese from a tape recorder.

Then we would pedal home, and in the evening I would cradle the book in my hands as if it were a prize I had fought to keep. I would read about how one night there was a storm, and how the windmill of the gloomy family was destroyed because there were no poplar trees to protect it. But the happy family went to help their gloomy neighbours, who stopped being gloomy. The two families rebuilt the destroyed windmill, painted it in bright colours, and decorated it with flags. That was the picture on the last page, when everybody was good and kind. I was there among them, in the world they had emptied of anxiety and filled with wonderment. They had done it themselves, and I was there too, with them until the darkness and the hum of the washing machine in our kitchen downstairs brought me back to my bedroom and the hot water of bath time, and left me wandering between the worlds I inhabited.

The closing of the book was my farewell to the happy people there. They turned their backs on me. I resentfully longed for yesterdays like theirs, which were mine alone to voyage through. But there were none. My time had been too short, the world a rainy day when we go out in the car along a dark road that is overhung with trees on one side, and on the other is lined by a metal fence with spikes at the top of a concrete slope that falls down to the grey slab of a reservoir.

Dad assembles a fishing rod. My brother Paul is holding it when the tangled line is reeled in and somebody notices the silver flicker of a fish twisting on the hook.

It is raining hard. There is anxiety. How will the fish be detached? It must be thrown back into the water. It cannot belong to us. It would be evil to let it die. It must be carefully unhooked and thrown back into the cold grey water, which is pocked by the falling rain.

We crouch on the concrete rim of the reservoir wondering if we are fishermen, wondering if we would catch another if the line were recast.

But then, from the water's edge, a wilderness opens up before me on the other side. There is an endless lake, where we live among trees, carrying knives and fishing rods, and breathe the mist and the rain as we stride through wet forests to a cottage on a moor where there is the smell of wood and a warm fire.

The fish, its gullet torn by the hook, is thrown back into the reservoir and the wipers slap on the windscreen. We drive home to the hiss of tyres on the wet road. And through eyes cast back to a time before memory a boy is fishing on the banks of a fast-flowing river which twists between moorland slopes of bracken and heather.

Then he is gone, and I look out through the steamed-up window of the black car and see a landscape that seems only to be nothing like the place it was supposed to be, that rugged and beautiful place where the boy becomes a fisherman and twitching silver skins fill a bag at the end of a cold wet day that turns the moorland to gold in the evening as the boy trudges home, his body humming with the bite of the air as he makes his way along a silent country lane that winds between fields towards a house high above a valley.

We crawl along in heavy traffic to the hum of the wipers, as orange street lamps ooze light onto the snake of cars. The streets of our town emerge around us from the rain. Our car engine stops, and all we hear is the rain as we reach the kerbstone on our square, and I imagine that the place I have been in my own mind must always be one of my secrets.

On a bright winter afternoon in December 1969, I found a place where I could hide my secrets.

We drive in the back of Mum and Dad's friend Adrian's convertible Hillman, down a wide avenue I had never before been along. Mum holds the knot of her silk scarf beneath her chin, smiling down at her young family as they laugh on the back seat, stung cold by the breeze as we speed through crisp air past a spire with a clock tower in a field of cows, to a house where we step through an old door into a new world.

The door has a dull, soft sound of age and many openings. We are new in somewhere old, where events have gone before us. We are arriving at our new home on the other side of town, long after the house's time had begun.

The bright sun of the day we travelled to our new home flooded my room. With magic, Mum and Dad had transformed what was old and familiar into a new, strange world, half recognizable, but with everything out of place, a home conjured out of what we knew: chairs, the woven, striped bedspreads Mum's eldest brother had brought from Algeria, the settee Dad had built with Uncle Mark, rich in the deep, bright cover Joan had made, and the chest of drawers where all things were, now standing along the wall of Mum and Dad's bedroom, where I could see it every time I mounted the stairs.

All is flooded by the winter sun, which glows beyond windows thick with dust and smoke engrained ever since the previous tenants had closed the Harlow School of Music they had run from the house, and had gone away. They had left their dust behind, and no forwarding address for the post which arrived for them. They left the feeling behind that somebody might still be lingering in one of those rooms off the stony clatter of the driveway and up the step onto the flagstones of the kitchen.

Then the cold silenced the world.

I shivered on the settee, dressed in all my clothes, wrapped in a maroon blazer my dad bought for me as winter settled in around us. The world became a harsh and silent place. I dared not even look outside at the endless back-garden, where nettles had grown into a towering wilderness I would be lost in if ever I stepped out into the winter freeze which each morning left a film of ice on the inside of my bedroom window.

We had heard that there were fields to discover, and that somewhere a river twisted across a land glittering with frozen grass. But the cold had silenced the world, our silent home so cold I could not move, the warmth of the coal boiler barely piercing the oozing draughts and the freeze of the frosted windows. Our new life seemed stillborn, December a place of steel light and the rare twitter of a bird in a frozen tree.

One: *Bloodlines*

A ship sails from Lisbon in the spring of 1942.

Somewhere in England a soldier waits on a quayside for the passengers to disembark.

Way out in the Atlantic, everybody drowns when the ship is struck by a torpedo.

But the soldier's family is not on board. His wife had refused to travel on this, the first available ship. It was full of children, who she said would irritate her during the voyage. So she, her two daughters and two sons steamed away from Europe a few days later.

To confuse the Nazi spies lurking in the Portuguese capital, the captain logged a course to Nova Scotia. But in mid-Atlantic he turned south, docking at Gibraltar. With her children, the soldier's wife – a woman good at securing favours by telling anybody who would listen that her husband was a 'very senior army officer' – convinced the captain of a Royal Navy frigate to give up his cabin for her family, until the skipper of a passing passenger ship agreed to take them to Britain.

The soldier waiting in England was said to have fought at Gallipoli during the First World War. It was said that as an officer in the Camel Corps he had been part of the last-ever cavalry charge mounted by the British army. When that war was over he moved to Paris and made it his home. There, he had married his first wife. Then, sometime in the 1930s he and his second wife moved into an apartment at 94 Rue du Bac, a fashionable street on the Left Bank of the Seine. They had met at a divorce court. Their spouses had been having an affair. Both couples agreed to split, and so went to the court to sign the papers. On the steps, the formalities over, the cheated pair chatted, took coffee in a nearby café, and agreed that marriage was the only solution to their loneliness. Thus, they became husband and wife, creating two families of siblings and half-siblings, who spent the rest of their lives haunted by their parents' betrayals.

The two who chatted in the café were my grandparents. My mum is the youngest of the two couples' numerous French, Belgian and British children.

Mum's birth in March 1940 in the village of Rogny-Les-Sept-Ecluses, 100 miles south of Paris, during a visit which had begun as a short holiday staffed by the family cook, the butler Isidore, and a special tent for my grandmother's dressing table, was part of the confusion stalking a world then fast-collapsing into pieces.

People always talked of 'Rogny', but I could never find it on a map. Then, when the war came, my grandfather left his family there, travelling to London to re-join what remained of his regiment from 1918. He mysteriously reappeared at Rogny-Les-Sept-Ecluses, staying for a day just before the German invasion. Then he was gone again, having assured his wife that there would be no invasion 'because they'll never make it past the Maginot Line'.

Nobody knows how he had reached the village, where Mum had been born on the first day of spring. Nor could anybody explain why he left his wife, four children and step-daughter alone to flee south through France. It was only later that Mum learned he had been living with his mistress in a London hotel while his family had been running from the Nazis, their convoy strafed by Italian fighter jets somewhere in Lot-et-Garonne, where they stayed hidden for a year, foreigners in their homeland, my grandmother working as a seamstress. After nearly two years on the run they reached Perpignan. A sympathetic American official somewhere in southern France gave all-but Mum's half-sister temporary US travel documents, which allowed them to cross into Spain. Belgian not British, the half-sister who would become my aunt, was left behind at Canet-Plage while the others crossed the border and began their journey by train to the Portuguese coast.

They survived on a water melon bought somewhere near Barcelona – or so the family folklore came to tell us. None of them ever freed themselves from the uncertainty of those times – times of fractured images and moments, which to this day have left the last few survivors remembering only what they want to remember.

And their memories have left me with nothing more than impressions – of which doorway might have been the one that closed behind them on the street that leads to Perpignan station from where they took their train to Barcelona. Today, there is nobody left to ask – though perhaps that woman staring from an upper window knows something of the Belgian lady whose husband was a British soldier, who had been trying to reach Lisbon with her children. Perhaps somewhere there is an ageing soul guarding the memory, somebody who could finish the story with tears and tea and 'Ah yes, I remember you, on your journey. You were not alone you know, though it may have seemed so at the time'.

*

So it would be that with a few photographs of that past carefully held in my shirt pocket, my own journey would years later become a part of what happened next.

Nobody stayed long in one place; everybody moved, hoping to find something, until the moment came when I realised that what I had been looking for was not where my journey might end, but where it had begun.

The starting point had the strongest hold, as the places of the imagination became places whose names were stamped on the fraying pages of my own numerous passports. I travelled the world – from Afghanistan to Rwanda, from Somalia to Guantánamo Bay – always knowing though for many years not realising it, that the place I truly wanted to end up was that place where I could find the people to whom my stories must be told. My journey started among the half-remembered stories of a family fleeing through France, among lives made fragile even before those who lived them had been born. Their legacies haunted me, just as fear haunted Mum, chance alone letting us live.

But then, there was always the possibility of happiness – a happiness fired in the early years by exuberance, which had soured since the days when beads of sweat glittered on the forehead of the bald man with the moustache who puffed resentfully through his nostrils while the boy glided exhilarated across the world, swaying as he balanced on the crossbar of a bicycle.

'Do take care', the man scolded, as the boy shuddered at his father's rebuke. 'Do stop wobbling, or you can walk the rest of the way.'

The boy held tight to the handlebars, touching his dad's hands until they edged away from his son's young fingers, and the pair rolled down the last slope into the shade of trees and homes.

It was there that I would have passed them – my dad and grandfather – some time just after the war, in a place for which I went looking, a place where the air was filled with the chatter of birds hidden among leaves which swung and fluttered.

Their route is history now.

Castlegate winds steeply past red-brick homes, then spirals deep into the shade.

My movements there, one summer's day more than half a century after the events of that time, when I happened to be driving close by and took a detour and sought a way back into their past, were a trespass along the pathway to St John's Church. A signpost stood against a shaded wall which marked the way to the cemetery, past an ageing German Shepherd that barked crippled in the doorway of the Castle Inn.

'How yer doing? Alright?' A builder nodded from among sand and cement then told the dog to be quiet.

Dad's parents had moved to the Lincolnshire village of Castle Bytham just after the war. I almost remember it well. They would etch me into their lives when I broke into the world and assembled the bloodline and grappled with the consequences of what we shared.

23

A man on a ladder was repairing a telephone cable.

A car passed with two women inside.

Nobody watched.

I was invisible, as I pulled away from the wooden bus shelter beside which I had parked my car. Each moment seemed poised to be that at which the man and the boy would appear on a bicycle over the gentle brows and dips of the long straight road out of the village. I was sure they were about to appear before me. I formed an explanation for my presence, then hoped I would not be recognised. If they spoke I would say I was lost and would ask for directions.

Then, no, I thought, I should tell them: this is what happened next. 'Where am I in all this?' I would perhaps call out to them as they cycled past.

But only the land could grasp the times it had witnessed and all that had passed it by. I drove on, wondering if we would ever disentangle the mysteries that made us such intimate strangers.

*

A photograph stored in a manila envelope in our home hinted at what had happened long after my dad left that place, after his parents had moved north to Manchester.

Mum's eldest brother is holding an umbrella over the newly-married couple – the sister whose departure he could not bear, the new brother-in-law he declared he hated. He holds the umbrella against an August storm, high above Mum and Dad's heads, his manner perhaps intended to mock the marriage he could not stop. He was the boy old enough to remember the journey of escape

24

across Spain. He had become a man before his time, when the soldier they called 'Daddy' died in 1947, leaving Mum's family penniless. He had watched his younger brother slip away into the shadows with strangers, and had seen the elder of his two sisters take holy orders and disappear to the far side of the world.

Dad's parents do not appear in the wedding photographs of that wet August day. Their son would be married by lunchtime, 'but we shan't be attending,' my grandmother may have said. Asked the reason by the neighbours, she would have remained silent, but would then perhaps have gone to sit with friends and explained: 'She is a Roman Catholic you know,' to the tut-tutting of those whose support she sought.

And within months of the marriage, everything changed again.

The time of war, life in the Paris of the 1930s, the past that was the bond – all of it fell into silence when the woman who had taken her children on a south-bound train across the Pyrenees, who had carved the water melon as they crossed Spain to the coast of Portugal and the ship that took them into the future, the woman who had held onto Mum, her brothers and sister as their world was torn to pieces, died.

Her children buried the secrets she had told them, never bringing them together as one, for fear that the magic they clung to would be shattered, as Mum and Dad watched the past slip into the present and become the promise of their own private future among the Yorkshire hills they moved to in 1962.

The moments on Mum's northward journey are still where they have always been – the stations, the streets. They have shifted and twisted a little, to make way for new features on the landscape. But the streets are heavy with her footsteps, passing through the stations where her gaze is held by steam belching from the groaning trains, where she watches women in hats, some alone, their young husbands now crosses against the dunes in the silent desert of North Africa I crossed years later when I went to live in Egypt. There are men wearing long coats and horn-rimmed spectacles. They carry briefcases and sip tea from cups. *Rizlas* droop from chapped lips. *Senior Service* are offered to deferential thanks. A bar beneath the arches is filled with smoke. There are men in caps, women's faces rich with lipstick smiles, raincoats wet, high-heels spattered, nylon laddered, half pints of beer warming in rough hands. There is talk amid the cackle of laughter.

Was it winter or spring? Was I being carried close to her beating heart, as she carried my brother Michael in her arms?

I imagine her looking for the room that would become my birthplace.

She crossed London with a son and a suitcase. The new life lay one final journey away, as she stepped out of Victoria Station, then looked for a bus or the underground train that would take her across the city to Euston, or perhaps Kings Cross, bound for the future.

Mum got off the train at Low Bentham some time in 1962. Dad took her home to a tall house close to the railway, where they lived for a year or more before moving to the house on the moors. The River Wenning rushed beneath a bridge. Steam trains chugged to and from Lancaster. American voices came over the airwaves. There was talk of nuclear war with Cuba and Russia, as the swallows darted across the skies and the moors turned from purple to brown.

There seemed no escape from war. Not even there, cradled by the sound of the flowing river and Michael chuckling as he played.

The crisis passed and winter came. With spring the cold stayed. The colour of the hills edged through the snow and the river flowed wild. Lambs-tails dangled across the torrent as spring became summer and walks with Michael became slower as the heat rose, and at the end of August 1963 the house beside the railway echoed with my new voice, crying into the darkness.

It was after my brother Paul had been born more than a year later that we moved to Gruskham, the house on the moors whose keystone marked the date of its construction as 1789.

The house is the beginning of time. The family was complete, and we five travelled up the farm track to our new home high on the valley side I walked up nearly twenty years and a lifetime later, after stepping off the train one December afternoon, and out of the station at Low Bentham.

We were not there long enough to discover what lay beyond the hills. To this day the moors of North Yorkshire are infinity in our eyes, because we left that land an unmapped mystery with which we could play and which would play with us forever, because we had no idea where its boundary lay or what lay beyond.

And every year afterwards we were told some more, to keep us informed of the moments that followed our departure. Each year after we left that place Joyce Cornthwaite wrote to Mum with her news from the farm at the end of the track that led up to the house we lived in. Mum has kept all her letters. They are her treasure.

And as I left the station behind and moved through that winter afternoon, I knew where I was going. With every step I knew the road. I knew the views through the trees, and the shapes of the hills. From a time before memory, the route up to our house on the moors lay deep inside me. It was a path lying open and empty. I was its guardian, just as it preserved the images I guarded.

I pushed at a wooden gate I had last seen swing open before my baby eyes. I was being cradled once more by the land – a track of stones winding past a mesh of hawthorns, a muddy bank topped with grass rising on a sharp bend where the track dipped into the peat and mud, a gate and a cattle grid breaking into the wet moss and lichen of a dry-stone wall. I knew every step, as if I had been there every day of my life, all the way to the brow of the slope where Gruskham House now lay dark against the darkening sky.

A short way ahead black roofs against the moorland hunched beneath the last trees before the open country. The possibility became real that if I could take one step into the infinity I would shed the years that had passed. The beginning awaited me at the end of this track. I could set off from here, out into the world, as I would do so many times before my life started all over again, beside a railway track in a Liberian forest.

A dog ran up to me barking then trotted back to from where it had come. A bare bulb on the corner of the low house was switched on from inside. Surrounded by the yard of the Cornthwaite's farm, where chickens clucked in wooden sheds and I heard the moaning of cattle, I stepped back into a life I might have led and wondered if the years had waited for me to catch them up.

I stood beneath a wooden porch and knocked. There was the sound of footsteps shuffling inside. The door opened and Joyce Cornthwaite stood framed by the low doorway. For a moment she was silent and wary, just as Mum had told me she had been when we had first arrived at Gruskham House and become neighbours to her own young family.

Whatever she said next would tell me whether I had ever really been there at all.

*

On an early January day of the new decade we walked out of our cold house, my brothers and me and Mum and Dad, and passed the neighbours' windows that still glittered with the last days of Christmas.

The gate of my new school was among wet moss and shadows beneath dark fir trees. The building was of old brick and had tall windows too far off the ground for anybody to look through.

At my first school on the other side of Harlow, I had joined the class at the beginning of the school year. This time I was joining months after everybody else. The kids all knew each other already. They would have no reason to want to know me.

The classroom smell was of sweet dust. The window panes chequered the sky like bars, light peering down on me where I sat in frozen fear among strangers I could never speak with. I would not be there for long. I was only there for a few minutes, then I would be gone. No need to take up my place. I would soon be away. Free.

I would soon be away, so there would be no need to speak or betray myself or my past, or even give my real name. I was just a visitor. My real home was a long way from here. I am really a stranger. My real home is far away. I am from Yorkshire. That's where I was born. I am really an outsider. I will never be the same as you. Never. I will always be different. We will never be quite the same.

I wanted it that way. It may even have been true.

My teacher had thin red lips. Her nose was pointed. She had long fingernails, like claws, which were painted bright red. There were thin brown lines above her eyes, where her eyebrows ought to have been. Her skin was a fine, soft brown. It was said that she had once become so angry with a boy that she had lifted him off the ground by his hair.

That first day I was certain that her dark brown eyes would injure me, or she would slice me with the red claws that curved out of the ends of her fingers.

I wondered if she would bite.

She smelled of perfume. I wanted her to say something kind to me, but I was too afraid to speak, and she only ever heard my voice when she called me up to her desk to read to her.

Then I would read her the only book I ever read in that class, a book I read over and over. It was a book on whose cover was a picture of a big train roaring across a prairie. The story was about a boy in America. He was a clean, eager boy. His dad wore dark brown suits and always wore a tie. They both carried smart suitcases emblazoned with their initials, and had smart raincoats, though the sun always shone. They had all the things that people needed.

One day the boy was taken by his dad on the big train. The train was sleek and silver and powerful, but clean, with thin red and blue lines running the length of its silver engine and carriages. The land it roared across was lush and green and bright. The train roared and thundered, and the boy was looking out of the window when he saw an Indian on horseback racing alongside. He watched as the Indian steadily gained on the train and eventually overtook it, while his dad nodded without smiling.

But the story wasn't over for the boy, because when the train pulled up in a town on the prairie, there was the Indian, pacing through the town mysteriously, while the boy and his dad watched but did not say hello, and instead went to a rodeo where the Indian was performing tricks for all the people in the audience who were all like the boy and his dad, smiling in the sun and the colours of the rodeo, after which the Indian disappeared without a word.

That's what I would do – disappear without a word, out into the frozen winter playground, where the girls were playing their skipping games and I wondered who had taught them their rhymes, and the boys were already in teams for playing 'He', and a black boy – Ali Jobe – the only black child in the school, ran and jumped near the classroom door as if playing a game of his own in a world of his own.

I had never seen a black person before. Our class had been told that he had come from a place called Nigeria. There was a war on there. He had come to our school because of the war. He played games on his own. He had a cream coloured jacket with 'The Incredible

Hulk' and a muscleman with a gorilla face printed in green on the back.

I wanted to wear his jacket. But before I could ask him if he would lend it to me, he disappeared from our school, and I never saw him again. I only remember him in wintertime, cold in his jacket, skipping on his own near the classroom door, like the children in Kaduna I saw twenty years later when I went to Nigeria.

A pupil rang a big brass bell as he stood on the path between dormant bushes which split the infant and junior playgrounds. The path led up steps to the stairs of brown lino and to the polished landing high up in the tower from where dark windows reflected the sky and hid the headmaster as he peered down on our games.

The bell cracked the ice air and the world fell silent until an order sent feet running and I was back in my class, arranging the things beneath the lid of my desk, lining up my pencils, stacking my books in a uniform pile, opening the story of the American boy on the train, reading it again and again, easing my way into the story and chatting with the boy and his dad. We would have such fine times together.

All the things I would tell them: about the long journeys I had made, mostly on my own, though sometimes with friends who were much older than me, whose parents let them travel on their own and who had smart suitcases with their initials printed on them. I would explain to them that when we arrived in America we knew where we were going, that we knew what you had to do at airports. I had things to do, so I had to spend quite a lot of time on my own, but I wasn't frightened, because I am not really as young as I seem.

Everybody tells me that.

But I'm quite alright on my own.

My parents are away somewhere.

They're quite international actually. They don't speak English. Well, they don't speak it very well. Well, actually, there are different languages spoken in our home. Some people, some aunts and others, are French. And there are some Germans. Well, one German aunt. So, we're quite international, and I can travel on my own. Nobody minds.

And then, when I woke, I knew from the brightness and the harsh cold that filled my room that something lay beyond the big folds of the linen curtains. I flung them aside, and beyond the glitter of the icy web of the window the world lay beneath a vast gleaming shroud of fresh snow that beckoned me away from the prairie town I had been dreaming of.

Now, before me, was a path that I knew led to northern forests where the only sounds were my footsteps on snow and a bird twittering among branches as I trudged homeward to my warm forest hut, my gaze cast into the deep of the forest where wolves lingered in the shadows.

We bounded down the stairs, my brothers and I, the rough carpet scratching underfoot, the snow draping the windows. All was changed. There was a new world all around us. Nothing would ever be the same again. Would there be a festival, we wondered, as we burst through the door into the warm kitchen, the only warm room in the house that winter. We ate quickly, put on Wellington boots and hats, gloves, coats, scarves, and stepped out into our own new world.

I knew nothing and recognized nothing. I could pretend not to know the world into which I was stepping, and could pretend we were in another land. I could pretend I had gone away, and that this harsh, unknown place was where I had arrived.

The road outside was empty. It was an early hour, a weekend I suppose now, otherwise we would have been preparing for school. We walked past the dark homes behind their trees, our young voices filling the air, a snowball thrown, laughter, complaints, the trickling cold. At the distant corner we turned and went further in that direction than I had ever been before. We were pioneers trudging across empty wastes to a distant place we might never reach.

Dad's friend Philip and one of his daughters joined us from the dark kitchen of their vast towering house. We were quiet, my brothers and I, a bit afraid of Philip. We followed. Men or boys? Dad's children? What were we on that landscape? We walked along a path beside a road, rose up the bank of a field, and the vast whiteness opened out before us, broken only by the wires between telegraph poles.

Philip knew where we were going. My toes froze. We rose into the swirling empty space where the sky and the land were one, the haze of our breath the only sign of life, six figures on a landscape, six lives at the brow of a slope in the January freeze of 1970.

The hill sloped down among the white frozen glitter of frost that spiked the dead twigs of forest thickets. A path of ice slid through a glade that led to the arch of a tunnel beneath a railway. Dark, long, the tunnel echoed with the fear a child alone can have of an adult's distant, receding laugh. Frozen mud ground and cracked underfoot in the gloom. Then, framed by the tunnel's mouth, the place I had seen when I woke to the sight outside my window opened up before me – a flooded, frozen plain, a single oak tree rising leafless from the dead land.

We stepped onto the gleaming white ice, and with a push slid across the world, the cold air rushing by as we gathered speed and slipped over the grass we could see frozen beneath the ice sheet. We glided to where the prairie rolled to the woodland beside a fast flowing river, where a boy filled a bag with his catch of twitching silver fish, then headed home to a house on the hills that rose high against the day. From the peak on the other side lay the northern forest, beyond the ice and the snow fields. I listened for wolves, but heard only the sound of voices.

A train clattered along the sharp line of the embankment we had passed beneath in the tunnel. I was along its journey to places, a local commuter train shuttling between towns, the faces of the lives it carried peering into distances passed, each gaze a scene snapped shut and swallowed deep, with me an image they remembered forever, of that cold day when they had passed the frozen water meadow and seen a figure sliding on the ice.

In the distance my dad and Philip and his daughter were disappearing. They had left us behind. I would never leave anybody behind. Not like that, striding through the frozen haze that oozed with the white gold of the winter sun. I must catch up with them before they disappear from view. Why had we been left behind? I saw my brothers across other distances. We were all alone, except Dad, who was disappearing across a white bridge with his friend, while I, wading wet and cold where the thin ice cracked, slipped onto cold grass and water and wondered if I would ever again be warm as, panicked by the emptiness, I rasped the cold air. I crashed through the ice as I ran and scrambled, wet hands cold inside my woollen gloves. Why had they left us behind? My brothers reached an embankment and a stile and joined the path that led to the white bridge.

Behind me the ice gleamed and glittered.

I ran up the embankment and leapt over the stile. Ahead, among dark trees overhanging the river whose flooded meadow we had crossed, Dad and Philip were walking towards us.

'Keep up. Don't get left behind,' they said.

No. I'll never leave anybody behind. That would be me. How I will be.

*

Sometimes, all the characters who ought to have been a part of my world seemed to have made their presence felt. Some were dead, some were mythical, and others were a telephone call away.

But it was not like that. Instead there were different worlds, which came and went in our house, occasionally mingling in our sitting room: young adults, old men from the war, professional people who drove new Fords, friends who shared secrets, smokers and non-smokers, hippy musicians, colleagues, challengers, idealists, teachers, business people, neighbours and favourite pupils – I watched them all, through the window that reflected the cherry blossom that in springtime exploded onto the front lawn. I sucked at its colour, which tangled with the vapour trail jets I watched passing overhead. I imagined that because of their altitude and the curve of the earth, the planes I could see were not really above me, but were already flying over parts of the world to which I would one day go – and that they may even be on their way to Vietnam, where there was a war.

From there, the war looked so clean, in the perfect soft blue hues of the sky.

The doorway captured me in its timeless shadow, and I stepped in among the voices gathered in my home. But instead of saying hello then leaving the room, I would sit and mumble my way through conversations, knowing I had nothing to say, lacking the courage to even tell myself I had nothing to say and that it would have been better to have tiptoed quietly up the stairs to my room and stayed there until the visitors had gone.

But instead, all eyes fell on the boy in the doorway.

'Ah, there you are.'

I knew I was not like the boys who lived on our road. I waited for the visitors to ask me why I was bad. Why I was so difficult – and so bad, because I was difficult. An easy child was a good child. But I stood in front of the strangers I must pretend to know, the old and the young, and stared hard at the smiles and expectations, as they waited for me to speak, while all the time hoping that one of them – some soft-spoken, kindly person who could see deep into my soul – would make space for me beside them, and say: 'Now, tell me about your life. Tell me how it's going, so far.'

Then I would have talked. I knew it.

But that person wasn't there, though somewhere inside me the feeling existed that one day they would be. All I had to do was wait, until it happened that I was drawn along by the need to go looking, a need which emerged while the words I spoke in those gatherings were tying me in knots as I tried to meet what I imagined were the expectations of the neighbours, the idealists, the professionals, the business people, the teachers and favourite pupils, while all the time wanting to escape to my secret world of forests and rivers and mountains.

Twice, I had the chance to play the part I imagined had been planned for me.

I rehearsed the role as we edged along the lanes through fields that led away from Nine Barrow Down, the Dorset hill beneath which we spent our early holidays, and made our way along the roads of southern England.

Traffic curled away from the coast. The soft green of the hills, the soft blue of the sky, were the colours of peacetime, a place to cradle the new-born generation that was my brothers and me. We would bury the past in our oblivion, knowing only what Mum dared to tell, that she had been there among the Dorset hills after the war was over. That was our role, when we stopped on the driveway of my godfather's house in Caterham. I would never know where he came from. I knew nothing about him, except that he had lived among Mum's brothers when they were schoolboys. Now he lived with his parents in a dark house of shadows behind a crooked fence softened green with moss. He was kind and soft-spoken, and had a pointed nose that hooked down over the long gap between his nostrils and his upper lip. He wore red leather slippers without backs. His ageing dad wore the same. His mother was old. She sat in an armchair, a teacup beside her on a table, as she spoke with Mum:

'And how is your mother now? Well, I hope. Is she well?'

Never before had my grandmother been alive. For a moment I waited to hear news of her. For a moment there was an expectation, even a possibility that something had changed.

'No. No. She died,' said Mum, as if delivering the news for the first time.

For me, it *was* the first time. The first time I had heard Mum speaking of the moment when the world had changed. Until then, the moment had been untouchable. Then, without warning, there it was in front of me, as if I were a part of the passing. It was my past too, not just another of the ancient days of which I was merely an inheritor.

I was left there, in that house of shadows, in a gloomy hallway from where a stairway led up into darkness. Its paint was not white like ours, its carpets not straw matting like we had. The door handles were high, the bed spread slightly musty. Mum and Dad and Michael and Paul drove away, and I waved as if it were normal that I should be left behind with long-heard-of strangers beneath the last shadows of a Surrey afternoon. It was my chance to pretend that I knew why I was there on the earth, that I knew what it was that I was a part of. It was my chance to prove my intimacy with the past that had brought me there. I should seem to know how to be, in a home where the sitting room chairs were allotted, where tables were ornamental, and the garden a trouble beyond the window.

How long would it be before they realised that I hardly knew most of the people through whom we were connected? There was nothing I could tell them about my grandmother, about my uncles and aunts, about their escape from France, about their hometown of Reigate as it emerged from the war, about anything that could explain why I was sitting at their dark table in a room of green lampshades, eating from a plate decorated with a faded floral design, the clatter of cutting searing the moments of silence. I wanted to seem authentic, genuinely present there among them. But to have asked them about themselves would have betrayed my ignorance and could have seemed intrusive. So I kept quiet.

Next day I walked in their garden, then watched the Olympic Games on the television.

'Do you like sport? Do you want to watch it? You can if you want to, if that's what you would like.' The Games were in Munich that year. I wasn't interested, but said I was, because I felt it was right to seem to enjoy sport like other boys did, so I sat for hours in the deserted sitting room, as blurred grey figures ran among the noise and glory.

My godfather took me out for a drive the next day, and showed me where a new motorway was being built. In a sweetshop he asked me what I liked, and I pointed to something at random, a sweet on a stick that tasted of pepper and which I had never had before. If I had pondered, and chosen something I liked, I would have given away something about myself. I could have chosen anything, and I picked out something nondescript, perhaps because it looked cheap and I would not seem greedy. Of course, I had no idea that that was what I was doing. Perhaps I just didn't want to have money spent on me.

Next day he and I took the train to London, crossed the city – I don't remember how – and caught the train to Harlow. Dad picked us up in the big Humber

Super Snipe we had bought. He had washed and polished it. I felt important being met at the station, as if from there we would be going to a place where an occasion was awaiting our arrival.

But we just went home, and I tried to think of ways in which the time away from my family had changed me, and whether I had brought something back that had not been there before. I wanted to show I could be changed, that I was a part of the world and could be changed by it. Instead I sensed that the time away had just been a test of how long I could play the part I had been given – a boy created from dust, moulded as clay, turned to flesh, now responsible for building new moments.

That role made me shudder, even after my godfather died, many thousands of days later, and I lay entwined on a mattress on the floor of a room without curtains in a Manchester suburb, torn between Mum's hope that I attend the funeral of a man who had always sent me a birthday card and the hope of a lover that I travel to see her in the city where she drowned my body, while a coffin was being lowered into the morning earth and the mourners dispersed, and she and I lay warm beneath the low windows, me wondering who I had disappointed, naked in the face of the past but uncertain whose past it was.

*

I moved on from the class of the teacher who had knives at the ends of her fingers. Our home was warmer now. The boys from the other houses along our road had not become our friends, and it seemed as though they never would. I began not to recognise them, as they grew into

41

young adults who wore tweed sports jackets and shiny leather shoes.

The nettles in our garden, which had been taller than me, were cut down. With mowing, a soft lawn appeared. Deep red roses grew in a flower bed outside the bay window of the sitting room. On warm bright mornings, the pigeons cooing invisibly, just as I would one day hear them outside the windows of my house at the oasis above Fayoum, Mum – shaking the leaves of the morning dew – would clip the thorny stems and gather them in foil to protect my hands. I would carry the velvet blooms to school for my teacher, embarrassed if I saw anybody I knew as I walked up the slope of New Road to the High Street, and on up to the school gate that stood in the darkness beneath the fir trees. My new teacher put them in a blue vase on her desk. That way, in my new class, a secret of my home was there, and I could suck the scent with my eyes and be far away, in the garden that was hidden from the world.

The classroom was at the top of the steps to the tall building from whose high windows the headmaster looked down from his office.

Down the steps during the break between lessons was a moment when there was talk between friends – casual talk between babies who were becoming children, kids who were neighbours or cousins, whose mothers were friends who worked in the shops or in the factories, their boys born beside each other in the hospital at Epping, all of them the children of families whose shared lives stretched back to the earliest times. Their talk went back years, on those steps between the classroom and the playground, where the chatter dispersed into corners from where old friends stared out over shoulders as if over walls.

'Can I play with you?'

'Naa. Ain't doing nothing. We ain't playing. You're it,' and with a tap on my shoulder a game would see the group run into new formations beneath the clipped limes and around the benches that lined the playground. Then there was laughter and dodging, tripping and cheating, and more laughter and scorn.

Then the game would, for no reason, be over, the group reformed, staring out as if over walls at strangers like me, from the place where last winter Ali Jobe had played on his own before he went away. Was there some sign that he had once been there? But the game was more important. The play. I could play. I would prove it, though I hated it. I hated play.

At the last kind bell of the afternoon I would run home. Then one day a boy called Johnny said I could come to play at his house. He lived on an estate of new homes set among huge oak trees, across the road from the school. In his sitting room his elder brother watched television. The closed curtains turned the room red and green. I thought it was smart and exotic, to have a room that colour, with a big television.

Across the road from him was the house of a girl from our class, Helen. One day after school when I was walking to Johnny's house with him he said that Helen wanted to meet him in a wood on the edge of the estate. She was there, waiting.

'Go on then.'

'You gonna or not?'

'What?'

'Chicken. Frightened or something? Go on then. Yer gonna?'

'No.' He smiled, red faced, and I stood a few feet away. Then he ran passed her and kissed her on her cheek, leaving her between me and him.

'You gonna or not?'

'What?'

'You chicken. Go on. You can do it,' he called from a distance, and I ran through brambles to get around her, as she cackled.

I hoped there would be a way of avoiding seeing her again. But she was there in our class next day, and I sat silent and embarrassed as she and her friends pointed at me and laughed. I wondered what Johnny thought of me, but he said nothing. I had no idea what anybody thought of me.

One hot Saturday he came to my house. Mum packed a fishing bag with sandwiches and fruit and juice, and we walked off down Old Road, across the fields, through the dark tunnel beneath the rail track, and out onto the water meadow where the leaves of the lone oak shifted slightly in the warm breeze. This is not play, I thought to myself, as we crossed the stile near the white bridge.

We stepped onto the riverbank and began our walk to Bishops Stortford in a paradise of humming and buzzing among the soft hues of morning, tranquil, at ease, with only our feet and breath carrying us to the place we must reach. We would return as travellers with a story to tell.

We walked until midday. Mum's sandwiches tasted of the sweet rich smell of our kitchen, drawing me home as we stepped further away. We walked on for some hours, to where felled willows blocked the path.

'No. I want to go back. I don't want to go on,' Johnny said. I refused. We argued. I had to go on. I could hear the trains coming from the station where we would wait on the platform and follow the glitter of the track then sit watching from the carriage that would carry us home as we crossed the tunnel and saw the lone oak in the water meadow. I had to look from the train at the walker standing where the ice had melted. I had to look back to see ahead, but Johnny refused and we turned in hatred, trod back in silence the way we had come and, as evening fell on the warm soft purple streets near our homes, said goodbye and never went to each other's houses again.

'See yer.'

'Yeah, see yer.'

*

Then the autumn came, stealing through my coat into winter, and I saw that the years were not time at all, but were mountains.

On the streets we kicked the crisp brown leaves the wind whirled and spiralled into corners. My grandparents drove their Volvo to our house, and my grandfather steered the roads we only ever walked along. I would have given directions, pointed out where we were, told him where we had to go, and he would have responded coldly if at all, not grateful, not proud of his helpful, knowledgeable grandson, just irritated, perhaps angry for reasons I was not entitled to understand.

He parked his car on the High Street under the canopy of Wasson's the greengrocers shop, and I thought for a moment that I should perhaps be proud that this was the car in which I had been driven, as I watched my grandfather stride among the shoppers and felt a little different and wondered if people were looking at me differently, as if I was somebody who had come from some distance away by car and would be travelling back there some time soon.

It was because of the rain that day that we had driven rather than walked. There were new and old shops, which together marked the times through which our town was passing. Somewhere I saw the past, with the present floating within it. Fred Scatley sold second-hand clothes. His shop was where my dad had bought the maroon blazer I wore that first winter when our house had been so cold. He was a quiet, short, grey-haired man, who didn't mind if people ambled through his shop and bought nothing, but was always grateful and a little surprised if they did.

Down the street was Brian, at a shop called Chattels. Brian was in his mid-twenties, wore striped tank tops, chunky modern shoes, purple corduroys and had long hair. His shop sold ethnic artefacts and model soldiers made of lead which could be formed into huge armies if the boys who bought them – always boys – had the money to buy and the patience to paint them.

Opposite Chattels was the greengrocer and his family, whose cheeks were the colour of their deep red apples, and beside them an ironmonger who peered suspiciously through his bifocals when customers set off an under-floor switch that buzzed the bell as they opened the door of his shop which smelled of lino. Further along was a supermarket of a strange brand called 'International', to which my mum would never go, and at the top of the street was 'jewboys' sweetshop where the ageing owner was rumoured to sell children single cigarettes hidden inside paper bags.

Fred Scatley and Brian at Chattels were the opposite ends of the world of our High Street. One, a sleepy shop smelling of old cloth and damp, perhaps opening up one day in the 1940s to sell clothes to men returning from the war, the owner leaning his bicycle against a wall after a journey before Old Harlow became the smarter district of the new town in which we had arrived when we parked our car on the waste ground beside the cinema and collected the keys to our first home. Then, down the High Street, up the steps behind a glass door, there was Brian looking anxiously as he judged the intentions of each customer who stepped into his fashionable shop, where Chinese paper lamps hung from the ceiling and customers could flick through posters of hippies in fields of daisies or shots of the pyramids in blue or pink.

'Are you going to buy that? If you're not going to buy that then do make way for somebody else,' he would say. Embarrassed, I would move on slowly, then slip out of the door, confused as to why the shopkeeper up the street who had greyed with the world and should have been stern and frightening was not what he ought to have been, while the young man with long hair and trendy clothes was brash and made me feel like a thief. It should have been the other way round.

Some time after my grandfather had parked his car on the High Street, it had been paved and closed to traffic. On a cold, wet Saturday we drove round it, away

47

past the school beneath the dark fir trees, along the wide avenue we had travelled along on the crisp morning of our move, and past the clock tower with its spire and red tiles rising out of the field of cows where people in post cards stood beside carts and bicycles in frayed sepia prints of how the landscape had once been.

We drove along the open road, following the slopes and twists between fields and the sound of our engine, Dad driving, Mum watching ahead, Michael and Paul and me in the back on the red leather seats fidgeting, bickering, and complaining that the journey was too long, then silenced by the darkness of Epping Forest. We would be gone forever if the car broke down there. As rain poured, the forest would not help us. The cars would surge past, we unseen in the darkness of the roadside, forever gone, lost among the oak and silver birch.

Then the road widened, and we passed a statue of Winston Churchill on the green at Woodford. The great man's name was a castle. I had never been in a castle. I would never ascend those steps. The height above me was too great, too distant. I dared not mention great, distant, magnificent things that were beyond the ideas I had been permitted. Churchill was a castle, a near-unmentionable magnificence, unquestionably a saviour, far greater than the life I could possibly even pretend I might be permitted to lead, as our car moaned in the rain across the cattle grid at the top of the road that descended the hill into Walthamstow from which London for the first time opened out before us.

We sped down the wet slope, passed Blackhorse Road, perched along the causeway between the reservoirs before Tottenham, and drove on into the barren lands of London, its streets seeming derelict, rain drizzling, small homes above shops, windows dark with curtains half draped, stores neither light nor dark between Tottenham Hale and the tunnel graffiti and leaking smears of mossy slime where our engine echoed beneath the tracks at Seven Sisters.

I was afraid to even watch, for fear of being trapped in the gaze of the cold, wet people who were walking there. I was afraid as if in the forest, whose darkness lingered. When would the darkness lift? Never, it seemed, as the wipers slapped the windscreen and we turned down Williamson Street and stopped outside a tall house where Suzanne, who had lived on Dad's street near Manchester some time in the 1950s, was now living the London of the 1970s with Jim and Sally Kate.

Pasts and presents met.

Here we are now, husbands, wives, children.

Who would have thought it?

Ha ha.

'Yes.'

'They're fine. All fine.'

'Yuh.'

'All fine.'

'The theatre.'

'Umm.'

'Nice.'

'The Young Vic.'

'Nice.'

'Very good.'

Where is the past in this?

'Now, don't do that Sally Kate.'

Outside, the rain poured over Holloway. We drove on past the prison, its horrifying gateway plunging its gaze into me, the thought of women doing things that would lead to them being forced screaming through the gate, an idea more terrifying than anything I had ever imagined. Forever I had to turn away as we passed there in years to come, and still today, the turrets and towers and darkness the cruellest thing I had ever seen.

On Camden's roads I watched men with long hair, people swaggering. The silence outside the window was tired and heavy. I had no idea whether what I was seeing was true. Could I see into people's lives by watching them as they walked the streets, windows dark, dustbins heaving, old bicycles locked to railings, rusting cars, no signs that people cared what their world looked like?

Fenced greens where people might have sat and chatted, were deserted, maybe because of the rain – the rain we had driven through for hours, the rain which glittered the brightening lights of Cambridge Circus and Charing Cross Road. Was it really us driving in the London traffic, among the buses and the strangers? It could not be us. What had we done that could bring us there? This was a place for other people – people we could only ever hear about, people who were castles, people who were not people at all, but who were the great and the magnificent. We were trespassing on the streets of the magnificent. When would we be stopped by a policeman? We are not permitted here. This was the city where the Queen and the royal family lived. We were far closer to the magnificent than was permitted. These people could only be seen from far away, from behind barriers penning thousands of strangers, perhaps us among them. We were not even members of the public, and had better not pretend we were familiar with the monuments that made the country great, for fear of seeming flippant or disrespectful. Better to stay silent, as Trafalgar Square flashed passed, then the Cenotaph, where the brave who died for me and all of us were buried under the street in the shadows of the great buildings of Whitehall which we must love to have ruling us with responsible decisions that we should not dare to question.

We crossed the great black river which lapped the Houses of Parliament, whose fearsome importance was overwhelming. The river curved into distances that I imagined must be England. On the other side the grand castles and towers gave way to low, dark streets that the rain had turned to headlamp beams and footsteps.

Bright lights marked the Young Vic theatre. Inside, there were young and serious people with long hair who dressed like Brian, the man in the shop on our High Street. Would they be like him? I wanted to pretend I knew their kind, because we had one like them back home. Would they be like him? What would actors be like? Would there be signs of a different life, when the drama started?

The red wooden benches filled, the lights went down, and a new world opened up in front of me. Words flowed as I had never heard them before. People stepped into the light and spoke truths as easily as they voiced their doubts, and made each other laugh and sigh. The world flew and curved and halted. The actors brushed past my seat. One threw a plastic glass lined with red plastic to make it appear filled with wine, which I picked up from the floor and which became part of the treasure I hid in my room at home. It was in the theatre that I would be safe, I thought, in the lights, where nobody could touch me. This was where people would listen and where I would always have something to say.

From then on I never doubted that I would be an actor. I would know it, even as the houselights went up and the magic was over, even as the cramped light of afternoon opened into the tree-lined avenues of dusk, and with what sounded like new confidence our car took us away to the soft glow of Uncle Mark's home on his smart North London corner behind the rhododendrons, where the dark of night could not reach. With laughter and smiles he ran through the menu, assuring Mum that a dash of alcohol was fine for children, and Gordon, the old man who lived there too, chuckled in his armchair as my uncle got everybody seated and chattered about 'Mummy', 'Daddy', his mum, the grandmother I would never see but who might have thought this and would have said that, the grandmother, the Mummy who might still be somewhere watching over her children and their children.

If only she was still there. I should be on my best behaviour just in case she arrived, as we sat among the lights and colours and smells of sizzling roast and steaming vegetables, of *paté* and *rillette* and *pomme dauphinoise*, *haricots verts*, red wine that I once said tasted sour and was scolded, of meringue and cognac and the chatter of a Frenchman's table deep within the city we had left outside beyond the shrubs and fences that hid us away in the home filled with photos of Mummy, and of Daddy the soldier who had ridden a camel through Palestine and fought at Gallipoli, who had then been in Brussels as Winston Churchill was driven in tears through the euphoria of victory. Was that once us? Was he one of us? He had died long before the story could really be known. But Mummy would be thinking of us, in the dead of night on the cold street, as we drove home into the darkness along the country road through Hertfordshire, our minds ringing with talk of strangers who were long gone, but whose lives I could pretend were a part of mine, whatever it was I was.

*

There was a boy who lived across our road, an only child in a perfect house which had a shining brass ring that hit the black polished front door with a thud, and beneath which my brother Paul and I waited shuffling on the black and white tiles of the porch. A lady who could have been a duchess opened the door and peered with an awkward smile in the soft light she allowed us to see of her home, as she considered which room it would be suitable for us to play in with her son.

He had deep ginger hair and always seemed to be in his school uniform. He was always smart. The house was warm and shining and soft and untouchable. I wished I was smart, like the woman's son. His dad was a doctor. He was there in the house when I went there, and I prepared myself to be asked questions about why I was there. He wore a dark tweed jacket, baggy, sharply-pressed trousers, and brown shoes that shone and had small holes arranged in swirling patterns on the toes. His voice boomed. His shining hair was black. It was combed perfectly, cut short and severe. He was like a soldier. He wore a tie, though it was a Saturday. He pulled back the sides of his jacket to adjust the waist of his trousers, and I could see he wore braces. He must be a soldier of some sort, as well as being a doctor.

He didn't ask me any questions. But I remember his voice and his face, where the black shading of his importance outlined his chin and cheeks and the gap between his nose and mouth. I thought that was something men like that had, so they could stare more sternly and say things that mattered.

The son talked about 'my father'. I had never heard that before. I wondered if it was something I could do. 'My father.' This was the way to talk now, in this new country, where other peoples' homes were warm and bright and soft, where garden paths that led to black shiny doors passed between rose bushes that emerged from winter in a disarray that a red-faced gardener who wore boots and a frayed tweed jacket and patched blue trousers held up with a heavy belt, would use his thick, scarred hands and cracked finger-nails to return to perfection.

The gate closed, an iron gate that shone with new black paint at the bottom of steps between two brick pillars on which the boy's house on its hilltop looked down. It looked down on me, and down on Paul.

Paul went back there, but I only thought about whether I could live like that. From somewhere we had the idea that boys of similar ages would have a 'fine time' together. A fine time. That was the idea. I wondered whose idea it was. After the war, when my mum and dad were growing up, they would have had a fine time with other kids, or at least said that it was so, or at least known that that was how things were supposed to be, so they could pass on the idea when the time came in the future. Boys back then would have been running into each other's homes, flying balsa wood planes, scratching their knees, muddying the shorts of their school uniforms. They would have had a fine time, laughing and chatting.

We could be just the same. That was the idea: boys teaming up in bright-eyed gangs with others of their own age, going on bicycles, chatting, arguing, running.

But it did not happen.

It was nothing that we learned that stopped us. Something held us back. Paul returned perhaps once or twice to the house of the doctor's son across the road. But he always knew when he was not really welcome. He stopped crossing the road to that house. Then the people there – the boy, the doctor, and the duchess – moved away, and we never saw them again. I imagined they had gone somewhere that was special, behind a bigger gate, to live in rooms where important voices talked about things that mattered, while the other kids who lived on our road sped past on their brand-new bikes. None of them went to our school. We were told they went to places that cost money. They drove in newer cars, and wore caps and shorts and new blazers. They smiled, and had rosy cheeks. They cycled fast on their racing bikes. They were growing up quickly. They seemed always to be glimpsed from far away, in the distance, on the way to somewhere, or closing doors behind them as they went inside their smart and perfect houses along the road where for no reason I would always run between the grey iron of the lampposts. When a car appeared behind me I would believe I would be captured by its driver unless I reached the next lamppost before the car passed, and would sense the relief at reaching the post just as the car passed at the end of a race between life and death that the evil driver did not even know was taking place, seeing nothing but a boy swiftly running from nothing to nowhere.

Had something happened in the world that – to use the phase that became the excuse for what seemed like every failure – meant we had 'nothing in common' with the people living around us? 'Nothing in common.' Was there something that set us apart? I never could ask whether this was the case, because the distance was far too subtle for me to even realise that was what it was. More strong was the feeling that we had arrived in a place where the things that mattered to people were already well underway – that we had arrived too late in the events that had formed this landscape, for us to be a part of it.

But I suppose I knew I was alone in feeling that way, because I never heard it said by anybody else. To me, life was at its beginning. But I knew I would be forever trying to become part of a world that seemed already to have happened.

*

I went away again, some time later, to stay with my uncle and aunt in Hertford. My uncle had been the one holding the umbrella above Mum and Dad as they emerged married from a church in 1961. He was the one who had brought the bedspreads from Algeria. I dared not ask why he had gone to Algeria, for fear of the answer. It was a place I could not imagine, though when I travelled throughout that country years later it was just as I had seen it in my mind.

I assumed he had lived there for many years, from the way it was talked about, and from the evidence of the artefacts that decorated their home, and assumed that they were just passing through Hertford on their way to somewhere else, perhaps to Nigeria or Vietnam.

It was because they would one day move on that I had better listen carefully. I might not see much of him and my aunt, the German woman who was part of my international family, if they decided they should find a new country in which their ideas for life and their skills and knowledge would be needed. I assumed that each morning the floor of the hallway beneath their letter box was strewn with envelopes decorated with stamps from around the world. They would perhaps go and work for the United Nations. People probably wrote and asked for their views and advice on the big issues of the day, which they discussed long into the evening around their table, after meals of cold meat and German sausage, black coffee and my uncle's cigars, dwelling upon reminiscences of the vaguely hinted time when he had shared a prison cell with Bertrand Russell after a protest against nuclear weapons.

I could not ask what was it like in prison, for fear of being questioned as to whether I knew who Bertrand Russell was and what it was that he believed.

My uncle told the story more than once, of his time as an activist. But the details never really seemed to fit, as he ran his hands through his long hair, and stroked the beard he seemed to have modelled on the one we saw in photographs of Alexander Solzhenitsyn. Books by the Russian who I never knew what to think of, were on my uncle's bookshelves. They had different books from ours – mostly modern writers, like Lawrence Durrell and Jean-Paul Sartre. Their house was modern, the furniture bright and new. They were living in modern times, confidently, while we travelled in our private world – one that made us seem to them and their daughters to be somewhere far away, in an agèd land which had yet to be infused with modern talk. They talked as if they were part of great events.

Then, one cold summer day, some time after I had spent those days with my godfather, I had been driven to my uncle and aunt's home in Hertford, across the road junction where once we had seen a car being towed and had watched as the tow-rope had snapped, then on past the factory where toothbrushes were made, whose pine trees in the factory garden were being grown to provide the bristles.

The bright modernity, the feeling that Algeria was not far away and that I should be aware of it, the books that I really ought to recognise and know and talk of, a feeling that I should have an opinion about Bloody Sunday, Vietnam, the royal family, the Soviet Union, and Georges Pompidou, and should know which newspaper I preferred – these were the towers of places and names bearing down on me as I edged into their house for my visit. But I knew nothing, and had no opinions that mattered, because for me the world was something that happened to other people – to my aunt and uncle and their two girls, my cousins, as I sometimes remembered they were.

Mum had packed my toothbrush in a plastic bag, and the morning after she left me there, my terror of being asked where I fitted in to this family and why I was there turned it into my sick bag. My cousin, the elder of the two, watched me from the door of the room I had been given, and called out to my aunt:

'He has been sick.'

My aunt, shocked that I might not like her food, responded with a mixture of embarrassment and disdain, while my humiliation was intensified by hearing my cousin refer to me only as 'he'.

It was nothing that I had eaten. It was just that I did not want to be there. Why could I not just tell her so? What credibility would I have had if I had said: 'Something in me hates being here. It's nothing that any of you have done. It's just a strong feeling that I have. Something is telling me that we are pretending to be acquainted, when in reality you mean nothing to me, and I mean nothing to you.'

It was because I felt like an intruder that I was sick. There was nothing I could possibly say to these people that could draw us close, bring us to share our secrets, build our lives together, or make sense of what it was that had gone before us.

It was only as my uncle lay dying, after I had taken my wife and children to see him in a Luxembourg hospital, said goodbye, broken every barrier that had ever been placed between us – by kissing him on the forehead as I was about to leave the room where his family had gathered – that Dad told me of the time my uncle had said that he hated him. But as I sat, drained, on the floor of the bedroom I had been given that time in their home, their image of me was one they had filtered through their attitude towards Mum and Dad. I knew nothing of this at that time, but it was all there, on that cold summer day, amid the lingering odour of vomit, my aunt's disdain winning out over her embarrassment.

So when what should have been a normal visit by a nephew was over, and I drove home with the four of them wondering what they would tell Mum and Dad, my mind dwelt only on the question of how quickly I could disappear from their lives. I could be nothing to them. But how could that nothingness be made real? Humiliated, confused, and resentful of their disdain: I had

had no right to feel any of these things. I should feel wretched and ungrateful.

But the truth was something else. I would never become what had been imagined for me. I was bound to disappoint my makers, as an instinct like the tide drew me surging out onto the open sea, and I sat on my bicycle leaning against a wire fence that was suspended between concrete posts at the end of a gravel path that ran the length of a playing field near my home.

A group of boys and girls were laughing and taunting each other a distance away.

One saw me there, wearing the bright red knitted cardigan Mum had made for me and which I always put on after school.

He suddenly called out, as if I was already a part of the group: 'Aye, d'ya wanna play on my side?'

Two: *Gangland*

A mound of earth, grass covered, left behind in the 1960s when we were all being born and the builders moved on from Chippingfield, was the citadel from where we looked down.

The hierarchy formed itself. Nobody said who was allowed to sit on the top of the mound, nor who should only linger on the slopes, or peer up at us from way below, where children played with baby brothers pushed out of home by mothers rattled by the noise of screaming: 'Take your brother out. I can't stand the noise no more'.

Below us, seven year-olds played parents. Girls preened, dressed in their best coats on a hot day, scraping the pavement with the blades of their mums' snapped stiletto shoes. Kids, muddy-faced, their frayed clothes torn, appeared from the house where a donkey was tethered in the garden and it was rumoured the parents kept a crocodile in the bath. A girl pushed a miniature pram, and arranged the edges of blankets around pink-lipped dolls, their cheeks cracked, eyelashes fluttering as they rocked across the paving we had transformed with coloured chalk into a worming path of garish graffiti.

'Bleedin' vandals,' a dad yelled. 'Anyway, what right 'ave you got to do it?' he bellowed, staring straight at me, ignoring the rest of the boys, who had been crouching on their knees as we chalked the path. 'Go back to yer own area. Go on, 'op it. Go an' pain' yer own pavement,' he told me, staring icily, before mumbling to himself and storming off to his house on the green.

We walked back up the grass of the mound the babies and children would never dare climb. Nobody would stop them. They just never would, unsaid why. The mound was ours, walled by the curving lines of terraced homes traced by paths between bushes, while we skinny white boys, stripped to the waist, flared jeans frayed, spring sunshine hitting our shoulders, long hair hot, watched down from the heights, as the curly-haired man who talked to himself as he shook his head and strode quickly past with his eyes cast down, went into his house, where he would stand at the window flicking his gaze from us to a record turntable on which a small box turned and turned, as we laughed at him and stared into the darkness of his room.

In the back of a blue Ford Transit van, the Irishmen who had been digging trenches for pipes sat and ate their sandwiches. We could see them through the window in the closed door at the back of the van. They sat in two rows, eating big slices of white bread.

'Fuckin' Paddies.'

'Fuck off,' said one boy.

'He's a Paddy.'

'Fuck off,' said the boy, flashing a nervous smile.

'Me old man had a bag of Irish peat for his allotment. Irish peat. Fuckin' Irish peat.'

'Fuck off,' said the Irish boy whose first name was Pete.

'Irish Pete.'

'Go 'ome,' the boy told his twin brothers, much younger than him, who were walking up the mound to tell him their dad wanted to see him. 'Go 'ome,' he told them, embarrassed in front of everybody else. 'Go on. Go 'ome.'

The hot sun made us itch. We were too young to sweat.

'Who's the Paddy in the van?'

We could see the men in the van talking. The closed door meant they couldn't hear us.

'Paddy van.'

'Paddy wagon.'

'Ha. Fuckin' paddy wagon.'

Shat ran down the slope and jumped onto the metal step at the back of the van. Staring through the window of the closed back door, he glared at the men eating their sandwiches.

'Paddy wagon,' he yelled at them, then turned and ran back up the mound. The Irishmen stared back without moving.

Polly ran down the slope.

'Paddy. Irish Paddy,' he yelled through the window, then leapt back off the step and ran away from the van, laughing.

I ran after him and jumped onto the step.

'Irish Paddy,' I yelled. I stepped away, turned, and walked towards the mound where the others sat.

The sun turned cold. The daylight seemed like ice around me. I could hear nothing but a dull buzz, and could only see Shat and Polly and Pete and Mick and Steve staring, after one of the Irishmen burst out of the van and threw himself at me with a fist which caught me on the back of my head.

He screamed. I turned and stood in terror, dwarfed by his massive size.

'Yer shut yer fuckin' little mouth yer fuckin' little brat, or I'll beat yer black and blue wi' me belt, yer fuckin' little cunt. Little fucker. I'll strip yer off and beat yer with my fuckin' belt yer talk like that again.'

Deaf and petrified, I turned towards the mound and smiled, as the Irishman got back inside the van and slammed the door behind him.

All holiday they had been there. We had talked with them a lot. We knew their names. They sometimes shared their drinks with us. There were old and young among them. The old looked out for the younger ones. There was a hierarchy. Some made the tea. Some dug harder at making the trenches. And in the evening their work became our battleground, our running feet cracking the rim of soil, sending it tumbling into the trench, so the digging would have to be redone the next day.

Then, one day they covered up the last of the pipes, and drove the van away from the mound and across the green. Nobody said goodbye. They were gone, and nobody cared or remembered that time when the big man hit me, while I remembered it forever, the pain, and the words he spat out then took away with him, those words that roared at what I was, a cowering, skinny white body with my frayed jeans and the sun on my bare skin.

I was new to that place, having only just ventured away from the road I lived on, to discover these kids who seemed to have known each other forever.

In those early days I never called them by their nicknames. Perhaps because they had given each other these names before I had appeared among them. I never knew where the nicknames came from. To ask would have marked the distance between us, as that year, 1973, edged towards summer, and I rode my bike every evening after school up to where they might be, on the playing field where I had first seen them, or – when the weather grew warmer – on the green where we sat on the mound which for weeks lay among the strips of bare earth that were the last signs of the Irishmen's work in the spring.

Sometimes I cycled around for an hour or more, and the streets would be empty. Seeing the streets empty was the worst time, as I imagined them in their homes, oblivious to me outside, they part of something – family, home, secrets – in which the outsider could never play a role.

I didn't know I was an outsider. I would keep going back there, as the evenings were falling. I would run or cycle down the slope of our road, on past the Catholic church where once a priest had given me and my brothers pineapple chunks after a children's mass on a Saturday morning, and on past the fire station, to where we had sometimes run when we were much younger kids, on hearing the wartime siren calling the part-time fire crew to rush to the huge red engine and speed off to an emergency. But we didn't do that anymore, my brothers and I. Then I would pass the cricket club where some of the boys from my road played, dressed in their white clothes, and linger along the street just beyond the wire fence and the lime trees on the edge of the field that even then seemed like a border between the boys who lived near my house and the boys I saw ahead on a corner of the road that looped through the homes of my new domain.

They never mixed, these different boys. But I didn't know that, until one evening when we walked past the cricket field – Polly, Mick, perhaps some others – and Mick began calling out and whistling at a boy who was walking slowly around the edge of the pitch speaking with a girl. The boy was dressed in his white cricket clothes. He was healthy and poised and confident, with red cheeks and a smart haircut, his blond fringe falling across his face until he flicked it back with a jerk of his head.

'Smart boy. Wanker. Such a wanker.'

At first, the boy and the girl ignored us.

'In love. Soooo in love.'

There was loud, provocative laughter.

'Ooooh. So in love. Darling, I'm so in love.'

The couple turned slowly. I stayed silent.

The boy in white lived close to my house. Sometimes his parents nodded at Mum and Dad. He knew where I lived.

I turned, smiling, awkward, hoping I would not be urged to join in the mockery. But the boy in the cricket clothes glanced directly at me. He gently urged the girl to walk away, to be out of earshot beyond the lime trees and the wire fence. He looked at me again, saying nothing. It was a look that bored in to me, isolating me from my friends, none of whom saw him pointing at me as he quietly spoke to the girl as they walked towards the clubhouse.

We strode along the narrow path that always smelled of dog shit, which ran between the cricket field and a long high wall topped with shards of glass that was broken by tall, locked gates leading into the fine gardens of some big houses whose luxuriant shrubs crept over the wall and gave us clues to the lives that lay on the other side.

'Fuckin' excellent apples in that one,' said Shat, as we caught a view of an apple tree. He had climbed onto the wall, arranging his fingers between the jagged shards.

'Go on then. Fuckin' get 'em.'

'Get 'em yerself, lazy cunt.'

'No point in fuckin' arguing.'

Shat pulled himself onto the wall and disappeared. A few seconds later big green apples started falling on top of us, littering the shit-smelling path. Mick pulled himself up onto the wall.

'Fuckin' dog. He's got a fuckin' dog on 'im. Get the fuckin' apples, you prat. There's some old bag seen him. Fuck off yer old bag.'

Shat crawled up the wall from the other side, crouching on the top to avoid the glass. He jumped down, ecstatic, red-faced, speechless with laughter in a way he sometimes became. He pulled three apples from the pockets of the flapping brown school trousers he always wore, and handed one each to Polly and Mick, gouging the third with his teeth. I had been a part of the laughter, but he didn't have an apple for me.

The apples were sour and unripe, so I shouldn't have cared.

'Get yer own,' he told me, in a voice I feared, pointing at the apples he had thrown, which lay on the path that smelled of shit.

We walked on. An ageing black dog which always barked from behind a gate in a rasping, vicious way whenever anybody passed it, snarled and roared at us. On my own I would have crossed the road to avoid it, even though it could do nothing more than bark. We passed the gate, and I winced as it roared.

'Fuck off mutt,' Polly yelled casually back at it, the others barely seeming to notice the teeth and claws that tore at a wooden board which half covered the gate. I walked on the far side of the pavement. Next time I would ignore it just as they did, I thought, my pace quickening as I strode slightly ahead, as if leading, as we walked up the slope to my house, the first time I had brought them to my home.

*

From: Mark P█ [mailto:█@gmail.com]
Sent: 22 January 2013 23:39
To: Mark Huband [mailto: █
Subject: From Mark P█.

Wow! Mark Huband - What a nice surprise. It must be getting on the forty years!

Well, it is me by the way. It's a funny thing, but I was standing in my brother-in laws mothers house quite recently and from her front garden, you can see that lovely old house that you and your family lived in and where we had so much fun. I remember the Guy Fawkes nights the most and playing in that little shed at the very end of that lovely long garden.

I actually still have a photo of Peter Munn and myself standing behind the 'decks' pretending to be cool D.Js. I remember that we got hold of two of the old fashioned mono record player, the sort that fold into a case. We unscrewed the lids and stood them next to each other and thought we were true pros. Though, I must admit, I don't remember doing any actual 'mixing'.

I have to say, it's really got me thinking of all those years ago.

Anyway Mark, I'll sign off for now, but feel free to right again and when you are next in London, or Harlow, perhaps we could meet up.

Cheers Mark - It's nice of you to make contact.

Bye for now ... Mark.

Dear Mark

It really is fantastic to hear from you, after all these years. Wherever I have been in the world, my memories of growing up in Harlow have always been with me; you can't imagine how important for me you were during those years.

I write a lot about those times – writing is what I do now, after years of covering wars for various newspapers – and it would be magical to hear whether we remember things in the same way, and to hear all about what you have done since we last caught sight of each other. I miss our old house – am glad that you remember the times we had there; childhood has such a powerful hold, and the house one grows up in becomes a monument. I am still jealous of the way you and your Dad painted that psychedelic tsunami around the walls of your room!

Let's meet, and talk more – I can't wait to do so.

Mark

On 26 January 2013 19:21, Mark Huband <█> wrote:
Dear Mark

It would be really good to meet up. I am going to be in London this coming week, and am wondering if next Friday 1 February might be a possibility for you. I can make any time from about midday, so maybe lunch, if that would suit you.

Looking forward to getting something sorted.

Best

Mark

Sent from my BlackBerry® wireless device

From: Mark P█ [mailto:█@gmail.com]
Sent: 26 January 2013 22:02
To: Mark Huband
Subject: Re: From Mark P█.

Hi Mark,

Thanks for the invitation. Friday would suit me fine as my wife has Fridays off. Just name the time and place and I'll be there. I've been looking at you books on the Internet and must say, I'm very, *very*, impressed. Real books - Wow! And such serious subjects. I love the poetic nature of some of the titles. Absolutely well done.

Anyway Mark - Friday it is then, as I say, just let me know where and when.

Bye for now – Mark

Dear Mark

I probably spend too much time with my nose in books, and not enough time enjoying myself – but there we are.

How about meeting at the Bacchus – 177 Hoxton Street, London, N1 6PJ – at 1pm on Friday? I hope that sounds good to you; let me know, and I will book.

Really looking forward to seeing you.
Mark

On 28 January 2013 23:08, Mark P█ <█@gmail.com>
wrote:
Hi Mark,
     one-thirty at the Bacchus this Friday. I know of
the place because I worked in the area a while back. I
look forward to seeing you. It'll be somewhat surreal,
meeting after all these years, but also rather exciting.
Bye for now - Mark

Dear Mark
That's great, am really looking forward to it. Actually I
booked for 1pm not 1.30pm - is that okay for you?
Mark

On 29 January 2013 18:47, Mark P█ <█@gmail.com>
wrote:
Hi Mark,
     sorry, 1pm is fine. I don't know why I got that
wrong. 1pm, at the Bacchus, this Friday. Yea ... I'm
looking forward to it to. See you then.
bye for now.
Mark.

                            *

I led my friends up the drive of our house and into the
garden.
     The massive lime tree swayed in a light breeze,
ropes hanging down from where Dad had climbed up and

knotted them high among the branches. Shat and Polly leapt onto the knotted seats at the end of the ropes and punched and kicked at each other, swearing and screaming in whispers as they swung wildly back and forth, higher than I had ever been.

There were apple trees, and beyond them a patch of ground where I had told them we could make a circular track for racing our bikes. We all had bikes, except Shat, who had nothing except a knitted blue hat which he rested on the crown of his head and only took off in school. He was violent if anybody touched his hat. We put planks of wood around the edge of the patch of ground, and by the time night fell we were talking of racing and stunts and the aces we would copy. We argued about the name of the track, Shat rubbishing the fantasy names because they sounded too American, Polly imagining it would be like California, where he would take blond girls to his camper van after the races.

It was afternoon when they came back next day to finish making the track.

I had thought they would not come, so in the morning my brother Paul and I had taken our red rocking horse from inside the house and put it out on the gravel beyond our veranda. We lined up chairs behind it and covered them in blankets, roped the rocking horse to the chairs, and attached buckets and shovels to the sides. Then we dressed in waistcoats and boots and cowboy hats with handkerchiefs tied around our necks.

Under the sun, the lime tree on a far distant hill of the American prairie that opened out in front of us beneath the towering white clouds of a vast, unexplored world, we whipped up the horse and set off on a trail into the unknown.

It was just as we set off that my friends appeared in the garden, looking at me as I slipped from the seat at the front of our wagon, hoping they would not notice my handkerchief, and would see only Paul's game, Paul's play, not mine, not my role, just my younger brother's.

'My brother's playing,' I told them, stepping away from where Paul sat watching to see which way I would go, as I took off my handkerchief and the green waistcoat Mum had made for me.

I stood among my friends, who looked at me and spoke, unable to detach me from the play. Paul listened. Then he went inside through the garden doors, leaving behind the rocking horse, the journey, the hours we had built up into the great adventure on which we had been about to embark.

The moment turned stale, like old breath. My friends were laughing. Paul felt only his loneliness. I, in the middle, felt only the deadness of the day, too uncertain and secretive to know what it was I might say to make that moment into what it was – a moment of departure, a stale, dead moment of departure.

My friends could not play, and I had to choose between them and my brother.

When we had painted the boards that surrounded the track as crash barriers and flattened the patch of ground, the boys from Chippingfield brought their bikes there. Many came, even some I hardly knew.

It was only a few minutes after we had begun our race that the tyres on our bikes started to burst. Our racing stopped. I saw on part of the course, in the grass and dust, small nails lying half hidden. They were there as if thrown deliberately. I said nothing, only wondered who might have put them there, and felt embarrassed and stupid and responsible. I was confused as to what might have happened, though somewhere in my mind I was also feeling the intrusion of our garden – on a patch of ground where Dad had sometimes grown potatoes – that our track seemed to be. I wanted my friends to be there, but now they were looking at me with resentment, as if everything in my garden was flawed, strewn with nails, blemished, half done, their plans for big games disappointed by what seemed like the false promise I had made.

We repaired the tyres. But by the time they were done the agitation had grown. My garden was not the place they wanted to be. We all cycled away, except Shat, who ran alongside, breathless and red-faced.

On the grass at the foot of the mound where we spent the high hours of those days, we made jumps and sped at ramps and leapt into the air, all a test of our guts, our age. We lived somewhere along a line that marked the sharp difference between the real and the imitation. That was the game – to show who was playing and who could hit the ramp at speed and, without fear, launch into the void, surrounded by the eyes of the baby brothers and the girls in their mum's shoes. We were split between the play of it and the void that opened up as the speed gathered and the ramp sloped up into the opprobrium – 'fucking crap' – or the applause – 'fucking mad'.

The run to the ramp became longer, reaching the length of a narrow path that led to back gates and gardens. We lined up along the path. I sped between the fences and alongside a hedge whose berries smelled of piss, and was emerging onto the green when a boy passed across my path from behind a hedge.

The crash of bikes and heads and hands lasted a second.

I tasted blood.

I was in a car, half-conscious. A man was driving. Polly was sitting in the front seat. He turned and spoke kind words. Nobody had ever spoken words of sympathy like that to me before. Nobody had ever needed to. His dad was driving. They took me home. Mum came out of the kitchen door and rushed down the drive to the roadside. It was the first of two occasions when she would meet Polly's dad. The next time would be when everything had turned bad.

She thanked Polly and his dad.

She took me upstairs and swirled warm water around me as I lay in the bath. I wanted that warm water always around me, and Mum's gentleness always looking down on me, and to hear Dad's words, soft as the warm purple evening that swelled and hummed in that late summer after I had tasted blood, as we closed the last gate between the hedges and strode the last mile in the shadow of Nine Barrow Down, the long hill to Corfe Castle we walked along each year.

'Well done. Well done. You did so well. All that way, and back again,' together, Dad and me, among the wail of gnats and the silent dark shape of cattle, the light shimmering in the farmhouse as it always did, our tents emerging out of the dusk beneath the hill's hollow darkness as we reached the soft embrace of familiar voices.

While we had been away on holiday, my friends had been in the garden. They had shaken the apples from the trees, leaving the thick summer grass strewn with bruised and broken fruit.

Wasps buzzed in the gashed flesh, turned brown with rotting. Dad was angry about the mess my friends had left behind.

I had told my friends they could pick the apples while we were away. I had wanted to share them, and to open my secret garden. I wanted to have no secrets, or at least to believe I had found friends with whom they could be shared. But the smell of rotting fruit and the menacing buzz of the wasps left a taste like the blood that had filled my mouth – brutal, helpless.

I didn't know it at the time, but it was the taste of desperation.

*

Then, with the end of the summer, I was a child again. Autumn dragged us through the school gate into the shade beneath the high panes of the windows, while home flowed with familiarity, though the hope always lingering that a new sound would break through. So, on the afternoon when I arrived home to find a huge French car slouched at the kerbside outside our house I was overwhelmed by the hope that something in our sitting room would be different.

I could smell cigarettes and hear the sound of laughter. There was fast talk that whirled in a breeze of enthusiasm. There were big smiles, as the smoke filled our sitting room with the light of Paris, where people smoked and talked ideas, where Simone de Beauvoir sat chatting with Jean-Paul Sartre at a corner table, at the heart of things, not distant, their books alive and dynamic, not intended to frighten me away, like the books on the shelves at my uncle and aunt's house in Hertford. Here, in our house, just like in Paris, people smoked and talked ideas and strode among the big buildings, at ease with the grand façades, because in France the famous people were not castles like in England. In France the famous people passed the time in cafés and drove cars that had long, sleek faces like the one I hoped our neighbours could see lying calmly on the road outside our house.

Who would they imagine had come to visit us, all the way from Paris? Our doors were closed, and now it was we who were hidden from the street with our family secrets.

My French aunt was famous. I was sure of it. She wore neat white shoes and stylish trousers and a crisp white shirt. She was tanned, her eyes sparkled, and she talked of her son and her grandchildren and smoked and laughed as she remembered.

Only Mum knew what there was to be remembered. My uncle smiled and laughed, leaning forward in his chair, a tall but slightly fragile man. He watched his wife, in awe as she sat back relaxed and filled the air with smoke and laughter. But only Mum really knew what there was to be remembered, because her half-sister gushed and enthused only in French, and we smiled and listened and asked Mum for translations, swept along by the hope that what was being discussed was rich in secrets that were ours alone.

My aunt – the half-sister who had been left behind on the coast at Perpignan, perhaps never to be seen again – was a woman who had secrets of a kind that perhaps become inevitable when the world is being torn to pieces. Her story was still fragments by the time of that autumn day when she and my uncle came to see us in Harlow, and it was only as she lay dying, and Mum moved to Brussels to be with her, that the secrets were finally spoken of. But that first time my aunt saw Mum with her young family was a time that was still too soon after the war for reflection or honesty. No one really wanted to remember, because then the laughter and enthusiasm would have been lost. What is her story, I wondered? I only really learned about it after she died in 2002, and the chance to be a part of that world into which I had been born was gone.

But I carried the fragments around with me, once she and her husband had driven away. Part of me lived the mystery made from seeing no reason why I could not be a player in a drama which might unfold one day, when somebody would take me aside and say: 'Now, Mark, there are things you should be told about what happened to the family in France all those years ago.' Then I would be able to feel that I had come from somewhere, that I had connections in distant places, where people thought of me as their family just flown in from England, and wondered what it was I might be doing and what direction my life might be taking. I imagined that one day the entire family would gather in a large house in Paris, and the laughter and the memories and the bonds between all the people there would draw me into a world that was awaiting me.

Then we would be a castle. I just had to arrive in their midst and I would be a part of it, striding at ease among the façades of Paris with cousins and friends who would consider me to be nothing less than one of their own.

Then the street outside our house was empty.

But the car would come back. French cars always lay on the road outside our house. We were the kind of family that had visitors from other countries. It was normal for us. The empty space was temporary. A fine car from somewhere else would come to fill that space. Then I would know that we were part of something larger than our neighbours could assume, and I could tell my friends about people they could not understand, but who were my family, the people I would walk with in Paris.

But I never did tell my friends. There was nothing I could show them to prove it was true.

Instead, autumn came, that year, 1973. But sometime – next week, perhaps even tomorrow – I knew we would be looking out across the sea as our ship sailed towards France. We would have said goodbye and moved away and become the memory of the family that lived for a while in the house with the rope swing and the apple trees. Then we would be gone, away, itinerate, mysterious. The only thing we would leave behind would be the question of what we did next, of which place we went to make a new home. It would be somewhere distant, a place people had heard of, a place that made us special, because that was where we lived now.

But I did not tell my friends about what might happen. Instead, the autumn was like no other autumn had been. The wind whipped the streets breathless with cold. Rain was steel. Our world shrunk under grey – always grey now, always grey, day after day, each day running into the next.

That year I had a teacher who rasped. He had grey stubble, and smoked in the store room at the side of the class. He wore green cardigans and strode slowly around the class. He had a stick that he banged on the desk when somebody gave a wrong answer.

It was not supposed to be like this.

Sometimes I caught a glimpse of my dad as he cycled along the road at the front of the school on his way to work. I had to run after him, and then we could go home together, to the safe place where we ought always to be. But he disappeared, me unnoticed. Why did he not see me? He was there, but I had not been seen. The only reason he would have passed was to see me. How could I not be seen? Was it possible to not be seen? I saw him again and then once more, and I told him in the evening that I wished he would cycle along another road, though I couldn't explain why. He said he would, and I didn't see him passing my school again, though for days I looked to see if he would.

The big, old trees in the playground were stripped of their leaves. There was usually rain, and wet clothes. The classroom smelled of damp and fear and the teacher's smoke, which rattled in the taut grey strings of a throat which was the voice of our timid class. We were preparing. We were the oldest in the school, the poor things soon to leave and move out into the vast place beyond the gate of childhood games, as we prepared to go to the secondary school. Then I became the boy who was given permission to leave the classroom just before the last lesson ended, who walked with special permission across the deserted playground where the sodden leaves clung to the drain grilles, who stepped up the path to the dark castle where the headmaster lived, pushed open the great door painted bright blue, and picked up the heavy brass bell from its place just inside the gloomy entrance hall where the brown lino had been worn into the perfect round shape of its rim.

I was the boy who stepped back into the grey and the wet, and who swung the shining bell until the ringing stung my ears.

It was me who brought the lessons to an end, who rang so as everybody could see it was me who cracked the air with time. That was me. It was me who did it, who stood there on the steps and filled the playground with feet and running. Then we were children playing, as autumn closed in upon the evenings, and mornings were strewn by the night fall of conkers that left knuckles bruised and sometimes bleeding as groups clustered in corner battles eyeing rough taut string stretched tight by small fingers loosed with hate in a vicious smile of crushed skin and yellow flesh swinging dead and cracked. Nobody cared about the loser, his prize smashed, his dad's careful work with a drill and his mum's careful cutting and knotting of string left torn in seconds, strewn among feet that drifted to another battle over there beneath the thinning trees, the shine of prize skins dulled by defeat as the season moved on to winter.

*

Every evening, after night fell and the wet cold hours of the day had been staked out by the BBC radio tune that announced *PM At Five PM*, and the news of the prime minister Mr Heath cowed us in towering voices that came from the world where decisions were made about our lives by the people who led the nation, and we heard of the war in Vietnam that had no end, of the Irish who were bombing somewhere as far away from our town as Vietnam, of the unions and the power cuts that were threatening the entire country, of all the world that ended in the radio tune that told us another day was coming to an end, every evening in the cold stillness of my room as I lay in my bed and my dad came to each of our rooms to say 'goodnight', I would ask the same questions: 'What will it be like, what will it be like this time? Christmas, can we talk about Christmas? What will it be like, this year? Can we talk about what it will be like? Will it be the same? How will it be? Tell me how it will be.'

I knew it was the time there would be magic, when the grey days slipped away faster, when our lives seemed likely to slip across the world, when everything would be alright because people changed when the kitchen dripped with the scent and smell of fruit and baking, when steam rose from bubbling pans as the rich mixture for Christmas cake and pudding oozed sticky around the wooden spoon and Mum called out: 'Make a wish'.

Would it be like that again?

'What will it be like this year?' I asked Dad, again and again, even after he said he was tired of discussing it and I demanded that he describe it again, tell me, assure me that we would again be going to that other world we always went to when the last light of afternoon had long gone from the winter day outside the wartime hut that was my classroom.

How could the rasping teacher make us work at our lessons when the festival was just around the corner, was just outside, gathering in the streets? Was he the strictest, the worst in the school? We would tell the other children he had made us work until the bell. They would pity us, and think of us as victims, martyrs even. We would pity ourselves, until he let me out to run across the playground to the castle door to grab the brass bell. Then the black winter night sang as, with a screaming joy filling my head, I told the whole world that it was time to stream out of the gate beneath the dark pines and into another land, where kitchens were bursting with the scent of the festival preparations, and every home was being transformed, like every life and voice and every smiling, kindly face.

Dad and I saw the lives and faces that Christmas Eve, after we cycled or perhaps drove to the towers at the centre of our town to buy the last-minute things Mum needed, and which were essential to make the magic. After dark, late afternoon, we walked across the market square, every stall glittering with bright white bulbs, fruit shining, voices calling loud greetings and happy wishes to the last-minute shoppers:

'A few extra fruit for free?'

'That's very kind of you.'

'Merry Christmas love – it'll only go off.'

'Very nice of you.'

The stalls were the other world. On autumn Thursdays, on summer Saturdays, they were there. But that Christmas Eve, walking across the market square with Dad as the sellers began to pack away their stalls and I thought I saw the homes and smiles they were heading towards, following Dad as we bought the fruit on Mum's list, that Christmas Eve it was all new again, this place of bright lights and colour and laughter, of calling voices under the stars of an evening whose night would end in a place and time the strangers who were gathered there, all knew. They were all heading to the same place, me and my dad there among them, all going to the same place – tomorrow, that day, where at dawn there would be the sound of running footsteps in our house, and we would look out into the early morning darkness in the hope that the world into which we had been brought was draped in snow.

But it never was.

*

The spring sun glittered in the currents that turned the leaves in our garden to shoals. Years earlier, on Mondays, Mum had clipped the velvet roses for me to take to my school. These days, my teacher would have laughed, his throat a rasping clatter of ashen spit grey stubble.

A hot weekend morning and a boy was wearing a black jacket of shimmering sequins. I tried it on. Everybody wore it, played Gary Glitter, then handed it back to the boy.

My friends from Chippingfield were not there. On Saturdays they went away with their uncles or their dads' mates, driving or taking the train to see their football teams, gangs dressed in their boots and scarves, claret and blue, red and white, blue and white. I could not imagine being with them at the football grounds of London, nor imagine how they survived the wars fought on the terraces and which we heard about every week on the news.

I crossed the field with the boys from my school. The boy with the sequined jacket went home. Ahead, an oak stooped over the grass where once I remembered there had been ice. Nobody knew that place. I mumbled of a memory, but we were not stopping there.

The railings of the white bridge were rusting. The towpath meandered, overhung by cow parsley. Beneath the river banks, where long grass strayed in the rippled breeze, shadows flowed. A moorhen darted into the midstream. A swan led its young out into sunlight. But we were not stopping there.

Somebody slid off the path and in among thorn bushes. We scratched and bled. The thorns were dense. There was no path. We pushed through backwards, into a long clearing where, for the length of a long dip in the ground which stretched into the distance, only grass grew.

'Bomb Dip. 'swat it is. From the war.'

'They bombed it. 'swhy i's like a bomb.'

'Bomb dip.'

'They dropped a bomb.'

That's where we stopped.

Everybody laughed and cackled when somebody pulled at the ragged torn muddy gloss pages of a magazine, rotting there so long that the grass had grown around the damp photographs of nude women holding their legs wide open.

'Fuckin' what?'

'Lookadat. Lookadat.'

'Fuckin' tits on it.'

'Size o' the fuckers.'

Screams of laughter echoed among the thorn bushes.

Anybody who looked too much was a 'fuckin' perv', and the damp, soiled pages were torn and flung back in among the slender strands of grass. We knew somebody must be there among the thorn bushes watching us, perhaps the 'perv' who went there to wank – maybe a teacher or a copper, or an older brother with a girl in a leather jacket who everybody knew wouldn't really mind if you grabbed her tits. There were girls like that. Some boys even had sisters like that. They might be there, among the thorn bushes, holding their legs wide open.

Somebody looked too much at the pictures, took a second look, or said stupid things, or stayed silent for too long. Then nobody knew what should happen next, except to run from there. So we ran from there, and at the white bridge some went back across the fields, and I went with two other boys along the river bank.

'Gotta see me old man.'

We ran – me, Paul, who had pale brown skin and slightly oriental eyes - and another boy, Theo, who had curly hair and had had a swollen lip ever since he had collided with a boy in the school playground months beforehand. Theo had laughed loud at the women in the magazine. Paul was quieter. We followed Paul along the river bank to where the open meadows gave way to willows, and elms that were dying of something Dutch.

'Gotta see me old man.'

Theo disappeared along the road that we reached at the end of the river path, and I followed Paul across the road which went to places I had not been, north, past the place where drivers watched two boys waiting for a gap in the traffic, standing in a glance before running to the other side and down a gravel track to the mill house, which was a hotel nobody I knew would ever stay in.

'Gotta see me old man.'

'He's in the ballroom.'

We stepped out of the sunlight. The walls were red paper flowers. Purple carpet spread across a huge, dim room, where chairs had been stacked on tables and a ball of mirrors hung from the ceiling. At one end there was a stage, and on floor-level beside it two men were sitting playing cards at a small table. One wore only a vest, shorts and slippers. The other had his shirt open. Both wore gold chains and were smoking. Their faces were faint in the gloom.

'Dad. Got some money?'

'Who's yer mate?'

'Mark.'

'Can yer play cards Mark?'

'Naa.'

We watched them play. They didn't look up at us. The other man said nothing.

'Dad. Can I 'ave some money?'

'What d'jer wannit for?'

'Buy summink.'

His dad sorted through some coins on the card table, picked one up and handed it to Paul.

'Ta.'

We watched them play some more.

'Go on then. 'op it.'

We stepped back into the sunlight, ran off up the road and caught up with Theo, the boy with the swollen lip.

'I'm going home now. You can come to my house if yer wan',' Theo told us.

We walked to Theo's estate and up a slope to his house where his mum, who had big eyes and whose hair kept falling from the clips she wore on the top of her head, gave us drinks and biscuits and looked hard at me and Paul, wondering if we were good or bad. Where had we been? Were we good or bad? She reminded me a bit of my German aunt. Their home was modern inside, like my uncle and aunt's house in Hertford. She looked at me and knew I was bad. She knew where I lived, and knew I was bad, even though I lived on a smart street.

'Goin' home now,' Paul said. Really he was going to the High Street shops, to spend the money his dad had given him.

'Can I come to your house?' Theo asked me.

We left his mum staring at us, as she wondered if we were good or bad.

Theo brought with him a small, framed picture of *The Blue Boy* by Thomas Gainsborough, which he held in his hand through the alleys and shortcuts behind the High Street. When we stepped through the doorway into our kitchen he gave the picture to my mum, who put it on the mantelpiece above the coal boiler between a painted statue I had made of Horatio Nelson and a clay model of Kaiser Wilhelm on a motorbike that my brother Michael had made at school.

'How very thoughtful of you. What a generous boy. That is very kind of you. Now, where did you get it from? I hope it's yours to give.'

'Yes. Yes, it's mine. I thought you would like it. Even though I don't know you very well.'

'Well, that's very kind of you.'

I hated that stark, raw moment of shame when Theo gave my mum the picture. I might be looked at, and may even be asked: had I ever been generous like that? When was the last time? Whose mum had I ever been so kind to?

Nothing was said, though it might have been. That was why Theo's picture mattered – for all that it said about me, and about my brothers. We had never done anything like that. We were takers, not givers. It never occurred to us that we had anything to give.

I was glad when Theo left our kitchen and I could walk the path to my friends in Chippingfield, hoping they

90

were back from football in London and that they wouldn't think it pointless having me around. I knocked on the front door of Polly's house. After some silence there were voices inside.

'Who's at the front door?'

'Dunno.'

'Who's that?'

''s Mark.'

''ang on. 'ang on a sec.'

Then there was silence. Polly peered out from the open side door.

'Oh, right. S'you. If yer gonna knock, knock on this door. No one ever uses that one. Fuckin' great game. Got on the pitch. Touched the great black man. Clyde Best. Fuckin' 'uge smelly black man.'

He was still wearing his claret and blue silk scarf around his wrist, his denim jacket and jeans, and his Dr Martens. He laughed as he spoke, gabbling through his slightly crooked teeth.

'Min' j'yer language,' Polly's mum told him as we walked, me following, along the passage and into their kitchen.

''ello Mark,' she said, the same smile she had when she saw me in the school playground she patrolled at lunchtimes. She lit a cigarette.

Polly's dad was smoking a roll-up, sitting at the kitchen table fumbling with his tobacco.

'Ever bin' t'a game Hube?' he asked me.

'Naa,' I replied, embarrassed that I called myself a fan – like Polly – of West Ham United but never went to see them, and that I had never touched Clyde Best, while hearing only that he called me 'Hube', a nickname this family had for me in the private kitchen into which I had

91

followed Polly without waiting for him to tell me I should.

'Don' yer wanna seat?' his dad said, and I sat opposite him at the table, wondering whether they saw me as the boy Polly's mum knew in the playground, or as a part of the world of rituals and form their life seemed to me to have. They knew where they would be on Saturday afternoons, and that on Monday evenings there was judo at the Sports Centre, for which Polly had the white kit and some coloured stripes on his belt. On Tuesday's his dad drank with the old men at the Working Men's Club. Sometimes a relative would come and see them from the East End, where they had their roots. Their lives were sorted. They knew where they came from, and knew where they were going.

'Yer gotta go to a game. Ain't a fan 'less yer seen 'em,' Polly said more than once. But he and his dad never asked me if I wanted to go with them. He wasn't mocking me when he said it. But for him everything that you had to do was 'obvious'. He listened to his dad, and his mum listened to both of them, drawing heavily on her cigarette, occasionally commenting, watching her son in quiet approval, as he stood, bubbling with enthusiasm, the boy who wore his football scarf and ran out from the shadow of the stadium stands where the crowds of East London jostled and laughed just as they had done when she had lived among them, and who joked about whether to wash his hand after touching Clyde Best.

She would never have thought the same of me if I had spoken like Polly. I could not be that kind of boy, swaggering a little, cackling with laughter at some weakness, nothing serious, no problems, no disappointments. They were safe in their kitchen, chatting, sometimes fighting to be heard, each being put down with a dismissive laugh by the others, but nothing of what they said really mattering, their language that of people who knew what they wanted to say, while I stayed silent.

All I wanted was to sound like them. The words almost came, but then I would stop myself, smile, shake my head, hearing the voice inside me as it resonated around the kitchen. Then the door would open, and Polly's sister – who my friend called 'Pud' – would come in, unsmiling, with some purpose, stand near her mum, her presence casting the family into calm, easing my awkwardness by taking the attention away from whatever I might have been about to say, Polly then breaking into the silence, saying: 'Ca' aan Hube, le's gaa.'

On the street the boys from the other houses would see us step out into the evening. We rarely needed to knock on the doors of their homes. Lives flowed at the same pace – tea after getting back from the football, then nothing to keep them indoors.

We strode to the mound beside the swings. The girls were there. Deena, and sometimes Joan, who was quiet, and Steve's sister Sharon. Deena talked loudly, laughing. She lived next door to Polly. Their mums looked similar, had the same hair, and I wondered if they were sisters. Deena always had the latest style of clothes: high waistband trousers, wedge-shaped soles on her shoes, and a long coat with a single long pleat down the back.

I never asked Polly what he thought of her. I had a feeling that they had something secret between them, which dated from long before my time there. Sometimes they would brawl, even punch each other – though only on the arms – and would argue in a way that I had not heard before, like two people who knew each other well. But there was nobody to ask whether they had something special between them, and I was left never knowing whether there was a story to this gang or not.

But sometimes it was good like that, when the feeling was that today was all, and I could swagger just like them, in the Dr Marten boots Polly gave me one hot Saturday afternoon, wearing my denim jacket and jeans as we walked out across the playing field and Gilden Way, past the strange silent wood that surrounded Dick's Pond, and further on, to the slaughterhouse, where once there was a chance to talk to Mick on an evening when his mum had told him it was his turn to take their Jack Russell to the dogs.

Mick was the eldest of four children, all of whom took after their small, fragile mum rather than their huge dad, who had massive arms and a loud voice. Mick was irritated that his mum wanted him to take the dog.

'Can't stand the dog. I'd quite happily have it put down, fuckin' mutt.'

'Why have you gotta take it there?'

'Get it up the duff.'

'What?'

'Don't you know nuffin?'

'Course.'

Ahead, beyond Dick's Pond, we could hear the hounds of the Essex Hunt barking wildly in the kennels in a dip in the fields where the farmers grew roses. The kennels were beside the slaughterhouse, and the smell of the place made us retch. The kids who lived there were at my school, arriving each day in a taxi paid for by the council. Nobody understood why they came by taxi, but despised them for it anyway, as well as for living at the slaughterhouse, and for wearing second-hand clothes and pink plastic glasses.

Mick and I hung around near the gate, and he let the Jack Russell off its leash. We didn't want to be noticed by the kids who lived there, who would know our names and would soon see what it was we were there to do, as Mick ordered the dog to go into the slaughterhouse yard and mingle with the Jack Russells that were taunting the hunting dogs by scratching at the doors of the kennels.

'Go on,' Mick told the shivering dog.

'What d'jer wannit to do?'

'You really were born yesterday, weren't yer?

'Well.'

'It goes in there and gets fucked, 'cos they got pedigree Jack Russells there. That's the idea. Otherwise it costs the bloody earth to get it pregnant. Then yer get a loada money for the pups. That's the idea. But this fuckin' stupid bitch bloody hates it. Reckon it's a lesbian. She never gets pregnant.'

We lingered at the gate for what seemed like ages. Darkness came, and the hunting dogs fell quiet, the Jack Russell running back towards us each time the pedigree dogs approached it.

'Go on, you stupid fuckin' bitch,' Mick yelled. But the timid animal refused, and we eventually gave up when a light came on over the door of the house where the kids from my school lived, and Mick and I hurried away across the fields, not knowing each other any better.

Perhaps their stories were too private, maybe even too fragile, I thought, as I knocked on Shat's back door on my brother Michael's birthday.

He had invited Shat, and some of his friends from our school, to a party we were going to have in our garden. Shat was the only one of my gang that Michael had any time for. He had invited him to the party partly out of generosity, because he seemed to have nothing. But Shat didn't want sympathy. He just wanted to laugh, and to have other kids to laugh with. He sometimes laughed ecstatically, almost madly, his face turning red, his ears turning the colour of beetroot. He could become lost in laughter, almost delirious.

But when the time came for the party, he did not turn up. I hated going to his house, and only knocked on his door five or six times in all those years.

Sometimes it was his brother Pip who answered, or his eldest brother Brent, or maybe his sister, or one of the two black haired kids whose dad lived there with Shat's mum, the man who Shat called his 'Uncle'.

The door opened suddenly.

'Yeah? What d'jer want?' asked his uncle.

Using his real name, I said: 'Um, well, I'm wondering if Paul is coming to my brother's party.'

'No, 'e ain't goin' out, and 'e ain't goin' to no bleedin' party.' Then he slammed the door, leaving me stunned in the passageway.

On seeing Shat a day or two later, he said nothing about the party. I told him: 'You could have come later, if it 'adn't been for that uncle of yours.'

'Don't say a fuckin' thing about my uncle. D'jou 'ear? Right? D'jer gettit?' I nodded, scared of him, as Steve, the eldest of our gang, and three years older than me, strode slowly, grinning, to the swings and the mound where the sound of childish voices mixed with the squeak of the swing chains and the occasional scream of a row erupting between the younger kids.

Sometimes I saw Steve's dad edging his way down the path from his house to his dark green Cortina parked by the roadside. He dragged his twisted legs behind him as he leaned heavily on two shiny walking sticks. Steve never talked about what made his dad like that. He invited me into his house once, into the kitchen, where his mum, who was short and smiling, stood smoking and chatting with Steve, his sister Sharon, who was in my year at school, and their much younger brother, while his dad sat in an armchair telling Steve what he should write on the football pools form he was filling out at the kitchen table.

His mum asked me questions while Steve called her by a nickname.

'Alright Chico. Thanks Chico,' he told her.

'Oy you mind yer lip,' his dad boomed from the end of the room. 'You show some respect for your mum, using name's like that.' Then there was silence, and Steve grinned, red-faced. 'In front of yer friend an' all,' his dad went on.

His mum stopped smiling and the silence hung in the air. Steve went back to filling out the crosses on the grids of the pools sheet.

I liked the sheets. I found a bag of them once, thrown in a ditch, and thought the grids of squares must contain some secret codes, or that they were a kind of money. Then, there I was in Steve's kitchen, watching him know what to do with the forms. I didn't want to ask what to do with them, because it would have said too much about me. I didn't understand the conversation they were having about which boxes to fill in, nor how they could know so much about football from there, in their kitchen, where Steve's mum gave me a plate of toast and baked beans and I hoped I wouldn't seem rude leaving straight after eating it, so I could run home in time for the dinner I knew Mum would be putting on the table in our house as evening fell and Dad asked why I was late home on the night before our journey.

*

The morning was bright and cool as we walked together to the station at Harlow Mill.

I watched, wishing I didn't need anybody to see us together as we walked out of town, wondering who it was I would be if I saw my friends and had to tell them where it was we were going, our family. I feared meeting them. I wouldn't know what to say – neither to them, nor to Mum and Dad – not knowing who I would be, there, walking, part of a family on the way to the station, pacing in a widening line along the streets that I must appear not to know too well, which I must seem to be discovering for the first time, in order to bring me together with my family in this journey of discovery that was ours alone. We had perhaps never walked there before, all of us together, my mum and dad, Michael, Paul. All was new. All was different – the path to the river, the road I had crossed to a hotel where I had watched two men playing cards in a big dark room. In another life I had followed those paths. But I was somebody else now, with my mum and my dad, stepping closer to our secrets as the train pulled away towards London.

None of us really knew where it was we were going, as we screeched and hummed and clicked time along the tracks. Who would watch over us now, through the first few stations of the map we knew, then past names on deserted platforms that were the unknown? Who would protect us from the stare of dark slum windows beneath bridges that flickered by and were gone, as we made our journey perched on high city embankments, through long tunnels that arched momentary shards of sunlight gleaming on the mesh of tracks arriving home from the towns of East Anglia, merging, parting, dimmed by the black brick of dead hands?

Our journey was the only one being made out into the world that early morning, as the city woke to the click of locks and doors that slammed in the cool breathless arching echo of space beneath the dead sky of dead smoke that peered down upon the trains worming to a halt at Liverpool Street Station, its timeless arrivals and parting moments burned into the years-browned glass of the roof and scored by the brush of shoulders on a pillar.

Ours was the only journey being made that day. But everybody, the strangers' feet dragging the flow into which we stepped with eager stares, everybody was there with us. They all knew where we were going. How could they not have known? They were there to see us on our way. They must have wanted to know why our journey was not like theirs. We were going much further. We were travellers, rising into the daylight from the underground at Victoria, sitting in the near-empty commuter train that clattered out of the station as if all was normal. It cannot have been known who was aboard, watching through the scarred dust of windows as the line curled among homes we had no interest in going inside, because this time we were going much further than anybody else. We were passing by. We were on our way through towns and across fields, towards the pale blue brightness of the sky which told of the sea that was just ahead, perhaps a mile away, beyond the next slope, no, the next, it must be beyond the next, until the waiting turned to irritation and the game was over at the moment when land and journey were drawn into the flowing emptiness of silent silver blue grey currents, which swept out beyond the finger of the sea wall that clustered the red funnels of blue ships belching smoke as they ploughed ripple shards through the shoals and shallows, dragged in the wake of the bright spring breeze gliding out across the sea to France.

There is a photograph of me sitting on a bicycle in the large courtyard that lay behind the tall grey wooden gates to my aunt and uncle's house in Gasny. It is one of the photographs of me that I didn't take one afternoon years later from the manila envelope in the chest of drawers where all things were, and tear up without anybody seeing, in an effort to have everybody forget how it was I had once looked.

In the photograph I am talking with the wrinkled grey face of my uncle's mother, who lived in the gatehouse on the other side of the courtyard. I am counting on my fingers.

On the train from the coast of France I had counted the poles that held the electric cable above the rail track. I had counted all the way. I could do that, or so I thought, in French, count the numbers quite high, counting the passing miles and the slow advance of our journey, which ended in the evening after hours and hours during which the excitement turned to uncertainty and boredom from the repetitiveness. It was uncertain what there would be for us after our arrival. Then we remembered that this was the place to which we were to come. This was the destination, the small Normandy village where, just after the war, Mum had stayed with her half-sister, my aunt, who had been left behind when the family members that could do so had fled to Spain, but who survived and came to see us in our house in Harlow, and had laughed and smoked and laughed. And here we were, behind the big gates, like a family.

How many years have I been riding a bicycle? How many children are there in my class at school? Is that what I am counting on my fingers for my uncle's mother, who gave us bland biscuits when she invited us into the kitchen of her house on the other side of the courtyard?

Her house was poor, and we wondered why my aunt and uncle didn't have it painted and made more comfortable. 'She likes it that way,' my uncle told Mum, who told us, as the days of family stories passed us by in translation.

It was there, during that spring holiday in Normandy, that I came to see that I was nobody's story, and was not a part of anybody's tale. But that village that had not been a part of my story, became so one hot afternoon, four or five days after we had arrived.

Michael and Paul and I had argued over something and – angry – I left the garden where we had been playing in the swimming pool in the garden of my aunt's house. I walked through the sitting room, where a policeman with a pistol at his belt was speaking in the sitting room with my aunt about a speeding fine she had been given when the same car she had parked on the road outside our house had swung too fast along the Normandy lanes and surged at speed through the village.

I walked quickly across the courtyard, quietly opened the big gates beside the silent cottage where my uncle's mother was perhaps dozing behind the delicate web of her net curtains in the dim cool of her kitchen, and stepped out into the solitude of the deserted street.

For those moments, hours – perhaps forever – the emptiness was perfect: a place where I could be alone. Nobody knew which way I had turned after I closed the gate behind me, took a step away that was made greater by the silence, and became aware of nothing to listen to but my own footsteps. I moved through the emptiness of streets that had no hold on me. It didn't matter where I went. Nobody was watching. I could burn in the hot sun. I could sweat and stride and burn. I could run and run and turn the ground beneath my feet. My eyes could stare into the hot sun. My head could swim in the heat. I could die, there, on the single line of rail track I found passing through tall grass that brushed up to my waist.

I stepped from one sleeper to the next, running on to the next the next the next, then one more, a rat rattling the stones beneath the rusting iron that curved ahead among pines, where there were buildings, perhaps a station, people.

I stepped off the track into tall grass on the other side, hot, breathless, stripped off my shirt, felt the pounding of the alien sun, a different sun, strange heat oozing, pangs, a wave's surge over and inside me. I was lost in the heat, mind and memory raw in the heat.

Who was the boy sitting raw in the sun, heat beating his young shoulders and his skinny white arms, and turning his red hair to a golden sheen? There on the grassy bank of a river where poplars shifted the breeze, who was the boy watching the water dimpled by dragonflies, as fish flickered in the mist of the shallows? Who was the figure on the riverbank, afraid of the story about the hot boy who dived into the cool flow of the river and died of a heart attack?

I believed the stories. But they never believed me. I had disappeared to where wet heat lingered in the summer air. I was hidden among strands of tall grass.

It was silent there, as my body roared and sang, there in the hot sun beside the river, as I stripped naked and lay for a second, exuberant, embarrassed by my nakedness, then dived into the river and was swallowed by the cold and for the first time felt my presence in the world.

Nobody asked where I had been.

The next day, my aunt drove fast as we surged up the spiral road into the shadow of the massive face of Chateau Gaillard, and stepped through gates and archways opening onto plains cradling times into which for the first time I felt my imagination could carry me, times of troubadours who sang of poet knights travelling these ancient lands.

Warm stone breathed the words to which my imagination clung, beneath turret shells and stairways worn smooth by steps that passed just ahead of me into shadows. Around the next corner horses would be heaving under the weight of armour, glaring at the sunlight that burned the coast, where turquoise currents rolled ships in white spray on towards the ageless stones of castles rising from the dry lands of Troy and Persia, lands where Alexander clad in gold rode the open plateaux, rising to mountains then falling to deserts twisted by the warm winds that rustled the olive groves on the hills above Jerusalem.

I saw the dry land and the terraced hillsides. For a moment longer I could be the young boy about to join the cavalcade as it journeyed the soft paths of Europe beneath the stars and the sun on its way to Constantinople and the vast lands beyond.

The land was dry, the people scorched by the sun, their skin seared by the lives they led under the pale, warm sky I woke to in my room, in our house, on the first day of the final term at my school, the cooing of a pigeon outside my bedroom window, the first soft and timeless sound.

But what should have happened next – the next step, which would take me closer to the heart of something that I could say was my own – that step never happened.

My friends and I would not gather in the morning, nor grow into men before setting off into the world, me walking with them past the mound of earth that was our place, past the classrooms of my primary school where each day I would feel the growing distance between myself and the rasping teacher with smoke on his breath.

Instead I would take my first step away from that world, when Mum and Dad said I would not be going to my friends' secondary school, but to the one where Dad taught, where Michael had been for the past year, where I would be a stranger again.

And when I arrived there, the strangest of all was me.

*

For the days of that first early autumn there was the chance to invent the boy in my skin. I came from the other side of town, a place nobody in my new class could know, and which they had no reason to know.

In the first weeks I fled in silence at each day's end. I fled as fast as I could when the last bells rang loud on the walls of the polished corridors, ran out into the cold air, slipping on mud as the autumn night sapped the orange evening oil of the street lamps, as car engines whined to the slapping rhythm of wipers on windscreens, as shadows clustered in a dark corner where a fight was had out beside the sheds of bicycles that perched rusting on hooks under asbestos roofs.

I wondered who might see me rush away, and who might be imagining what it was awaited me as I took my route home, a different journey from theirs, different from everybody else, a bike ride away, spray from the tarmac spitting grime, my clothes wet with the grit of the old road which passed among trees behind the factories belching sweet, sick fumes, where people were carrying heavy bags from J Sainsbury Ltd, back to homes where the warmth and the light were safe.

In the classrooms there was no chance to sit silently as I had done when I had arrived at my previous school in the dead of winter, where I had hidden behind the flap of my desk and read and read the book about the American boy who had travelled across the prairies and watched an Indian race his train on horseback. In my new school we changed class for every lesson, and in each room there were tables in rows and everybody swarmed in to sit with the kids they had known since long before we had driven from Yorkshire and parked on the waste-ground beside the cinema at the beginning of our new life.

Sometimes I would sit on the edge of a group and the boys would know that I was pretending to be a part of something they had created years ago in secret in a part of town to which I would be afraid to go, where people would stare at me and know I did not belong. But I would sit there, waiting.

'Get out mi fuckin' seat. Get off mi fuckin' chair.'

I would stand and eye the tables, asked by a teacher where I was going, and would mumble under my breath and sit next to whoever had nobody sitting next to them – a fat kid, or one who was small, or a girl who everybody laughed at because she had the face and the hair and the voice and the clothes that must mean she was ugly. Then the gangs would laugh some more, until the morning stepped a little closer to the break, and the bells in the corridors pierced the air and they strolled or swaggered or scarpered to the door and stormed out into the heat and secrecy of the coat racks that lined the corridors, where some gathered muttering in groups as they swapped cigarettes from open palm to closed fist dug deep into pockets, eyes screwed for signs of betrayal.

When the morning ended, and autumn rain clattered across the windows and the sky and the light were grinding blades of grey, then the gangs cowered scowling in the bogs, down by the bins, or among the coats, in the hidden secret private worlds of the brothers Neil and Dennis – loud, tough, every word stabbed out like a blade, to defend or attack - or Ralph, short, a deep laugh, broken words spoken always on the attack – 'Wha' d'ja fuckin say? Tell me wha' yer fuckin' said,' – every word a punch out into the hot damp air of the corridors, the doorways, or the queues into the common rooms where the cooks laid out big dishes of steaming food.

The gangs sat at tables with their mates from years back – their neighbours, their brothers, maybe their cousins. Rivermill boys, Tanys Dell, Little Parndon: to the outsider these were the names of childhood territory.

Paul – the boy whose dad I had watched playing cards one summer in the dark ballroom of the riverside hotel near my house – was there. He had moved away from my part of town and was now among Neil and Stephen and Andrew and Tony. I could try to know Paul, if he remembered finding magazines with photos of naked women with their legs wide open. He might remember the Bomb Dip and that other world of a summer or more ago. No, there was nothing left of that. He was in another gang now.

But I sat at his table at lunchtime, as there were no other empty places.

'Can I sit 'ere?'

'Yeah.'

'Naa. 's Dennis' seat.'

'Yeah, you sit there.'

'G'is yer pudding.'

'Naa, I wannit.'

And I would eat, wondering what I should say, as the kids threatened each other unless food was swapped and hunger satisfied.

"Oy, is 'uband your old man.'

'Yeah.'

'Right.'

'Mr 'uband?'

'Yeah.'

'Wha's 'at like then, 'avin' yer old man a teacher 'ere?'

"salright.'

'D'yer wanna veg for a meat?'

'Naa.'

'Yeah, I'll 'ave it.'

'You owe me then. You owe me, a'right? You owe me two puddings.'

'Fuck off. Don' owe you nothing.'

'Fuckin' right you do,' the words muttered in a vicious whisper, a bell piercing the damp, hot air, rain spitting at the window, the warmth inside sickening in its pretence of comfort.

'What d'jer gonna do now then?'

'Dunno. Nuffin.' Then, their lunch sitting over, the bell silent, their gang would melt away, knowing what they had planned. Half an hour later, when the bell rang for the end of the lunch break, I would see them again, pass them in the corridor, and would smell the smoke that clung to their lank wet hair and the sodden frays of grey jumpers that sagged with rain.

'Where yer bin?'

' W'as it t'you?'

'Dunno.'

Our teacher took the afternoon register, and for a few minutes we were just names on a list – Kenny, Jeremy, Steven, Tony, Richard, Mark, Sherman, Peter, Andrew, Jeremy, other Mark, Neil, Martin, and on, until the girls' names were called – Mandy, Karen, Beverley, Dawn, Sonia, Valerie, Wai and more, names and responses, me wondering what they heard when I answered my name, and whether it said anything. There was no chance to tell anybody where it was I had come from. I was nothing special to look at. There were no signs that I came from a place that made me different.

In the first weeks, when the class gathered to be registered, when gangs gathered in corners and I stood against hot radiators, I would tell anybody who asked that I had been born on the Yorkshire moors, in a cottage, and that I was one-quarter Belgian. But, just as it had been with my friends in Chippingfield, being from some other place was a bit weird. It didn't mean anything to anybody. Nobody was impressed or looked at me differently or asked me if I spoke Belgian. One boy, Stephen, didn't believe I had been born in Yorkshire, because I didn't speak with a Yorkshire accent. I didn't know what to say to him, and shrugged and wondered if perhaps he might think I was lying about where I had been born. Most of them had been born in Epping Hospital, because that was where Harlow's babies were delivered before Princess Alexandra opened her hospital among the pine trees on the far side of the towers at the centre of our town. Maybe where I had been born was slipping away from me anyway. I didn't even know what Yorkshire looked like, and hoped nobody would ask me what my life had been like up there, where there was snow all year on the mountain tops and people spoke Belgian.

'I'm French,' one boy, Tony, said, laughing.

'You ain't fuckin' French,' Andrew told him in a voice that twanged like a wire being snapped. Everything Andrew said hit hard. He was sad, but nobody could see it at that time.

'Course I'm French.' Tony said, enunciating his surname, which sounded French. He didn't care if Andrew or anybody else believed him.

I liked that about Tony – that he didn't really care – and he smiled and laughed, and was laughed at by the gang he had arrived with from his primary school. They laughed at him, but he was still part of their gang. They walked home together, through the Town Park, which opened out just beyond the school boundary. There was nothing they had to explain to each other. They understood who was in their gang, and Tony was a part of it even though they laughed at him. Perhaps it was because he laughed at himself that they liked him. Even the big brothers of the boys in my class laughed at Tony, and he laughed back, sometimes nervous when it was Neil's brother Dennis, who usually only laughed to mock and seemed embarrassed to laugh when there was no victim.

'I can be French if I want,' Tony told Andrew.

'You're a right prat you are,' Andrew's voice would twang, a slight rural lilt lingering in his tone. 'You're a right prat. You ain't French,' he insisted.

'Come on please,' Tony would exclaim with mock protest, adopting an air of fake pomposity, before breaking into a smile and laughing, while Andrew scowled, unable to laugh, resentful at Tony's jocular attitude, almost hurt by it – that ability to laugh, that sign that Tony had something that he didn't have.

I hoped Tony was French. Perhaps there was another outsider there, though I knew he was only joking about where he might have come from.

'He might be French,' I told Andrew, the son of the teacher coming out in me. 'You don't know.'

'Fuck off 'uband. Snobby little prat.'

'Bu' 'e might be.'

'Just fuck off.'

Then I was afraid.

Andrew was shorter than me, skinny and pale, with long hair like we all had. But I was afraid of him, and went quiet. Nobody cared about Tony's name. What mattered was his fantasy, the vague hint of a world outside. They knew Tony better than I did. They knew he lived in Rivermill, near the Sports Centre, with his mum and his dad and his twin sister and his two younger brothers. They knew he didn't come from France, and knew that there was nothing more to his life than there was to their own.

I went quiet, wanting to stay out of Andrew's way. Whatever he might think of me, or might say, I was nothing. In my own mind I was nobody – I was none of what he said, nor anything else. But to him I must have seemed to have it all. I sat on the edge of groups because I was a snobby prat; I ate my food at a table where I sat with boys who made up a landscape that Andrew hoped belonged to him, but on which I imposed myself when it suited me; I had so much confidence I could be a part of whatever I wanted, or so he thought.

'An' yer old man, a teacher an' all. Cocky prat.'

Tony laughed.

The other Andrew in my class laughed too. I could see he was clever, but he only showed it when he was manipulating people. He could have conversations, but was one of the gang, and never wanted to show how clever he was. I didn't know why I thought he was clever. It was just a feeling. But he coaxed his namesake, pushed him, found it funny that he said provocative things to me – the teacher's son – and swung between malicious laughter and stone-faced menace. He saw the fun of forcing me to prove myself. He knew I knew nobody, and perhaps could see that I had resigned myself to needing to be a part of something.

'You gotta fight 'im. You gotta' do it. Yer gonna do it. You ain't gonna stand for that,' he told me.

'Don't wanna,' I said.

For weeks he pushed me, as autumn turned to winter.

I started coughing badly, then rasping and feeling nauseous when I coughed. The cough went on for weeks. Mum took me to the doctor, but he said it was just a bad cough, though my lungs felt as though they were full of stones that were crashing around inside my chest. My throat would dry, and in the cold sheeting rain of the empty winter playground I would always be outside after lunch when I felt my cough coming on. It was only when I was outside that I knew where to run to when that dryness hit my throat and I would rattle a rasping cough and then vomit, nowhere to hide, hoping no-one had seen me.

'So, when yer gonna fight him then?' Andrew whispered, almost intimately, on a wet, grey morning in late November 1974.

We were making small boats in the woodwork room, all the boys in my class making the same boats. Before us, other classes had made these boats. They were six inches long, had three indentations where the cargo lay, and a funnel.

The woodwork room was warm and smelled of sawdust. I liked it there. It felt safe, having the smell of a place where fine things were made. We had one of the boats at home. It lay on the rim of the bath, painted green by Michael. He had made it the previous year when he started at the school and had stood where I was standing.

112

I imagined him standing where I was standing. I saw the boat beside the bath at home, thought of home, and wondered where my dad was in the school – somewhere a long way away, where he couldn't see or hear me.

"s gotta be today. I'll write that yer gonna fight 'im.'

Neil and Stephen joined him.

'Chicken. Yer gonna be chicken?' Neil said, cackling with laughter, his rolls of flab swinging slightly around his chest and belly.

'You can beat him,' said Stephen, slightly red-faced.

The warmth of the woodwork room turned to stifling heat, the smell of the sawdust becoming sickening. My throat dried, their eyes on me – on me, as if I mattered. As if I mattered.

'Yeah. Alright.'

'Right,' said the Andrew who had been urging me to fight, grinning wide. With a pencil he wrote on a piece of wood shaving that I would fight. He handed the note to my rival, and then told him what the illegible note said.

The big brothers were there, at the bottom of a muddy slope that ran down from the playground's metal fence and onto the playing field. Just beyond a line of trees was the Town Park. Perhaps I could run to the house in the park where Mum and Dad's friend Joan had lived before she had moved to Portugal. By chance she might be passing, somewhere far off in the distance, where I could see the chestnut trees we used to cycle beneath on Sunday afternoons from our house in Primrose Field, Dad at the front, then Michael and Paul and me, then Mum, all together, rolling fast down slopes, until the end of the day when we turned to go home and closed the door behind us and sat at our kitchen table for a supper of tomato soup as day became night and the terror grew inside me of what might happen in school next day.

He hit me hard, once only, on the side of the head, with hate in his eyes and anger in his look of a kind that I had never known. My throat turned to bone as I felt the rattling in my lungs and the burning heat that had flowed through my veins each time that cough shook me. I watched the big brothers, heard them laugh and jeer, and I ran, up the mud slope towards the trees that marked the boundary of the school, where the cough turned my belly upside down and I stood weak and empty as kids watched.

*

'Yer gottit in yer?'

Cold rain drifted across the mound beside the swings.

'Ain't yer?'

Deena was laughing loud.

'Leave 'im alone,' Polly told her, awkward about intervening, not wanting to give too much.

'Ain't yer gottit in yer?' she went on.

'Listen to 'er. What the fuck's it gotta worry you for, any road?' Polly asked her.

'Bet yer ain't gottit in yer?' she screeched, her broad smile revealing her mouthful of big teeth.

'Naa.'

'Wha'? Yer ain't gottit in yer? Oy, Hube ain't gottit in 'im. Yer ain't gottit in yer? Oy, Hube ain't gottit in 'im.'

'Shut yer fuckin' row,' Polly told her, as Deena walked off to tell his sister.

'Oi, Hube ain't gottit in 'im.'

'Really?'

' 'e admitted it. Oy, who else ain't gottit in 'em?'

'Do shut yer row,' said Mick.

'Mark's gottit in 'im,' she assured everybody, looking at Polly, using his real name, the only one of them who did.

'How d'jer know that then?' Steve asked, laughing at her. She grinned, red-faced.

'I told yer to shut yer row,' Polly told her through clenched teeth, punching her arm as she tittered and giggled and blushed and gabbled words to which nobody was listening anymore.

I wondered when everybody would turn to look at me again. I waited for them all – Polly, Mick, Steve, Shat – to tell me they had somewhere else to go, that I was too young to go with them, now that I had admitted something about myself. They wouldn't tell me that it was because I didn't have it in me, though that would be the reason.

But instead, the rain became heavier. Nothing was said, and everybody drifted away to their homes.

'Le's go, Hube,' said Polly, and we walked past his house and down towards the cricket pitch. 'D'jer know 'ow to wank?' he said, in a matter-of-fact way, no hint of anything. 'Yer can either 'old yer thumb and finger round it, or yer kinda stick yer prick in between all yer fingers, an' do it like that,' he said, demonstrating the two methods by contorting his fingers. 'But yer do it too much and yer prick'll swell up like a balloon.'

'Yeah. Right,' I said, as if perhaps half hinting at something I might already know. But I didn't want to talk more, in case he realised that I hadn't known what Deena had meant when she asked me whether I had it in me.

We walked past the tin-roofed shack where, during the summer, the cricket scores were hung up in big white numbers, and saw a boy with long hair sitting on the corrugated roof staring out from among the lime tree branches that overhung the rusting iron and peeling paint.

'Fuckin' weirdo, that boy Tim. Right fuckin' weirdo.'

We looked at the boy, his dark complexion staring out from the trees. He lived near Mum and Dad's friend Philip. I knew him, I suppose. I had been to his house. His dad owned a shop where one warm Saturday morning Dad and I had bought the table and chairs we sat at every day in our house. I wondered if he remembered that he knew me. We walked on in the rain.

When we reached my house Polly said he was going further on to see somebody else, somebody from his school who lived around the corner. He didn't suggest I go with him. I watched him walk away, wondering if he would come back.

It was still raining when they knocked on our front door as evening was falling. He was with a boy whose long blonde hair was spiked on the top. He was wearing a long denim coat, and on his feet, half hidden by flapping flared jeans, he wore cream coloured platform shoes. His voice was drowsy, as if he had just woken up. As he stood there I noticed he scratched his cheeks with the knuckles of fingers whose nails had been well bitten.

I don't know why I noticed these things about him. Perhaps it was because he stood there with Polly on the doorstep of our house as if he had stepped off one of the record covers whose fantasy world we all secretly hoped we might one day wake up in. He must have been to London, down a side street, to basements where people didn't say much but just stared and had long hair and smoked in cold rooms near deserted parks where rusting bikes were chained to railings and curtains were half-closed across dark windows. That's where he must have been to buy his long coat and his platform shoes, because you couldn't buy things like that on our High Street. You had to go a long way, to places that only a few people knew about.

He strolled as we walked in the rain, me and Polly in our Dr Marten boots, our jeans and denim jackets emblazoned with 'The Hammers'. We were short beside the boy with his high shoes, who strolled, set the pace, and didn't care about walking fast.

The rain poured, hair turning lank. With a hand the boy carefully brushed the drops that clung to the spikes of hair on the top of his head, then patted the spikes so they were all set neatly in place.

Polly mocked himself for not having long hair.

'Right fuckin' prat, me. Had all me 'air cut off 'cos I was gonna be a skin'ead, just before the 'ole fuckin' world started growin' it long.'

He had painted his room since I had last been in it. For a few months his grandfather had been to live in his house, and Polly had been obliged to share his room.

'Can't stand the old man. Lies in fuckin' bed fartin' all the time, tellin' me 'ow to run mi life. Ain't even mi fuckin' grandad really.'

I wondered what he meant by that, but didn't ask, and he never told me that he and his sister were adopted,

117

as I learned it years later from somebody else. When his grandfather had moved out to live in an old people's home, Polly and his dad had transformed the room. Now it was purple, and had a multicoloured wavy line which flowed like a ribbon circling the walls.

He closed the curtains and switched on a coloured light and laughed at the gloom.

'Fuckin' psychedelic,' he said, putting a record on the turntable.

When I got to know the blond haired boy better he said he was changing his name to Rick, because the name he had been born with was no good for the rock star he was planning to become. He stood in the gloom of Polly's purple room and moved his head from side to side, eyes shut, his long hair swinging across his shoulders as the mesmerising music roared form the turntable, a scratch on the record clicking in time.

I sat against the wall in a corner, on the bare floor of the room.

I had no records at home. My mum and dad listened to classical music and folk songs, and sometimes one of the people my dad worked with came to our house and played his guitar and sang, and sometimes Dad played on a big recorder or on his violin with the daughter of his friend Philip. I hated to hear them play. I was jealous that they could do it so easily and smile as if it was natural. I wished they would stop because I hated so much to hear them, in their ease, standing there enjoying themselves while all I could do was listen and applaud when they had finished, and feel jealous and angry that nobody realised how much I wanted to be able to stand up in front of everybody and sing and act and create something that was beautiful but that I didn't know how and didn't know anybody who could show me and didn't know who to ask.

Polly changed the record and the thunderous screech of a guitar swept through the room and a pained voice yelled a story about somebody burning a building to the ground and smoke pouring out across the water of a lake.

Rick shook his head even more, his long denim coat swaying from side to side, his platform shoes tapping the floor.

Polly looked awkward. The fantasy was just a laugh for him. No need to take it too seriously. I sat silently in the corner, watching the two, aware that I had been silent for too long, seeing only the distance between me and them. I moved towards the music. The noise was ugly, but I didn't know how to make beautiful sounds, like my dad and Philip's daughter, or like the man who came sometimes to play his guitar at our house. But if I couldn't do things that were fine and clever and beautiful and which made people listen, I would sit in dark rooms until my body hummed and I was deafened by the noise in my head. These were the real sounds. This was the sound on the street, our street, where we walked in our jeans, skinny kids going somewhere. Ugly was real. That's what I would say. That's how I would be real, by echoing the words of songs that were raw and hard and tough. I would be tough. I would live on the streets as buildings burned. I would live under the sun or in the driving rain, a survivor, just like the tough men in the songs, screaming, pained, soaked, burned, meeting strange women.

I sat in the corner as Polly turned off the record player.

Rick left and Polly said he was going to see his Uncle Gary and that I could come with him if I wanted. We stepped into the wet darkness of another gathering autumn, as the time I was supposed to be home passed and I didn't care because I could never be what was wanted of me, could never do fine, beautiful things, so I would walk the streets at night and find my own way.

We swaggered past closed shops, boys on the town, on our streets, our territory, which we would defend, though we didn't know how or against whom. If somebody passed us they would shatter our illusions with a word. But we wouldn't hear and wouldn't know whether what they saw was more or less real than our swaggering and our tough words.

Gary looked tough. He was young, had long fair hair, and lived in his flat with his stylish wife. Polly said they had it all. They lived on an estate I had only ever seen from a distance. They had everything their lives needed – a warm flat, a big colour television, a soft settee and armchairs. They had made a home.

Gary let us in, though his sister-in-law and her husband were there, and just turning up on their doorstep at night didn't seem right. We were breaking into their world. They had things to talk about that only people in their twenties talked about. I wished we hadn't gone there, and sat silent and awkward until Gary's sister-in-law whispered to Gary's wife and pointed at me and his wife asked me if I was alright.

'Yeah,' I said, embarrassed because I couldn't think of anything else to say. What was there to say? What could I tell them about myself that would be worth saying? Only lies, and Polly would know. Perhaps I could tell them that I was only living in this town for a while, that I was born among mountains in the north and had family all over the world, even on the prairies of America, and that I had an aunt who sometimes sat in cafés with famous writers when she was in Paris, which was where my mum used to live before she had to escape from France because of the war.

'You sure you're alright? You're really quiet.'

'Sorry.'

'No need to be sorry. Just wanna make sure, tha's all.'

'Yer don' fuckin' say much,' Polly said, after Gary had closed the door behind us and we were walking back into the night. 'Bit fuckin' weird, you sittin' there like a bleedin' dummy.'

'Yeah. Sorry.'

'Must o' scared yer. They ain't gonna bite yer 'ead off yer know.'

'No. I know. Jus', yer know, didn't know what to say, 'as all.'

'Well, yer don' have to ge' all clever an' serious. Jus' 'ave a laugh.'

'Yeah, yer right.'

'Anyway, I'm off. See yer,' and he crossed the road at the end of the High Street, and I ran through the orange streetlamp light beneath the looming of the great trees that swayed autumn naked against the ink blue-black of a sky aglow with the cut glass of white clouds that drifted across the silver watching gaze of the gaping moon.

*

October nights were always the worst, when summer was still a memory. As the cold bit, friendship came or went in the tone of parting words. The whole world seemed caught in the last words uttered, in a call to follow a friend home off the street, in the closing of a door, in the silence of being left on the emptiness of the street, no territory, no gang, only the steel chains of the children's swings squeaking faintly in a cold gust that rushed with a shiver through the bushes beside the pavements. Then the silence brought the unravelling of bonds, of that vague hint of something shared, of whatever it was that connected us that was more than just words. The silence of the time after nightfall, when the last cars disappeared, was the time when the emptiness drowned our land, when the land that we thought had become our territory – for which we might fight, might even die – stared gaping at our tiny steps and sent us into our homes.

Why go home? Why run from our streets? We could make fires and crouch gathered beside the flames beneath the ancient trees whose shadows the moonlight carved on the still black waters of Dick's Pond.

'Loadsa wood under the Scouts hut. Just lyin' there. Easy to nick,' somebody had said, a week before Guy Fawkes.

We built the bonfire with the wood they stole early one evening. I felt that I had let them down, not being there with them when they had taken it. I had been too late back from my school to join them. The following evening we walked to the playing field where our fire had stood, to find it lying in ruins, wood strewn across the grass, the Scouts having destroyed it – we assumed – when they retrieved the wood after realising where it had gone.

'Right fuckin' wankers. Fuckin' Boy Scouts. Right bunch o' poofs.'

At 'jewboy's' shop on the High Street, where kids of any age could buy single cigarettes, which the owner handed over to them in paper bags, we bought bangers and a handful of rockets. We walked across the playing field and through the line of trees to the field of long grass beside the Scouts' hut. In the darkness, the cold night air carrying the vague smell of coal fires, the squawking of bats the only sound that broke into the rush of cold wind in the trees, we crouched low in the grass, put the rockets in milk bottles and pointed them at the hut.

The Scouts were talking loudly inside. The bangers were lit and hurled at the hut. I watched as my friends launched the barrage, and as the noise inside fell silent the rockets fizzed and roared, a torrent of blazing sparks ripping through the darkness and crashing into the wooden walls of the building.

'Fuckin scarper. They're comin' after us.'

We ran, some through the line of trees, me and Shat through the tall grass of the field and towards a long embankment which rose up in the shadow of a wood.

We were the only two they chased.

We heard them behind us, voices, as we ran into the empty cold void of the darkness. The darkness would save us. The darkness, the black void, would be where we could hide. Nobody can be seen in the darkness. We could slip back into the emptiness from which we had come. Back and back, into instinct, back into light and dark, into nothingness, into a dream of disappearance, into the voice inside saying that if we fled far enough we would reach the very start, the time before time.

My throat and lungs and heart rattled. I rasped the scent of lush damp grass as I slipped to the ground and drank and tasted the earth that would drain my shivering frightened limbs into its currents and hide me from the shadows that were gathered in the lighted doorway.

I should have run into the wood.

But I lay, too afraid to move.

An engine started. Then another. Two motorbikes, their beams scanning the field, lingered. Then the beams glared across the damp grass, sprayed the field with light, and roared towards me.

Run. Run fast. There was still time. Run into the darkness which had swallowed Shat as I had slipped to the ground. Run.

But it was too late. The lights were nearly upon me. I couldn't bear to run, to have the lights at my back where I could not see them, drawing closer like claws, like teeth. I was in the soft, cold, damp embrace of the earth, a shadow among all the others, a bump on the ground which the motorcyclists would steer around. They wouldn't see me, but would speed past without noticing me lying there. They would miss me. They wouldn't hit me. The lights would pass.

My breath stopped, the lights glaring at the ground on either side of where I lay as the engines roared so close I felt the exhaust and saw the drivers' faces stark, clear as day, as they eyed the black trees I knew lay behind me.

They circled, feet away. Then they were gone, back to the hut, their red lights glowing, then dark.

Then silence.

A silhouette stood in the doorway of the hut. For minutes he was there. Then slowly he began walking towards me. Now I must run. But I was gripped by the damp earth I had made warm, my body a part of it, gripped by an earth that had always been so kind. There were names for what the world had been, the woods, the towns, and places on maps. Now it was a cruel, dead place. It was rock under a cold night sky, footsteps on thick grass drawing closer, closer.

'Right you. Get up.'

A police car arrived. Two of my friends were sitting on the back seat.

I sat between them. In our car I never sat in the middle, always next to the window.

We drove through the night along our streets. There had been snow there once, when I had followed my mum, or was it my dad, on the first frozen day at my primary school. Would the dog behind the gate bark as we passed? I caught a glimpse of the cricket pitch. The smart boy and the girl were gone. I wish I could see them. I'll be late home. My mum will be worried, wondering where I am. My mum will be worrying about where I am. Can I go home now?

'Mum.'

'Hello darling. Where have you been?'

She was sitting or standing out of view as I went in through the kitchen door, the policeman behind me.

'The police are here.'

'What? What on earth have you been doing?'

Would she have understood if I had told her? How would I have sounded to the policeman, as he stood in our kitchen shattering all that was safe in our home just by standing there? My fault. I was bad. All I had to do was admit it. I was bad, for some reason or another. I had not stolen the wood. I hadn't thrown any fireworks. I had only watched. Is that why I was bad – because I had just watched?

I saw the glare of lights in my eyes, roaring towards me where I had lain on the cold earth.

What was my story – my true story? Nobody would believe me if I told them. So I told nobody, and so never believed it myself, and can only think it now, though it became a part of the myth my friends created for that time and talked of for some time afterwards, that if one of the motorbikes had hit me where I lay, that night would have been my last.

*

On 4 February 2013 09:13, Mark Huband <█> wrote:
Dear Mark
It was pretty magical meeting up after all these years. Something rare and special, and I really look forward to meeting again soon; lots more to talk about.
See you very soon
Mark

From: Mark P █@gmail.com>
Date: Tue, 5 Feb 2013 15:35:34 +0000
To: Mark Huband<█>
Subject: Re: Friday afternoon
Dear Mark,

My head has been buzzing with childhood memories since our meeting. I got back quite early from the gathering I attended on Friday evening and, although a little tipsy by then, started reading your book. I got through about a third of it, did the same on Saturday evening and finished it on Sunday evening. Wow! My mind is spinning with memories. To be quite honest I thought of little else all weekend. I had forgotten how crawl children can be. When I asked you what we were 'in to' all those years ago well, now I know; we were just trying to survive and be excepted by each other. Obviously, when you came along, I had a well forged place in our little gang and can see now how difficult it was for you trying to fit in with us estate kids and how brave you were to keep turning up. I must say, I am rather proud to have been the one that invited you in and, at times, defended you. I'd forgotten how gobby Deanna could be. You are obviously a bit of a romantic and that is how I see myself. It's probably, although I didn't know it at the time, what I saw in you back then and the same goes for Rik. I love the seen when I go off and come back to you house a while later with Rik. It's almost like I was saying, 'look Hube, look what I've found - this is the future.' The other boys - Shat, Mick, Steve, etc, were not and never were interested in breaking out into a world that had nothing to do with our parents. I was quite obsessed with this exciting cultural shift and continued to be so throughout my life. To us you were this shy, slightly nervous, even sometimes frightened posh kid, but at the time we never understood the courage that it took for you to be hanging out with us. And of course, in our own ways, we were often frightened ourselves: I wouldn't have wanted to have had to fight Shat, even though he was two years my junior, and certainly wouldn't have liked to fight Steve. The passage about the Irish workers was great and so to was the part about the race track that we made in your garden. I was deeply ashamed of the part about wrecking the apple tree in your garden, though, I doubt if this was planed. It was probably just a game that got out of hand as we became over-excited. It probable started out with one of us throwing a rotten apple at somebody else and then all hell would have broken lose. You Dad had a great deal of patience.

Mark (or should I say Hube) I still have lots to say about it all, (there are a couple of very minor details that do not ring quite true, but they aren't important and I will run them past you when we next meet, which I look forward to, but will sign off for now. Very well done Sir.

p.s Being an avid reader it is very exciting reading a story of which I am a part. Exciting and rather surreal. You write beautifully, by the way. Your style does put me in mind of Laurie Lee which is no bad thing.

See you soon - Mark, or should I say - Polly.

On 10 February 2013 19:18, Mark Huband <■> wrote:

Dear Mark

At points in the past few weeks I have felt that I am being taken to a place which doesn't exist in anywhere but my memories and imagination, and which had perhaps never existed except in the way in which I remember it. But your memories of those times – specifically, the ways in which you have been inviting me back there, by talking and writing about what went on so long ago, and your response to my making contact – have been a confirmation that I wasn't just imagining things or romanticising or doing anything more than looking back and trying to follow the trail wherein lie the clues as to how a character develops, how a boy becomes a man, how a son becomes a person free to entwine what he inherits with what he then goes on to experience, alone in the world.

Your last comments – about the memoir of which you have read the parts with which I left you – are the first time I have ever in my life heard – as it were – a 'witness' speak. It's hard to explain how moving it is to hear of the memories and perceptions of the one person who was in a position to know; I never thought I would hear any kind of account of how it was I was perceived, what were the currents and relationships and fears and hopes that were swirling around us, how it was that such young people were taking in so much, and storing so much inside that is still there, perhaps awaiting a moment like this for it to be articulated.

For me, also, it has been made all the more magical by the way in which you describe what you remember; you use a different language to the one that I remember you using, which is why our conversation when we met and the notes we have exchanged, are so overwhelming. The ways you have remembered and explained and reflected have authenticated my own imaginings and fleeting memories and – even though I have written hundreds of pages – my own writings (I am looking forward to being corrected, where I got things wrong). For me to be remembered in the ways that you have described – for you to sense the risks and uncertainties which dogged my childhood – perhaps jogged by what I have written and what you have now read, is momentous for many reasons, as I never imagined I would ever hear you speak of those times in the ways and with the impact you have. Why so? Because I never imagined that we would meet again.

Perhaps you would like to know what happened next – the memoir as it unfolded. In the meantime we have, as you say, much much more to talk about, and I am really looking forward to meeting again to do that.

Mark

From: Mark P [mailto:█@gmail.com]
Sent: 18 February 2013 17:50
To: Mark Huband
Subject: Re: Friday afternoon
Dear Mark,

sorry to take so long to reply, I have had a busy week because my wife caught a bug so looking after my daughter was my responsibility alone and it was just about all I had time for. That was a really interesting email. And of course, I can't wait to read more of your memoirs. I can see how those day in Chippingfield link up with your future as a journalist and the precarious situations that you had to face. By the way, I Googled Charles Taylor and read up a small amount about him. He must have been a scary character to have to deal with.

I have been thinking about it all a lot of late. It's a shame that we got into that spot of bother in Sawbridgeworth that time and our friendship cut short over something so silly, something that, for us to play a part in, was out of character for us both. Believe it or not, I feel that I could have done with your influence a little longer back then. I think that I valued education and intellectualism, but, though this sounds a bit daft, didn't know at the time. Anyway, it was great meeting up after all these years. Next time you come to London we must meet up again. Just let me know when.

See you soon - Mark

On 11 March 2013 17:13, Mark Huband <■> wrote:

Dear Mark

It is an incredibly perceptive link that you make, that between the me that you met one summer evening in 1973, and the me who 16 years later went off to write about wars. You are the first person – other than me – who has ever made the connection; it really is amazing me, how much we have been able to identify the faintest signs of characteristics evident all those years ago, which went on to become unfolding stories.

Maybe it's good that this immense number of years has passed, until now when we have met again; perhaps it's what has given the subconscious time to turn over and over, to bring things to the point they are now at. In so many ways I am experiencing – for the one and only time in my life, I am sure of it – the rewriting of the past, because all these comments and observations mean that all that seemed to be the past is having inevitably to be seen in a different light.

I can't wait to meet up again. It would be great to meet in Harlow, in your mum's kitchen. How about it? If you can bear to, I would love to send you the chapters of my memoir which follow what you have already read (there is also what precedes what you have, but that may be less interesting for you). Maybe I could print it out and post it?

When shall we meet? How about the week after Easter?

Mark

On 22 March 2013 14:59, Mark P <■@gmail.com> wrote:

Hi Mark,

Sorry to take so long to answer your email, I've been very busy of late and, believe it or not, I'm always the last one to get to use the computer in our house - what with my daughter playing games on c-beebies and my wife, who paints most evenings, using the computer for reference.

I'm looking forward to reading more of you manuscript, like I said before, it very surreal reading something professionally written that you can get quite lost in, almost forgetting that you are one of the characters, and then coming across your own name. It strange though, it gets the heart thumping in a way. Like somebody calling you name in a crowd.

I'm looking forward to our next meeting. To be honest though, I don't facing doing at my Mum's, but you seem to have guessed that. The line in your email "... If you can bear to," is the giveaway, but as soon as you come to London again, let me know and, if it's alright with you, we can meet in a pub again. We must have been in that pub for almost four hours. It sure did fly by.

bye for now - I look forward to our next meet.

kind regards - Mark.

On 22 March 2013 15:44, Mark Huband <█> wrote:

Dear Mark

Great to hear from you. Meeting in a pub would be really good - what about the same one in Hoxton? Would Friday 5 April be good for you?

Really looking forward to it.

Mark

On 26 March 2013 21:02, Mark P <██@gmail.com>
wrote:

Hi Mark,

Friday the fifth is good with me. One o'clock in
Bachas it is then. I look forward to it. I'll probably email
you a day or two before, but will defiantly see you there.
Bye for now - Mark.

*

Red and green flashed in a blur through the wire mesh
that caged the tall frosted glass windows of *Speakeasy*.

By day, within the deep red brick of Victoria
Memorial Hall, people went to vote at election time. The
big double doors onto the street were opened, and the
shoppers on our High Street, neighbours, men going to
work on their bikes, Mongy Joe in his blue Mac who
plodded around the streets with his ageing mum, his
fingers twitching and mouth cackling as he pretended in
vain to be making it with girls, all stood for a while
outside the hall, some wearing rosettes of different
colours, as kids watched from outside wondering what
went on in there, where they were not allowed to go.

Election Day was when neighbours who didn't
look as if they were different would admit that they were
not all the same. They became rivals, on opposite sides of
the world. Would they fight? Who was good and who was
bad? That was all that mattered. That was all that could
matter. Wasn't that right? There was no middle ground
between good and bad. All the troubles we heard about
on the radio would be sorted out after people had voted.
Then the miners would go back to work so we wouldn't

have to take baths by candlelight, and the bombing would stop in Belfast, and everybody would be good.

There was a lady who did good, and who I often saw walking our streets. She was always smart and purposeful. She had a wrinkled face that always had a deep tan – a face that smiled like a politician's, like Barbara Castle's, like somebody about to shake your hand and ask you for your vote, if you looked old enough. She had a huge pile of hair, sculpted like a walnut whip, but which never moved in the wind. She looked as though she must be important, perhaps a councillor. I wondered if I was supposed to know who she was when she walked past me in the street. She was usually pushing old women in wheelchairs or chatting with other smart women outside *Bardot's Beauty Box*, the hairdresser's salon that was always bathed in strong smells that oozed out of the open door through which I could see women in the afternoon perched primly under big cones. They were always covered in towels and reading shiny magazines as if it was normal to be sitting like that outside their homes, just off the street where anything could happen. Did they know that anything could happen? Something bad could happen, and they would be in their towels, trapped inside their cones, unable to escape.

But the women didn't seem to notice that the street was like that. Perhaps I should tell the lady who pushed the wheelchairs, whose blue rosette caught the wind at election time when she held leaflets and a clipboard outside Victoria Memorial Hall and smiled at me with what I hoped was sympathy. I wanted her to see that I wasn't really bad, just curious, as I peered past her to where grown-ups were voting.

'Oh no, you can't go in there. Not for a few more years yet,' she told me, her smile fixed, guarding the democracy that lay inside beyond the arch and the big wooden doors, and which I might damage, if I went inside and upset the tables.

Then, at night, when the hall became *Speakeasy*, the woman was gone without leaving a trace. The big doors were closed and the political rivals were far away in the warmth of their homes, as we fell silent in the rain at the side door, where a man sat smoking behind a table, shouting over the music to ask us how old we were.

He hardly cared that we were lying.

Boys wading on high-heeled shoes like Rick's stood sharing cigarettes in the hallway, staring through long hair, watching us for signs. We were the gang that had a story, who had seen danger in the night, who had nearly escaped from the cops at the Scouts' hut but had then been cornered and were now being watched. Our futures might be harsh and we might not even survive, because now the world was against us and we could only live from day to day. We might not get home tonight.

We moved on, into the main hall.

From a raised platform, where there were pool tables, and boys stood leaning against a red railing, we looked out over the near-empty dance floor.

My friends dispersed among kids from their school who I didn't know. Polly, in his platform shoes and high waistband trousers, stood among the pool tables then went down the steps and onto the dance floor with Deena. They were the only couple dancing, holding each other, kissing hard, their eyes screwed tight shut in the gloom of the coloured lights that turned and blinked out of two banks of bulbs which stood on either side of the turntable, where older kids were selecting the records.

The songs filled the cavernous room: '*My baby love my baby love…,Take me in your arms, rock your baby…I'm gonna make you a star…*'

Deena was quiet after her kiss with Polly.

A boy had a packet of ten cigarettes.

'Gotta snout?' Polly asked. He knew the boy. 'One for Hube?'

'Fuck off, scrounger. He can get 'is fuckin' own.'

'Mean cunt. 'ere Hube,' and Polly handed me the cigarette he had scrounged from the boy, who took a lighter from his pocket.

'Ain't givin' yer another.'

' 'ark at 'im. Mean little git.'

The boy was holding a flame to the cigarette, whose damp filter had already started to sting my lips. He held the flame close and I sipped at the filter and felt the burst of hot smoke surge down my throat as I swallowed hard.

'Don't fuckin' swallow it.'

' 'e don' even know 'ow to do it,' the boy told Polly, who took the cigarette from between my fingers.

'Look. Yer breathe. Just like normal,' he said, two perfect lines of smoke flowing from his nostrils. 'Reckon I'll have the rest,' and he walked back to Deena. They went back down the steps and onto the dance floor, where Rick was now standing close to the speakers, eyes staring up to the high roof beams, foot tapping the wooden floorboards, his long denim coat swaying as the music grew louder, guitars pushing aside the high happy voices of the singers that yer Mum played at family parties. Now, those 'summer day' sounds were fallen into the night and the rain and the cold that we could feel inside the red brick hall. The sound now was loud. Women didn't sing the sounds we had in our heads. Only men could sing of the place we were in – fast guitars, drums, lost words, *down down deeper and down*. Nobody cared what was said, just as long as it was loud and fast.

'Ca' on Hube,' somebody said.

I followed.

Rain swept across the road outside, through vast trees that lined a green. Beside the building was an alley that fell away into the dark wet blackness along the length of the garden ends. Some boys stood in the shadow of the wall, out of the glare of the street-corner lamp.

'Want some?' A boy passed a rolled cigarette to another, who took a long draw.

'Wan' it?' he said to me.

'Naa.'

The smell mingled with the odour of the leaves in the rain.

The boys passed the cigarette between them. I liked that – sharing, from lip to lip. Inside the hall they had stared at us. Now, I imagined for a moment that they had no idea where I had come from. In the silence that became all that I would be remembered for, among the kids I knew during those years, I heard myself say that whatever they could see in the rain of the dark alley, they didn't know anything about me. They didn't know where I had come from.

'Don' wannit?' said one of the boys. 'Ain't never 'ad a spliff?

'Alright,' and I took it and drew hard, just like breathing, and within seconds I was away from there, the pelting rain warm and the black night a soft breath, the voices murmuring gently, nobody looking at me, nobody looking, just strangers talking softly in the darkness, the strangers I was among, people whose names I didn't even know, passing a spliff from lip to lip. I can be among strangers, I thought – people who know nothing about me, and who won't ask, but who will share a spliff in the wet darkness of the alley.

Mum woke me before I had fallen into the depths of sleep, and I heard the rain flapping at my bedroom window.

'I really think you should stop this job. It really distresses me that you don't get enough sleep,' she said, as my eyes fell shut over breakfast.

I cannot remember how I replied. But I can see how it pained her to see me tired, cycling out into the rain at just after 6.30 in the morning to deliver newspapers. But I had to be there – cold on the empty streets, some money in my pocket, the newspaper round something that was mine, something that I knew.

I cycled down long empty roads that only months beforehand had been forbidden worlds – the land of unknown gangs and strange kids who might throw stones, or worse.

But in the early morning light, when the curtains of the town were still closed, car windows sleeping blind with the glitter of night rain and mist lingering over the land, there seemed no danger, except at one house, where there was never light or sound.

It was a big house set back from a road lined with wartime bungalows. Tall trees kept the land around it in constant shadow. In what might once have been a garden, wrecked cars lay in pieces amid the junk of years – rusting prams, wooden crates, old bonfires soaked by days and nights of rain.

The front door was at the top of some steps. A shiver always passed through me as my route reached the gap in the hedge that marked the driveway to that house. The curtains had been closed for weeks, through autumn and into winter, up to that Christmas holiday in 1974, when my pockets filled with tips from the people who had bothered to get up early and press their loose change into my hand and wish me a happy Christmas and thank me for always getting the right newspaper to them each morning: 'Good an' early. Nice an' early.'

I stepped off my bike and let it fall to the ground then bounded up the steps to the front door of the silent house. As I quietly lifted the flap on the letterbox and was about to ram the newspaper through quickly before turning and rushing away, the door burst open. I slipped back a step, staring into the gloom inside at a long-haired man with a beard who stood staring at me from the doorway. I dropped the newspaper and was frozen to the step, staring, waiting for him to grab me, pull me inside and slam the door behind me.

'Thanks,' he said. 'Happy Christmas.' He held out his hand and I picked up the newspaper then leaned forward to hand it to him from the distance of the lower step. 'This is for you,' he said, and held out a fifty pence piece, the biggest tip and I had ever had.

'Thanks a lot,' I rasped, throat dry with fear, handing him the newspaper. 'Thanks a lot,' I repeated. I wanted to apologise, as he turned away and gently closed the door, and I stood watching as the winter sun melted the last of the mist and I rode quickly home, the strange world of my early mornings suddenly jolted into the timetable of uniform and books and school.

*

For weeks, kids had asked me if it was true that I had run away from the boy who had hit me, after one punch. Mostly I shrugged and said nothing, embarrassed, and my cough would come back and I would wonder whether I was going to vomit.

I stopped following Andrew and Neil and Stephen and sat nowhere in particular in class. I wondered for how long I could slip away from the gangs that moved together, and where it was I could slip away to, in that place which became the smell of polished corridors. I knew that if I was not part of a group I was nothing – an outcast, reminded of his isolation by the odour of the changing rooms, where I hated to strip naked as we changed into clothes for sports, where voices mingled with the steam from wet clothes as the December sky ground like stone over the cold empty world.

Each morning I arrived back in the smell that told me where and who I was. I was just one more body there, and when the Christmas holiday finally came and the door closed behind me as I ran to my bike and sped fast away from that hot place and out into the cold and away along the road behind the factories, I knew that the further I got away the more pure the air would be. I was sure of it, that only in our house could I breathe, where my mum and my dad made magic, and all I had to do was believe in it and want to let myself believe in it. I passed my friends' homes, passed the mound where we had so often gathered, which now was silent and dark in the light of the winter evening. I passed the cricket field, and went down the path where bare twigs hung over shards of glass that gashed out like savage teeth to guard the rich privacy that lay behind the wall. I wheeled my bike past a silent gate where a dog sometimes growled and barked ferociously at anybody who was passing.

The Christmas lights were on in our neighbour's house, and in all the windows I could see trailing off into the distance. Everybody was preparing for the festival, making the same food, decorating their homes, sharing something. I imagined faces smiling in the dusk light of the market square where I once walked with my dad on Christmas Eve. Was it there that I had listened and watched, heard and seen the clamour and colour, and floated among the kind voices wishing well as if everybody knew the same thing? I dreamed I was there with my dad again, among the voices, buying fresh fruit and the last few things Mum needed to make the magic we would slip into when we woke to find parcels at the feet of our beds, our running feet breaking the silence of the time before dawn as we burst, my brothers and I, into the sitting room which was still cold with night, to find we were somewhere else, on another stage, in a dream of colour and light, laughter on the faces of Mum and Dad as they watched their family, safe, hidden away with our secrets as we tore at the wrapping of presents we were never quite certain we deserved.

At first light we feasted on breakfast and our house was filled with the singing of angels, delicate, fragile, praying hands in reverence to the babe lying in the manger painted on the record sleeve against the landscape

141

we would only see and hear on that morning of the year when all was happy.

That wonderful, luxurious feeling lasted until we heard the sound of the back door being opened, and looked into the face of my grandfather.

He strode into our house with gift-wrapped parcels in a well-used plastic bag.

'This one's for you, Ann. And David, here's something we can take back if it's the wrong size. And here's something for you boys,' he would say, as he thrust small brown envelopes at us, which neither Michael nor Paul nor I dared open in front of him, in case doing so made us look greedy.

Then we had a duty to laugh, because this was the season.

'Merry Christmas dear,' my grandmother chimed, and our times stopped as we held our breath, waiting to hear the words that would bind us, the story of us, the tale that had brought us into the same warm room for the festival. My brothers and I held our breaths, listened, and said nothing, as my grandfather stared with an air of disdain intended to discipline foolish children, who of course he knew all about because he was a part of their creation. No, nothing could be hidden from him. Oh no. Who would dare approach him to talk?

Mum's summons to our Christmas table was the magic sound that broke his sinister spell. It was our table, not my grandfather's. Our table, loaded with crisp turkey, steaming vegetables, roasted chestnuts, bacon rolls, delicious sauces, all laid out on the fine white cloth woven with lace sewn by the grandmother I had never known, overlaid with the woven patterns in red and green on the delicate cotton Mum brought out from a secret, special place we would never dare seek to find.

The colours and the richness they gave our table were a secret we could keep from my grandparents.

'Lovely lunch,' my grandmother would say.

'Mmm. Quite good,' my grandfather would add, to make clear that he knew what constituted a satisfactory Christmas lunch.

But they would never know that they were not a part of us. They were eating at a table whose colours and cloths came from Mum's world, across the sea, in France, or from Mum's parents' honeymoon in the Balkans during a distant time of kings and princes. These icons were from a past that was ours, not theirs. These were not our people at all. We were from somewhere else. Could they know, or would it be rude to tell them? Would my grandfather stare viciously through his glasses if we told him that we – Michael and Paul and I – had another family who lived a long way away, in places he had never visited?

'Oh you do, do you? Well, I think you'll find that I have seen rather more of the world than you three. I think you had better remember that there's not much you can tell me about France. Some of us have been going there for rather longer than I dare say you have.'

Then there would be silence, the put-down having had its intended effect, we boys cowed into silence, Mum and Dad the same, the day slipping away from us, as my mind wandered off into thinking about telephoning my friends to see what they had been given for Christmas.

But to have called them would have torn me way from the day that was ours, and which I wanted to be ours alone, with my mum and dad and my brothers. How long could we keep the day to ourselves? We would stay off the street; we would play with the presents Mum and Dad had so carefully wrapped in shining gold paper, our names cut and arranged on the boxes and packages that were ours alone.

But I wonder what my friends had been given? I should just step outside for a moment, into that other world, that life on our streets, and walk towards the mound of earth that was our place, where we could talk as we did, and mention only the presents that were something like the things we ought to have been given. Things I never got. I got other things, from a world of which my friends would never be a part, and which I must leave behind if I were ever to live the life they could live.

'Yeah. Christmas. Yeah. 'salright. Yeah. Got a few things. Nothing special.'

I heard my voice. I heard my voice tell my friends about the day. Then I heard my voice fall silent.

There was no magic in my voice. There was no happiness. No laughter. I imagined they believed me. I talked to make them believe me, that my Christmas Day was nothing special.

I talked in order to sound and be like them.

I talked, and felt the dull pang of the wound I inflicted with my words, as with every sound I uttered I heard the laughter and saw the magic, but could do nothing to suppress the betrayal. It was my mum and dad I betrayed, and I felt it and could do nothing to stop it, as I imagined telling my friends the false story of the day that had begun with laughter and magic and the singing of angels. My friends would not want to hear that story. I wanted to tell them the story I imagined they wanted to hear. Laughter and magic and angels were not a part of that.

*

The sharp cold bit into our smiles as Mum locked the back door and we strode, breath steaming, out into the Boxing Day morning, then stepped into the enveloping mesh of deep voices and laughter, music upstairs, the clatter of plates as the door opened onto the tall, dark house of Mum and Dad's friends Philip and Carla.

'Happy Christmas. Happy Christmas little ducks,' said Carla. She was tall, broad, smiling, and had a deeply tanned face and silver hair. Her eyes always glittered with what might have been tears that would not fall. 'Beautiful hair,' she said, pulling at my long ginger hair, which reached down to my shoulders. 'You must never cut it. It's beautiful, beautiful, long like that,' her strong Dutch accent filling the low dark kitchen where people, all adults, were gathered, drinking wine and sangria, eating off plates painted in dark blues and greens.

Carla had made the plates in a clay oven in an adjoining room that was lined with shelves cluttered with mugs painted with the names of her children, of Philip, of other people who may have been the ones she knew when she was in Holland during the war and had worked secretly for the Dutch Resistance, by whom she had been given the codename 'Carla'. I wanted to see my name on one of the mugs, and the names of my mum and my dad, so that we could see that we were thought about even when we were not there. Then we would know that we had a special place among all the people gathered there, and that we were more a part of the place than the

145

women in kaftans, brightly striped tights and coloured sandals, than the men with long hair who wore leather sports jackets, than the neighbour in the blazer who worked for *The Times*, whose Japanese wife was out of place in her chic business clothes.

Conversation rose like bubbles through water, laughter piercing the air like the sudden sharp cries of birds.

'Lawrence would never have seen it that way,' went a conversation above my head.

'Oh Lawrence Lawrence Lawrence; can't people move on from Lawrence? The man's been given far too much importance. Dirty old sod.'

'Well, really, I don't think that's very fair. He's marvellous.'

'But it's as if nothing worth reading has been written since 1930. Very outdated. What about Henry Miller – much more modern?'

'But Lawrence is very modern in his outlook. Think of *Women In Love*.'

'I'd rather not. All that questioning. I want certainty in a novel. All he ever does is have his women reluctantly submissive, and his men either terribly fey – or macho bastards.'

'Oh come on. That's all rather simplistic. Rupert and Gerald are both far more complex. And think of the world Gudrun and Ursula are struggling to break out of.'

'It's amazing that Yorkshire ever managed to produce anybody like those sisters.'

'That's rather snobbish, isn't it? Anyway, it's Derbyshire not Yorkshire.'

'Who cares? It's all the same. They're all miners.'

'I'm not sure I like that attitude.'

'Oh do come on. More wine?'

'No thank you. Well, perhaps just a little.'

'And where do you teach?'

'Oh, no, I don't teach.'

'So, you're the wife of a teacher. I can always tell. That must be why you have all these views about D.H.Lawrence.'

'Well, I have my own views about D.H.Lawrence.'

'Mmm. Well, I think I'll go and see what's going on upstairs. I hope there's some heating up there – it's a bit nippy down here.'

Upstairs, friends of Philip and Carla's daughters had gathered in the sitting room, where tapestries and shadow puppets from Indonesia hung from the walls. They were the mementoes of where Philip and Carla had begun their life together. Some time in the 1950s they had both taken a ship to Indonesia, he to teach, she to work in a courtroom. They had met on the ship, and fallen in love. Indonesia was the past now. It was their Yorkshire. Their Algeria. Everybody had a place that played on their minds, which became holy, a place that clung to the walls in the glare of the winter sun.

The youngest people there – all of them five or six years older than me – had long curly hair and wore flared jeans, suede desert boots, and multicoloured hooded coats that Carla had made for them. I wanted to be like them, to be bohemian like them, though I didn't know what the word 'bohemian' really meant, though assumed it must describe the men in that room, whose hair reached down their backs and whose bewildered looks and mysterious silence was what I hoped I seemed to have.

I hovered, half with them, wondering if my hair was long enough for me to be seen as a part of their world, wondering what they had that I didn't have, and told one of them the name of a record I had bought with the money I had saved up from my newspaper round.

They all laughed.

'Oh. That's an awful record. They're an awful, noisy bunch.'

'Total crap. Like a bunch of mechanics playing music on bits they tore from a car.'

'You don't really…like it, do you? That kind of music.'

'Umm. Well. Some of it. Some of it's alright.'

'Gawd. It's real caveman stuff.'

'Caveman. I do like that. Caveman. What a great way to describe it.'

They all laughed, their long hair shaking, their pale faces staring out from their world of music and colours and exotic ideas and beautiful explanations which I knew I could share and believe, but which I had missed by being born a few years too late. I imagined that I could step into the past I assumed they had hidden somewhere – a place they cradled in secret, in their rooms, in the theatres where some of them acted, at the pop festivals under the sun that brought the poets and singers and the perfect, beautiful people together. I could be like them. I wasn't really bad or silent. In my mind I was all the things I imagined they were, as they sat in their exotic colours, calm, all-knowing, nothing desperate, a guitar strummed, a song sung, confident fingers at ease gliding over the frets, a clear voice people would love and applaud.

But instead, I froze into silence, embarrassed and out of place, wondering why they laughed at my record.

They all had the same long hair and look of bewilderment as the band members whose photographs were printed on its sleeve. They should have been the same. I said nothing to defend my record, the first I had ever bought, which I had gone with Polly and his dad to buy, in his dad's car. If Polly had been there in that room with me he would have told them it was a good record. But there was nobody like Polly in the room, nor like Rick.

The long-haired men were well-spoken. They all knew Carla, and some of them called her 'Mrs P.' They were all going to be actors, just like Philip and Carla's daughters – actors, or musicians. They were all going to do things that would make them famous, and I would not have dared tell them that I had once wanted to be an actor too, for fear of being asked for the name of my favourite playwright and for a list of the parts I had played. In time, I and my friends would perhaps hear about these people, long after they had left our town and become famous and admired, their names flashing up on television screens – 'I knew him once. Do you remember him?' – or mentioned as part of experimental rock bands that were doing interesting things. Some might move to the Hebrides, or be last heard of living with foreign girls in the squats of Notting Hill or some other part of London that people in our town could refer to as if it were familiar, but which they could never pretend to know or be a part of.

My brothers and I left my mum and my dad in the hot throng of people, and stepped out into the cold silent dusk of the winter afternoon, not really knowing what kind of kids we were supposed to be in that place, where everybody knew so much and where nobody had any doubts, or so it seemed to me. They all fitted in so well,

149

while Michael and Paul and I ran home to the cold darkness of our house, which was soon warmed by the gas fire, safe but silent after the noise of the party had fallen away.

The silence meant that after all our waiting and expectation, another Christmas was over. Soon the streets would again just be cold and grey, until the springtime.

But at weekends there might be visitors. Perhaps Uncle Mark would be visiting, with laughter and stories and new jokes, like the one about the Irishman who laughed as his car was smashed to pieces – laughed and laughed, because every time the man smashing his car turned away from the chalk circle in which he had confined the Irishman, the Irishman jumped out of the circle.

That was when we laughed. Then, after delicious sandwiches and apple tart, it would be time for my uncle to leave, and we wondered why he had to go back to London, to his elegant ground-floor flat hidden behind the rhododendrons.

'Can you spell rhododendron? Do you know the joke about the Irishman who laughed as his car was being smashed to pieces by a man who made him stand in a chalk circle?'

'Wha' yer fuckin' talkin' about?'

'Hube. Wha'tcher fuckin' ga'an on abaa?'

I would forget that among my friends nobody cared how you spelt the name of a flower. The joke was nothing, because the Irish weren't funny.

We had laughed in our house. Laughed and laughed. And now I was pretending I had never laughed, that it wasn't funny after all. I fell into silence, waiting for my words to be forgotten, waiting for the chance to disappear and arrive again. They would let me. They would let me, and I envisioned myself back in my home for a second, hearing the laughter and the stories, and then we were swaggering to our High Street, our gangland, where the late afternoon spat rain in the steel gloom of the day's end as we walked, our gang, looking to be looked at, down the High Street, where shopkeepers were rattling down shutters, where Saturday was about to give way to the cold silence of Sunday, where the Old Town Christmas tree stood with the few coloured lights that had yet to be stolen.

'Ga'an home. Gonna watch *Lawrence of Arabia*. 'bout some fuckin' poof who tosses off little boys.'

'Mi old man says he ain't gonna let me watch it,' somebody said.

'Loada crap anyway.'

'D'jer wanna watch it a' my 'ouse Hube? Hubie Hube,' Polly asked me.

'Yeah, alright.'

'Well, le's 'ave a bit more enthusiasm.'

'Thanks. Yeah. When's it on?'

'Half seven.'

Polly's mum and dad were in their kitchen smoking when we stepped off the cold, dark street and into their safe home where I might one day belong. His mum asked me how my new school was going.

'I's alright thanks.'

'Thanks,' Polly said, mimicking me, with a laugh. 'Thanks.'

'Shut yer row,' his dad told him. 'Wha d'jer go there for, then?' he asked me.

'Mi dad, yer know, he wan'ed me to go there. Dunno really.'

151

'Wha'. D'je think i's better than Mark's school?' he asked, looking at Polly.

'Naa. I dunno. 'e jus' wan'ed me to go there. Tha's all.'

'You got some nice friends?' Polly's mum asked. 'You gotta bad cough too, in't yer?' she added.

'Yeah. They're alright, some of 'em,' I replied, her mention of my cough a reminder to me that I still had it, though it seemed to die down when I was in familiar places.

'Bi' young for this film, in't yer?' his dad said to me. 'I's all about this bloke who goes off to the desert and tosses off little boys.'

'Oh. Right.'

'I's startin',' said Polly, and for the first time I was taken into the sitting room in the house of one of my friends, and given a seat on a settee where I imagined they gathered in private times and discussed their family affairs. And there I was, among them, one of the family, warm in my place on the soft settee, accepted there as if it was normal, while hoping that they would not see that I didn't really know what the film was about if the scene they were waiting for suddenly appeared on the screen.

I watched spellbound, as the landscape opened out in front of me. But I would never go there. There had been a world like that. But it had gone. Anyway, we could never be like those people. Nobody we would ever know was like Lawrence of Arabia – imagining life, then living it. Never happened. Impossible. Big stories never happened. That's why it was a film – because it never happened. Not like that. And I needed to show that I knew it was just a film. Nothing real. Just a film. I would not be as I had been in the early spring last year, when

Monday nights were cold and we had never missed an episode of the story about prisoners at Colditz castle. When the English became the winners and the Germans lost and I assumed would all die, I cried as the last programme came to an end, when the castle commandant said goodbye to the Englishmen. I cried for the commandant, because he had not done any bad things, but he had lost, and now he would be shot or tortured, and I wanted him to be alright.

Paul had turned to Mum and whispered: 'Mark's crying,' and Mum said: 'It is rather sad,' and I wonder now what she thought, seeing me cry for one of Hitler's soldiers.

They were quiet in their sitting room, Polly and his mum and dad. I was quiet too, and gave nothing away, except for laughing with them at the accents of the toffy-nosed gits. They were waiting for the scene that never happened, and when the film was over I ran out into the cold ooze of the streetlamps, into the rush of the wind in the black trees I would still be watching grow fifty years from now, because this was all there was of the world. The streets from my friend's house would always be my path home. Always. Don't think anything else. This is everything – all that the world can ever be.

Then I would be at their house again, hoping that we would sit together, me thinking all the time about school, wondering why I worried when Polly never seemed to worry or talk about his school. Maybe he was better at his lessons than me and had no worries. Perhaps he understood everything his teachers taught him, while I was wondering when the kids at my school would forget that I had run away from the boy who had only thrown one punch. Would anybody from my school meet my friends from Chippingfield and tell them that story? Then I wouldn't know what I could be anymore. Anyway, Polly never asked me about my school, and we went up to his room to listen to a new record he had bought with money he saved from his newspaper round.

'Fuckin' kitsch cover,' he said. 'Look at 'em fuckin' shoes. 'ow could yer walk in 'em?'

We listened, reading the lyrics that were printed inside, wondering if we should like the gaudy colours of the record cover, which opened out onto a pink fantasy world overlaid with photos of the drab musicians slouched on uncut grass in the garden of a suburban house that was imitating California.

'Yer can lie on 'ere and read the lyrics of yer want?' he said, and I lay next to him on his bed and we followed the words of Elton John as he sang about funerals, a sinister wind effect making me shiver, a candle blowing out, a man leaving privileged society behind and striding in his sparkling high-heeled shoes to a place where he went hunting for toads, leaving us wondering whether leaving the yellow brick road was a good thing or a bad thing.

I wondered how Elton could have seen all these things, and then the bedroom door opened and Polly's dad stood in the doorway and blew kisses at us and said we looked like a 'right couple of poofs' lying there on Polly's bed.

The last song played, the crash down from the fantasy made stark as we stepped out onto the street, the heavy sky that had been threatening all morning bursting onto us where we stood with the rest of our friends, half-on half-off the pavement.

We crammed into the shelter of a wall beside the path that led to the wartime brick and windows of the public toilet opposite the Post Office. Sheets of rain drifted across the rooftops and the roads.

'Fuck this. I'm ga'an in 'ere,' said a girl from a village a few miles away across the fields, who had become Polly's girlfriend just before Christmas. The other girls followed her into the ladies' toilet.

'Ca'an le's gaa an' take a look,' Polly said, following the girls inside.

The rain was leaking through the roof, leaving the damp, cold place flooded, almost sinister.

'Alright. Le's 'ave a competition. Whose tits are biggest?' said Polly. The girls giggled, red-faced. 'Ca' on. I'll be the judge. A fair competition,' he said.

'Alright then. Who's goin' first?' said one of the girls.

'You all go at the same time,' said Polly.

The girls disappeared inside two of the cubicles, closed the doors behind them, and then stepped back out into the cold gloom. They were all stripped to the waist, shoulders hunched, pale skin shivering, one with her hands covering her breasts, all looking at Polly, wanting his approval, their faces exposing both ecstasy and humiliation, confidence and timidity.

' 'ang on. I ain't gonna tell just by lookin'. Needs a bit of a fondle,' he said, and he fondled each of the girls with his two hands, as they laughed and screamed and he delivered his verdict, his face red with a mixture of exuberance and embarrassment, which evaporated when we ran from there as two elderly women wearing clear-plastic head-scarves and smart raincoats walked into the toilet and stared at us with disgust as we emerged into the daylight.

The rain eased.

The warmer weather came, as 1975 edged towards summer.

Sometimes Polly's new girlfriend was at his house when I knocked at the back door and went into their kitchen.

It was not the same, her being there. She had two friends who went everywhere with her. One had freckles and a rasping voice. She never smiled. She would have been mistaken for a boy if she had worn boy's clothes. The other one was loud and friendly.

'It's all gonna be a lot easier if yer go ou' wiv 'er,' Polly told me. 'She ain't bad. A bit of a laugh.'

He was talking about the freckled girl with the rasping voice. To me she seemed cold and ugly. I would never say so. Who was I to say things like that about a girl? Polly wanted to create a group – two couples. He imagined the four of us having lives like his Uncle Gary's, comfortable in our own homes, sports cars parked outside, trips to the soccer on Saturdays, maybe even holidays together, Spain or Majorca, sometimes a bit of trouble, a few new mates who might enter our lives then disappear, each evening walking out of the factory gates in boots, donkey jacket with a company name across the shoulder blades, back to the women at home, warm, smoking in front of their favourite programmes, Mum on the telephone to complain about Dad, the sick old man. The music would all be forgotten, those bleedin' old days and school mates not really thought about much…'don't see 'em much now. Saw this 'ansome bird in the canteen. Might ask 'er out. Wife's a bit of a fuckin' nag these days, just like 'er old woman. But given 'er old man got us mi job through some mate of 'is 'e knew from 'is pub, ain't gonna leave 'er. Naa. Just 'ave a bit on the side. Nothing serious. Fuckin' ansome chick though.'

'D'jer remember that time when your wife got so pissed on gin she passed out, an' yer old man 'ad to carry her to 'is car and drive 'er all the way 'ome?'

'Naa. Don' remember that.'

Three: *Strangers*

'Are you Mark?'

For all they knew, this was what happened next –
a chance meeting on a cold wet night in 1996 as I was
waiting for a northbound train at Tottenham Hale station.

A strike had brought the London Underground to
a standstill. A replacement bus hissed and blasted through
the rain to this station, from where I could take a train out
into Essex.

That evening's journey through London had been
a familiar one made in unfamiliar circumstances. Grilles
caged the dim-lit entrances of closed stations along a
route I had left behind so many times and so long ago,
before new roads had opened my way to Africa.

I remember who it was I had been to see that
evening. But that's another story. Then I was on a bus
winding along the road from Camden Town through
Finsbury Park and Seven Sisters, looking out for a car
passing into the wet black night, parents silent behind the
rushing slap of the wipers, the deep-sleeping faces of

children tilted in dreams on the back seat, stroked by the ooze of orange light and darkness.

The empty bus lurched away into the night, and I walked slowly into the darkness at the end of the platform, turned, then ambled back towards the gathered silence of the travellers waiting in the light.

'Yes. I'm Mark.'

'You don't remember me. I'm Neil.'

Where there had once been a short, fat boy there was now a tall thin man.

Immediately self-conscious I wondered what it was that he remembered of me, as I looked into an old face, the tight curls of his curly hair greying, the gaps between the teeth of his smile visible in the dim light of the platform. Whose becoming was marked by this chance meeting?

'Of course I remember you. How are you?'

But I hope you don't remember me, beyond whatever you might have heard about me since I left England, since you perhaps began to see my name in the newspapers, or hear of me on the radio from places on a map. Monrovia, Kinshasa, Mogadishu, Kigali, Casablanca, Algiers. Of course I remember you. I can see how you are – tall where you were once short, your folds of fat shaking as you sneered and mocked in our classrooms all those years ago. Do you want me to remember you, or should we just remember what we hoped our lives would have become since we last saw each other? Shall I tell you that since I last saw you I have been to the places I dreamed of visiting, when the rain poured outside our classrooms and we breathed the sweat and the smells of young boys and girls? Which story do you want to hear – the shared memory, or what I became?

Our voices were drowned by the clatter of the train as it arrived at the platform. We could pause, and think about where to sit. Would we sit together, and spend the forty minutes or so of our journey picking up the story where we assumed it had ended? What will you want to know about me now, I wondered, as the train pulled away, its rhythm setting the pace of the conversation, both of us aware that our story could only last as long as it took to reach Harlow. Then we would be gone, forever, the likelihood of another chance meeting impossible to imagine.

'I heard about you in Africa,' he said. 'Yer got kidnapped. Is that right? Is that what happened? On a train in Liberia?'

'Sort of.'

'Was it dangerous?'

'A bit. But it was alright in the end.'

'Wha' d'jer wanna go to Africa for then?'

'Ahh. Yer know. I wan'ed to see the world. Yer know – see things. But, what about you?'

'Not much really. Nothing like that. D'jer see Tony in Africa.'

'Yeah. I did. I went to see him. It was before I went to live in Africa though. I travelled from Kenya to South Africa, and went to see him.'

'When was that then?'

'Ten years ago. 1986.'

'Oh right. I saw 'im after that. When 'e came to Harlow. He knocked on my door. He 'adn't changed. Just the same. Did yer see him then?'

'No. No, 'e didn't...I didn't know he had come back.'

'Oh, right. I thought 'e would 'ave told yer. After all, 'e was really your mate, weren't he? I would 'ave thought you would 'ave been the first one 'e would see.'

'Yeah...'e was my mate...,' and my mind wandered away from the shock of fully seeing in the brighter light of the railway carriage Neil's face – aged, worn out, though he was my age, 33. Then the fragmented words suddenly clamped together, as the pieces of time, of the years that had passed glided into place, and I learned by chance how it was that a story he knew of me had ended.

Tony had chuckled when he heard about the one punch the boy had landed. Then he had laughed and wished he had been there to see it.

'Oooh,' he had said, half-mocking. 'One punch. And he's such a weed.'

But it was obvious he didn't care. He laughed, but without judging me or having an opinion. That was all that mattered to me – that somebody didn't care and didn't think it said anything about me.

It gave me air to breathe, the feeling that what I had been for a moment – frightened, shocked, and above all worried about what it might mean for my dad if the fight was seen by a teacher – was not what I would always be or seem to be. Tony had grown up with all those boys. He knew them, and didn't take them seriously. But for me, the outsider who had yet to prove himself, there were walls between us, and old stories into which I must somehow try to be written.

But Tony seemed outside their story. His was a different voice – not bad, no bad elder brothers whose footsteps he would be dragged into at our school by secret words and the suspicious eyes of teachers looking for signs of bad blood. He seemed good natured, a smiler, an athlete and a gymnast. People disliked him for his good nature. Some people were even suspicious of his smile.

For me what mattered most was that Tony had survived the tough kids, but without becoming bad. They mocked him. But he could be in their gang when he wanted, because they had grown up together. I could see he had survived, but that he wasn't bad. That's what I wanted to be like, though in class nothing was ever said that spelled out what connected us. Friendship had no voice. There was only laughter and jeering, as accusations flew through the hot dry air.

'D'jer fuckin' fancy her?'

'Course yer fuckin' fancy her.'

'Sitting with the girls now are yer?'

'Right fuckin' pansy you are.'

'Wha' d'jer call me?'

Tony laughed at the waves of insults, which died down during the desperate moment at the beginning of lessons, when the shape of the world was formed for crucial seconds by whose smell you found yourself sitting beside, as the chaos slumped to the scrape of a chair and a last chuckle.

But then, slowly, in the early months of 1975, the currents of the ocean in which we were wallowing seemed slightly to shift. The boy who sneered might leave a seat empty beside somebody he knew was another's friend. Everybody knew that I would sit next to Tony, just as Richard would sit next to Jeremy, Karen would sit next to Mandy, Andrew would sit next to Stephen, Lorraine would sit next to Beverley.

Kids who had once been jealous and scathing now looked for signs that they were not alone. The gangs were there, but they were gangs that couldn't survive the presence of outsiders. In the classrooms, in the corridors, running in the din of the bells, kids were torn away from paths they had thought would always be there. But now, who could run fastest? Who wanted to stay a kid? Who had hair around their prick? Did somebody have a secret to tell about the girl who looked and smiled at them in the morning?

'Tell us. Ga'an, tell us. Yer ain't done nothing, yer ain't.'

I learned to smile and laugh like never before, or so it seemed, Tony coaxing me into a smile as we laughed and joked and laughed some more. Laughter had never been like this, with girls looking at us with what we thought was awe, and teachers unable to stop the flow of jokes and quips and ridiculous faces pulled to break the monotony and pointlessness of study. The class would roar, bells would sound in the corridors, and we would become the main attraction, the new gang, flowing with words that could reduce teachers to furious silence and bring laughter to the menacing faces that had watched me beaten down the slope on the edge of the playground. Now, they and their elder brothers had to pause before they threatened or snarled, before they stole food from my lunch plate, demanded my pen, told me they wanted to take my bicycle at lunch time, tear sheets from my exercise books or use my coat when it rained. They knew we were being funny now, that we had sharp tongues and that we weren't afraid to sting them with words. They were afraid of words. The only words they had were 'fuck', 'cunt', 'poof', 'wanker', 'cunt', 'cunt' – ugly words,

166

which some boys never used. Sometimes it even seemed that the days were just a short ride away from the shy childish moments that we all remembered from the time before our childhoods had been trashed by ugly words.

There was something still left.

At moments I felt I could even remember what it was I might have become by now. I was going to be an actor. Remember? People would listen to my voice flowing from a stage, they would see my body flooded with light and hear my words – clear, bold, all-knowing, somebody else's words, a writer's words, which I would learn so well that I would become the character, and in the daytime, in the corridors, in lessons, people would see the change, as the characters I played became part of me.

But when the chance came, in a childish play about animals, the words were not like that. There was no part of me in the character. The words said nothing of me. Nobody could hear my real voice. Instead, a broken, stammering noise stumbled over lines that meant nothing to me. I could barely remember what I had to say, and stared out into the darkness from where the shadows and silhouettes of the world to which I wanted to speak and make listen to me, stared back in silence.

I wondered how it was that great actors could command the attention of an audience. And when they did, what was the point? In our class, Tony and I joked and laughed and people listened and laughed. That was our stage. We never did any work, nor learned anything. All we wanted was to be heard.

But really we had nothing to say, because we didn't know anything.

Our stage disappeared when the last bell of the day sounded and I cycled home fast, along the track behind the factories that always smelled of something sick-sweet in the late afternoon. After the rush of wind in my hair there was only silence, as if no voices had really spoken that day. Downstairs, Mum's kitchen was the only warm, safe, perfect place. But it was a place now sniggering with the noise of *PM AT FIVE PM* – the tune and voices that staked out the purpose of days that happened just because they happened, the same tune every day, the same voices, mocking with a tone that implied that every day could be the same, and at the end, at 'FIVE PM', the day sat back to consider what had happened, out there, in a world that only happened to other people – people who were a long way away and always would be.

The world perhaps came closer at the weekend, when people gathered in our house. Uncle Mark would visit for tea on Sunday, and perhaps arrive with some of his friends, and Tony was going to cycle over from his house near the Sports Centre. Would we joke and laugh like we did in school, or would we be other people? Would he ask me why my uncle didn't have a wife, or would he just chatter and say 'thank you', as Mum cut larges slices of gleaming apple tart and covered them with thick cream?

'Thanks Ann,' Tony said, his familiarity all that I wanted, something everybody could see. They could see that I could have a friend who could be in our house just like us. Uncle Mark could see it – and my mum and my dad – that I had a friend who was a sign of what I could be or might already be.

We played board games, then cards, *Happy Families* beside the warm glow of the gas fire, everybody laughing, the delicious sandwiches and cake and apple tart all finished, the chatter loud and happy. We played quiz games, competed on general knowledge, and our ignorance about the world that in our school we pretended to have at our feet, did not matter, because we were not there to compete. We were there to be warm, our curtains shutting out the black night which only broke through when the unfamiliar thud of the door knocker meant that Tony had to go, because his dad had arrived to take him home, with his bike in the boot of their car.

Then the room seemed broken up, the cold draft from the open front door never seeming to dissolve into the warmth, the glimpse of the night outside lingering still. I wanted to draw the afternoon along with me, into school tomorrow morning, to preserve what had been created. Would Tony talk of apple tart and *Happy Families* when we gathered in our classroom for the morning register? What could be left of our day, of my uncle's laughter and jokes?

But when the corridor bells roared the day into running bodies, into the casting of a glance, into the cackle, the jibe, the stink of fresh floor polish, the scrape of a chair, the memory of yesterday seemed less fragile. Take or leave the memory behind, remember or forget the day past. What was there to remember anyway? Nothing had happened. Some people came for tea. Who were they anyway? What did it matter? They could come anytime. All they had to do was say they were going to be there. There would always be food. My mum would make it. And what then, after the food? Perhaps a game. My uncle might be there.

'Why don't your uncle have a wife?'

'Dunno.'

'Yer must know.'

169

'No, dunno. Never asked him.'

'Can I come to your house next Sunday again?'

'Yeah, sure.'

'Would yer mum mind? Better ask yer mum.'

'It'll be alright.'

'Right you lot, shut up.'

The Welshman who taught us mathematics had long curly hair, just like Leo Sayer, and wore light brown three-piece suits. It was in his class that Tony and I – unspoken, even to this day, more than forty years later, as I look through the letters he sent after he disappeared from our school – sensed why the question answer question answer of the man in the suit with the Leo Sayer hairstyle never could tell us anything that would stop our minds from wandering. Our attitudes were surly and rude. There was nothing that could explain where our manner came from. Confusion underlay everything, though we were too cocky to betray it, and when the girls looked our way we hoped it was sympathy they felt, as the teacher turned on us, intent on inflicting humiliation – us his victims, the victims of his cruelty.

'Shut up you two.'

'Shut up you two.'

'What did you say?'

'What did you say?'

'Come 'ere.'

'Go there.'

'Oy, shut up.'

'Oy, shut up.'

'Get 'ere now.'

'I'm 'ere.'

'Got two ears 'ave you?'

'Right, get 'ere then.'

170

'Right.'

'Right.'

'I told you to get 'ere.'

'But I like my ears.'

'Enough of your lip.'

'You want my lips and my ears?'

'Shut up you two.'

'Right sir. Shut up Tony.'

'Shut up Mark.'

'I'm trying to work,'

'I like maths.'

'Me too.'

'Enough of your lip.'

'And your ears.'

'What's wrong with my ears?'

'Get 'ere you two.'

' 'e wants your ears.'

'But 'e's had enough of your lips,' and the class laughed, and the teacher stared, seething as the banter died down, we unable to keep the stupidity going, he clawing back the attention of the agitated class, among which only the immigrant kids hunched over their books to work, as fear like a drop of poison seeped through my veins.

It was a fear of the teacher's knowledge, though a fear I could barely discern, and which haunts me to this day, if only because the first drop was shed during those strange days. It was a fear born somewhere I had never been – an inheritance from somebody I had never known. But it was a powerful fear, that the world might just be comprised of the Welshman's perfect, baffling, logical theories. His numbers became the terror he wielded before my eyes, a terror that my 12-year old instincts told me I must fight – in defence of the pure air and moorlands that were the landscape I must return to and walk on to survive. My dream world had no numbers. All I had was the fast-receding past, which I must recapture on the breath of my imagination before all was lost and the numbers had won – before the death of the words that I had not yet even begun to write or speak.

*

The train Neil and I had boarded at Tottenham Hale slipped back into our past, winding into the night towards all that should have been familiar to us both – all that should have drawn us into reminiscence, laughter, old times, old times.

But instead, Neil eased his way around my questions.

'What's yer brother Dennis doing now?'

'Oh. No. No.'

'What's he doing?'

Neil just smiled.

At the end of a corridor, in a common room, in the playground, the sight of Dennis swaggering with Ralph or Danny, his gang, turned childish noise and play into subdued muttering, into the worry of raising suspicion, into the fear of catching an eye or attracting attention. Never attract the attention of Dennis – much better to fade into the gloom among the coat racks until the danger had passed.

'Where is he now?'

'Naa. Naa.'

Neil would not say. He just smiled.

'And what about Andrew?' I asked, referring to the one who had coaxed me to fight his namesake, and who I had sometimes sensed was more clever than he pretended to be.

Oh, 'e's right serious now, 'e is. 'e don't talk to anybody else no more. 'e went off and did his exams, and now 'e don't talk to us anymore.'

'What d'yer mean?'

'Naa. I mean, 'e left school, same as me. An' 'e 'ad a job. But then 'e went off and done A-levels. An' then 'e went to university, an' got a degree in English. So, now, if I see 'im 'e don' talk to me no more. 'e got all superior. Don' see 'im now. 'e don't wanna see me now, nor anyone else.'

He smiled.

Once, Neil's smile had mocked and sneered, jeered at me when I had run away to be sick in the bushes beside the school field after one punch had been thrown. Would he remember? Now his smile was timid. He didn't want to tell me what had happened to his brother. I assumed the story would have been a sad one. Perhaps Dennis was dead. I wouldn't ask him again.

'Andrew was always more intelligent then he pretended to be,' I said, immediately regretting my tone, regretting that I sounded like a commentator. This was our shared past and I wanted to be a part of it, to make it mine, there, in that conversation.

'Yeah. Dunno. Maybe. Don' see 'im. 'e don' wanna see me.'

'What about the other Andrew?' I asked, referring to the boy who had hit me.

'Dunno. Ain't seen 'im for years. You're really asking a lot of questions. No one's done anything like what you've done.'

'I want to know what happened.'

' 's only Andrew who went off and did his university. And Tony. Weird that 'e didn't go to see yer when 'e came back.'

And we were back there again.

At the end of the summer term of 1975 I cycled fast away from the school, along the track that was bordered by cow parsley and dappled with sunlight that poured through the big trees that cast late afternoon shadows over the factories. It was the distance between me and the lives Neil and I were talking of – the lives I was written out of during the holidays, when I went back to my part of our town many miles and territories away.

My own sense of that half-presence in the lives of the kids in my school lingered still, as our train edged towards Harlow.

That summer holiday I saw Tony only once. All of my days at home were spent with my friends from Chippingfield, and I wondered some days what it would be like when school started again and I had to find a way back into that other life.

But for Tony I had never really been away.

When the new term started, the autumn rains did not seem so bad. We, older, had new days to stake out, until the bells drew us to our classrooms, where the same fear gripped me as had been there before with the Welshman, and the autumn edged its way into the gloom of late afternoon, and the time we had perhaps thought might never end slid irrevocably towards its close.

'Mr Huband Saa, you will stay behind at the end of the lesson. Then I will explain all that you have failed to learn.'

My new mathematics teacher's command, stated so casually, on the last day of term before Christmas that year, was the order of a man commanding a firing squad. A bird perhaps sang beyond a high wall. Were there clouds? Would the sun die today, with the end of a life? How could it continue to shine? Bring out the prisoner, hands bound. Guide him almost gently to the place against the wall where time will stop.

Time will stop at a wall. There, the end will happen. That is the place where it has been decided that a life will end, where a man stops. The world is a man in a blindfold, the tapestry once imagined perhaps as holy now lying torn, leaving no witness but whatever it was that was last seen in the eyes of his executioners.

My helplessness was that of a body bound in chains, as I struggled to hope that the last bell of the day would never sound. I would be left standing there, as all the months of friendship disappeared through the door and were gone.

Nobody really knew how to say goodbye to Tony, on that wet, dark evening. It would be the last time we would ever see him. Tomorrow he would be on an airplane to South Africa and a new life as an émigré, with his mum, dad, sister and brothers, gone forever to the sun. We would be left behind, to say goodbye among the desks, amid the home-time clamour and the zipping of Parkas.

'Mr Huband Saa, where is it that you are going? You will stay behind.'

The boys lingered, edging slowly towards the door, uncertain how long they could stay and how they could defy the teacher by – perhaps – trying to drag me along with them for the goodbye on the landing, the goodbye on the stairs, the goodbye in the warm damp of the corridor, then across the playground for the last goodbye beneath the trees near a slope where once we had gathered on a wet morning more than a year beforehand for a fight that ended after only one punch had been thrown.

'Off you go, out of my class,' the teacher told Tony and all the boys who lingered, watching me as I hovered between the desks, half shifting towards where my friend was watching to see if he would be allowed to say goodbye to me.

'Mr Huband Saa, you will stay behind. Your friends will go.'

I saw the rain. I saw the end of my world. I saw all that had brought me out of the shell in which I had been hiding when I arrived at my school – I saw it passing out through the door and away forever as my friend left.

And I was being told I could not say goodbye.

I looked hard at the teacher, unable to believe there could be a person capable of this cruelty. Unable to understand how I had ever found myself in that place.

The doorway was filled with my departing friend and the other boys, my sense of whose freedom to leave with him weakening my legs and punching at my eyes. My throat dried to bone, and there, in front of the departing class of girls who had laughed at the jokes and larks with which Tony and I had entertained them for so long, there in front of the teacher whose mercy lay between me and the order to shoot at the body standing alone against a wall at the end of time, there, as the eyes of the last witness watched the wrenching apart of a friendship, my tears burst into the warm dry air and I looked into the eyes of the man who had denied me a last goodbye and hoped that he saw the innocence of the hatred, anger and despair that only my tears could show.

*

Was silence her judgement?

I knew that I had waited too long, but still wondered if my time had now come, as she turned the typed pages, her booted feet motionless among the strewn waste of the story that had begun so long ago that I could not begin to explain. Whatever I said or wrote, it would always somehow remain hidden, and she and I would reach our end, drifting away from the dream that we could write each other into our pasts, there, beside the red-orange glare of the bar heater.

She was still wearing her coat. I wished she would take it off. Then I would see the woman to whom I wanted to tell my story. With her coat, her boots, and the West London cold, she seemed a stranger, lingering in the story room where a small window above the bed let in light beneath the tilt of the roof that drew the eye towards the corner shadows of a time on many now-forgotten streets, which would end at Heathrow Airport a few years later when we said goodbye forever and I started my life again.

How long could I remain silent as she read? Her hands were different, holding me there. Would the story take her to its heart?

Her eyes moved quickly across the lines. So quiet I heard her breathing. I wanted her to cast an eye at me, to see if I was watching, see me caress the body whose judgement I awaited. My story. Are we one, she and I – one, or perhaps nothing?

I never told her I had cried when my friend had left. Which boy could she see or want to know? She looked up and smiled, then cast her gaze down again. Would she become past, present and future – beginning, middle and end – by becoming the voice and body of what my story became?

Did she remember the letters I had sent her?

I wonder now if she kept my letters, sent along the journey that would never really be told of in the telling, its voice left among all the others, in the house of a strange family whose pick-up truck had stopped by the roadside in an early morning storm in 1986, when I was on my way through Zimbabwe to the South African border?

'Where are you heading?'

'I'm hitching rides to the border, hoping to reach Johannesburg by nightfall.'

'You'll need a good breakfast, but you should make it before nightfall. Who are you staying with down South? We have good friends down South who can put you up. They're just outside Louis Trichardt, on a farm. I'll call them to let them know you might pass by.'

'Thank you. That's kind. But I think I'll try and get to Jo'burg in a day.'

'Who'll you be staying with there?'

'A friend. He was at my school in England. He left in 1975, to live in South Africa.'

'Well that's sweet. And you've not seen him for eleven whole years? You'll be having a reunion then. I'll bet that'll be quite a party. But I'll call my friends in Louis Trichardt. Wouldn't want you getting stuck on the way. Gotta talk with them anyhow.'

'Well, thank you. Thanks. That's very kind.'

'Don't mention it. Hey Jack, it's me. Haa iz it? All good? Won't keep yer. Picked up a hiker. He's passing your way later, on the way to Jo'burg. Might drop by. Thought you'd say that. Name's Mark. O' course. Yeah. O' course he's white. May stop. May not. Says 'e wants to reach Jo'burg tonight. Bit ambitious. Will give him yer number. Take care. Love to all. Bye. Sorted then. Rain's stopped. Better be on your way if you wanna reach Jo'burg before dark.'

Trucks stopped. Raw hands hauled me up under tarpaulins in whose shadows men crouched smiling, sharing cigarettes.

Across the border, white women edged their saloon cars along straight roads that crossed the grasslands and the hills, and the journey that I will tell of some other time ended among the midnight lights of Johannesburg, when an old Afrikaaner man cranked through the gears of his rusting pick-up truck and left me standing at the sparkling marble entrance of a luxury hotel, said 'goodbye, good luck', and rattled off into the night.

I dialled a telephone number. Waited. Waited. The click and hum of a line, a voice, a laugh I wondered if I knew, a tone – was it familiar?

'You wait right there. You've come far enough already, friend. I'll come and pick you up.'

179

'Friend.' Tony had used the word a lot. In one of his letters to me, in 1983, he had signed himself: '*All the best, life-long friend, Tony.*'

'*Life-long.*' We had shared months. Perhaps I was visiting him because those months had now been reduced to curiosity about what his life in a pariah state had become. How could anything remain of what had been, other than my own hope that there was no end and that the story would go on forever? We had barely started to grow before he had gone. In the end we had shared little. Perhaps, when I had cried in our classroom on that last day, it was from despair at being denied what I sensed might have become the possibilities – despair of ever seeing something that might go on forever.

'*Life-long friend.*' Our paths had crossed momentarily, and now they were about to cross again, late one night in the vast marble lobby of a Johannesburg hotel, where black bellboys wearing white gloves ran and stooped before white people who drifted in and out of the light of sparkling chandeliers and, across the space, a man with a paunch, wearing shorts and a tee-shirt, strolled in flip-flops as he twisted and untwisted a chain around his finger that was attached to a set of keys.

The smile was the same. A short laugh I knew, like the slightly hooded eyes. But now also a moustache, which I had seen in a wedding photograph he had sent, and shoulders that had once been slightly hunched now thrown back in a sign of confidence.

Would we embrace? No, we shook hands.

We did not linger there. We strode, grappling for words, listening for signs of a common language. Was the story one of my months spent travelling across thousands of miles of Africa, or his tale of what happened after his family woke one morning eleven years earlier upon the landscape of a new world? I wondered if we were thinking the same things, and wondered if we ever had.

I regretted not re-reading his letters just before reaching the place at which we were to meet.

He had written ten times over the years, always with the same enthusiasm, always with not too much to say, but never losing the sense of life having been left behind rather than a new one having been gained, his first letter saying that he would record a message for all the friends he had left behind…'*I'll write to Mr Robinson* (our house-master) *asking if he would play it in the first and second year assembly…Tell the tutor group that I am waiting for a letter from one of them, tell them I will write back if one of them writes a letter…Now I've got to get ready for bed it's 5 to 7 and it's 5 to 5 in England but we have to get up at 6.30 when it's 4.30 in England, bye for now…P.S. Look after yourself. See you soon over here. Please write back.*'

'*…As I am ill in bed I thought I'd write…Does your Dad still teach English at Burnt Mill. And does that Indian guy take you for Maths? He did not like us two, do you remember…It's hard to write lying in bed. I have got some illness the doctors don't know about and my blood has to be taken to the big doctors in Johannesburg…Don't worry, it's not that bad…keep smiling.*'

'*…I don't get much time to myself anymore. I started writing this letter at midnight…I've just got in from work. Yes, I have left school and I am working now…for Holiday Inn Hotel group…Are there many people left at Burnt Mill who know me. If there is, tell them I say hi…I am going to sleep now, and I'll finish this letter tomorrow. I can tell you this now, England, yourself and all my old friends will be in my dream. I miss you all, and the growing up we did together.*'

181

'…Sorry that I have not written for such a long time, but I am not the type of person who can write a letter…My company decided to send me to a different hotel, in the middle of nowhere. I want to go back to England for a holiday somewhere around June (1980) if I have the money, that seems to be a big problem. I tell you when I do get home I want you to get all our old school friends together and we'll have one hell of a party, just for old times…'

'…From next month, the 12/2/83 it will be Mr and Mrs B. and jnr, that's right the man is getting married. Got a little girl the name is Nicki. Can't believe it… Do you see any of the blokes from school, if so say hi. Have you seen Neil, if so give him my address and tell him to write me a letter…All the best life-long friend.'

'…How long has it been, what 8 years! Shit, it's a long time. I can still remember our last day in school when that curry-muncher of a Maths teacher gave us all that shit…The wife's working and the little one goes to nursery school…Shit what else can I tell you. How's university going and them lovely dolly-birds up in Manchester. I hope you haven't turned out to be a Manchester United fan. Come on you can't let the side down. Come on you Spurs.'

'…Well it was really good receiving your letter, and even better hearing you are coming to South Africa…just think, together again after 11 years…Since I received your letter I haven't stopped thinking of all the things I want to do when you get here and all the places I want to show you. I'll take some time off work so we'll have more time together…Say hi to your parents for me and tell them not to worry…South Africa is not a dangerous corner of the world. We only have a few small problems, but who doesn't.'

His letters – years apart – had told me something of his changing moods, of what he had become. For my part, perhaps I had given back too little in my letters to him, leaving him uncertain about me.

182

But I had also told her little of him, before she read of my visit when I returned to her and England in February 1987. Only now, years after that visit, have I re-read what he wrote. All she – for whom I wrote of what happened – could have known of him was what I told her. Something in me wanted my account to show her I had moved on from my schooldays. She would not want to hear about the boy who had cried, nor of my friend's recollections of the mathematics teacher who *'gave us all that shit'* on the last day that *'I still remember'*. She would not want to know how much it mattered to me that he remembered. She would not want to hear that I was in my friend's dreams, that he missed the England he had left behind, and that he wondered if that place still existed.

But she was what the world might want to hear of my journey. She would be the recipient of a version of my life, of a rootless glimpse and rapid glance across the years. In that version, all the people would be wrapped in a beginning a middle and an end. That was how I would tell my story, to her as to anybody else who had not been there when the story began – the strangers who had not been there, the readers of the *New Statesman*, which published my story of the reunion with my friend. They were the people who were now the landscape of which I had become a part, for whom I wrote about how… *'In this country never trust a kaffir. They'll always let you down,' said my friend's South African-born wife as she stormed through the living-room the morning after I had arrived in Vereeniging. The black maid had failed to turn up and there was a coffee morning to organise…By 11am the maid still had not arrived and the small bungalow, an hour's drive from Johannesburg, was filled with young mothers holding up their children for inspection as they sipped coffee…*

A short drive away, at the illegal squatter camp of Mushenguville on the outskirts of Soweto, 400 families were watching bulldozers tear down the shacks which had taken them months to save up for... The young mothers in Vereeniging began to gather their children together and haul their prams out into the quiet street. At Mushenguville, women of the same age sorted through the wreckage of what had once been their homes... I asked my friend what he thought of this taking place in the country he had made his own. 'Well, you know,' he said, in a drawl which came and went depending on whether he was talking about South Africa or England, 'they knew they shouldn't be there... What happens if you get a load of squatters together?' he continued. 'There's a problem of security, isn't there...Any more people and there are bound to be more problems...'

I had no idea what had really happened to the boy who said he missed the friends he had left behind in Harlow. But I could not tell him: 'You don't have to say these things, to show us that in the end you became a man, with opinions.' Sitting there in his house I couldn't bring myself to ask him why it was he felt the need to say these things about a country he did not dream about. England was the place he dreamed about – the place where he wanted me to say 'hi' to anybody who remembered him.

But there was nobody left to remember him, except me, and when I went to visit him I reminded him of things he would rather forget, and all I could do was write down how...*Next day we went for supper at my friend's parents' plush bungalow. The cramped Harlow housing estate they had left behind was a distant memory... 'This is my country now,' said my friend's mother. 'I could never go back to England. It's too cold.' I wondered how many people there were keeping apartheid alive simply because they enjoyed the South African weather...She turned to her husband. 'I think the pace of life in South Africa suits us much better,' he said, sourly, without looking up, the swimming pool, the drinks bar and the maid they delighted in calling the kaffirmatic – all these were part of the dream home which allowed them to forget the past I reminded them of.*

But there seemed no past of which to be reminded. 'All we are is what you see around you,' they seemed to be saying, while eyeing me suspiciously as if, beneath the horror I could not hide when they talked of 'kaffirs', I was hatching a plot to deprive them of what they had created, perhaps by telling them simply: 'I knew you before you had any of this.'

I gradually sensed – there beside the pool, or at the drinks bar in their sitting room – that we did not know each other, that the years meant nothing, and that we had attached so much importance to the time we had been apart that we had failed to see that it had divided rather than united us. They could not see that I wasn't going to patronise them, or remind them of the place they might still occupy if they had stayed in Harlow or decided to return there. *'This is my country now.'* Who was I to deny it? But all evening they were expecting me to shatter their dream of home, eyeing me suspiciously, as my friend's mother *explained to me what a kaffir is.*

*

I was shivering with cold by the time the waiting was over, as my friend put aside the papers on which I had typed my story.

She took off her coat and sat on the arm of my chair.

185

'It's brilliant,' she said, her wide mouth broadening into the smile that I loved. 'It's really good. You're so clever.'

She unbuttoned my jeans and slipped a hand inside. 'My writer, so thin and gorgeous,' she said, pushing my jeans and shorts to the floor and pulling up my shirt. I trembled with cold as she stripped and sat astride me, our eyes open, watching, listening for the quickening of breath, our perfect moment, electric, our body, the soft shape of us bound by the flood of fire licking the heat of our beauty, our slowing breath, the hum like a struck bell singing in taut limbs.

'Right. That's enough of that. You must find someone to publish your story,' she said, smiling broadly, her face now hot, her nakedness dry but for a sheen to her shoulders.

We talked.

We always talked. On the street. In cars. In the bath when we lay tangled as two bodies made one. We talked in bed before we made love, and afterwards. We talked, lost in the confusion of not knowing if the body we made into ours alone was the moment, the fruit, the sacred text we had been born to create.

Had our separate stories been drawn together? The question lingered always in mind. Perhaps now it did not matter. I had written my story for her. I had told her the story of my visit to a friend in South Africa. I had told her the story in a way that would make it a story of her and me. The style, the point, the impression would be what she would understand. Everybody knew about South Africa and its odious regime. Only one thing could be said about South Africa and the white people who lived there, particularly the émigrés who knew what they

186

were heading into. Judgement was easy, and I wrote a story about a character whose path had once crossed mine, but who was now a long way away and who would probably never read the story anyway. Then I would be somebody else. Nobody would know about the boy who had cried for his friend, or perhaps had just cried for himself. People would comment. My career would move forward. My lover would be a part of the story by being a part of my success, by being a part of the new world of me, I thought, as we showered and saw nothing but the future together.

But really she knew nothing of his story.

Tony and I had gone back to our separate worlds since that moment when I had sat waiting in the hotel lobby in Johannesburg as he, immediately recognisable, approached me swinging his car keys around his finger.

'Horrible horrible people,' she told me as we dressed.

'But who wants to know about this kind of experience?'

'Everybody. South Africa's always a good one to write about.'

But it was not about South Africa. It was about me and my friend. My friend. His words had killed the past. There was no past.

For him – and even more for his family – there could be no present if there was a past. He would take time off work *so we'll have more time together*. I was a part of the past they could not have if they were to build the life they sought. The time we spent together in Vereeniging, or water skiing on the Vaal River, or eating at an Italian restaurant, and most of all at his parents' home, were days lived outside of time. They were days spent looking through glass.

All those years earlier, in our school classroom on the day before he left, my tears had been real. But my tears did not fit into the story I was going to tell her – the story she would be a part of, because it was a story about today, not about the moment when today began, many years ago.

But there still had to be a beginning, a middle and an end, so she and the strangers who had not been there when the story began could feel they knew my friend and knew why he had been my friend, even after it had become clear that discussion of politics could not be avoided, and he and I had talked of children – teenagers and younger – being arrested, imprisoned, and tortured in South Africa's jails. *'Even though in England they might be seen as children,' said my friend… 'I see them as enemies of the state. You know, anyone who is old enough to throw a stone is an enemy of the state.' We looked at each other in silence. His four-year-old daughter came in to the room. Even he did not seem quite able to believe the truth could be twisted that far.*

*

Perhaps I should have told this story to Neil while there was time, before our train reached his destination on that night in 1996, a decade after my journey to see Tony.

Did Neil remember my tears? Perhaps his memories of those moments were what lay behind his surprise that Tony had not come to see me when he had visited England. But knowing how sad I had been on the day that Tony had left, Neil might well have understood why I had then written as I did about my visit to South

Africa. Perhaps he would have understood my shock and disappointment. Perhaps he would – his dad being Jamaican – have appreciated me writing so openly about my disgust at the talk of '*kaffirs*'

Cheshunt, Broxbourne, Roydon. His journey was about to end.

'I spend most of my time at my girlfriend's house now,' said Neil. 'Her parents like having me around. They live right near the old school. Not far at all.'

The train began slowing as we passed the mill house that had become a pottery, passed the familiar embankment, the lock on the river, and the poplar trees near the place where boys I never knew went canoeing.

'Well, this is my stop,' Neil said, smiling, perhaps wondering whether I remembered that it would be, as the stories we had not told each other were drowned by the squeal of brakes and the sound of doors being opened.

Our meeting had been neither past nor present. What could we say, now that finality had been reached? Was the story that a tall, thin man had replaced the fat boy who had sneered and cackled? I had not asked him enough about himself. I should have been more insistent, got some answers, been the observer, the commentator. I had moved on, away from all those days. I had interviewed rebel chieftains and dictators. I had seen genocide, famine and wars. But I had told him nothing. Nor could I have asked him more about our past. What *had* happened to his brother Dennis? I couldn't ask him that again. Did he remember that I had cried that day when Tony left? Something in me wanted him to remember, as then I could have told him how I had changed and about what had happened next.

He opened the carriage door.

'Well, see yer then,' he said.

I wanted him to leave me with a last clue, to hint that nothing was the same?

And so he did.

The cackling fat boy who sneered and laughed, who had the bullying brother he tried sometimes to copy but whose fearsome reputation could not really be emulated, turned, smiling, and peered for a second with gentle, sad eyes that had aged a thousand times beyond his years.

'God bless,' he said, then slammed the door and disappeared into the night, as the train flickered past the last station light and I wondered – an anxiety revived, even after so many years had passed – if I had betrayed Tony and betrayed our past by writing of those days in South Africa, and wonder if I am doing so again by writing of them now. I never told Tony I had written anything. Nor have I heard from him since receiving a short note telling me how much he enjoyed me coming to see him. But I still wonder if he one day discovered what I had written, and whether if we met again he would say: 'Don't worry, life-long friend. It was different then. South Africa has changed, and me with it,' and wonder if I should write to him to explain that I had been trying to tell the story to somebody else, but that now she was long gone out of my life.

*

Tony had left nothing behind in England, though there were a few places that would always remain his. He had worked on a market stall in the Town Centre, selling greetings cards. I had sometimes seen him there on

Saturday mornings, when I had passed by with my friends from Chippingfield. He and my friends had eyed each other suspiciously, then we had walked on, our gang striding among the shops, wondering which gangs we would come across and whose territory we were in.

Another kid took over his job on the market stall. I would see him there wearing the pocketed belt Tony had worn, where he kept loose change. I never knew who it was you had to know if you wanted to get a job like that, on the market where I had walked with my dad one Christmas Eve when all the world seemed magical. The new kid on the card stall didn't know me, and Polly and I swaggered past with Mick and Steve and other kids who drifted in and out of our gang, past the café where families ate burgers and spaghetti and drank mugs of tea, then up the steps to Pépé's Saturday morning disco.

There were girls from my school there, because this was their territory, whereas we were from way off, on the far edge of town. Sometimes I imagined I could be the bridge between the kids there, because I was different, knowing kids from all sides.

'What's 'er name? That one.'

'Sharon.'

'She going out with someone?'

'Yeah. That bloke.'

'Don't fuckin' stare at 'em.'

'That one, with those kids over there.'

'D'jou know 'im?'

'Yeah.'

'Looks a right prat.'

'Yeah.'

In the gloom beside the dance floor I saw kids from my class and others they hung around with in our school. I wondered if they would tell Polly and my other friends about the things that happened in our school. They might tell them about how I had cried when my mate Tony had left and gone to live in South Africa. I nodded their way but didn't approach them. I didn't want any stories to be told. They stared at us from across the dance-floor, and I wondered what they were saying.

Pépé, the disc jockey, who had Afro hair and looked like Jimi Hendrix, spoke smoothly over the speakers, perhaps sensing the tensions between the kids from different parts of town: 'Nice and friendly. Here's another great sound from last year. 1975's fabulous favourite...10CC...*I'm not in love*...yeah, *so don't forget it*...but maybe you are – so take to the floor and show it.'

The dance-floor would slowly fill, Polly with his girl, nodding at me to pick a girl to dance with, as I stood on the edge and watched, until the lights came up, the fire exit opened, the sun streamed in and the disco was over. Then we could go back to our homeland at the other end of the 801 bus route, gathering loudly on the back seat of the upper deck as we edged our way towards our own territory at this odd hour of the early afternoon, after a morning spent doing things that we knew were supposed to happen in the depths of a big city at night.

Aside from *Speakeasy*, nightlife never really happened, even when Deena had a party in her parent's front room one Saturday night, then Rick had one too.

It was only as the summer approached, and we could stay out all day and late into the evening doing nothing in particular, that we felt less like the imitators we were.

On a summer morning Polly's girl and the louder of her two friends stood rasping in the warm breeze that rustled the deep red of the leaves that drifted across our front garden. They cackled, their eyes rolling, the soft air oozing with the stench of the gin on their breath. They knew where I lived. I was happy: they were the first girls like them ever to have knocked on our front door and asked for me. I was the boy of the nickname they used for me, the boy of the street, the boy striding away with his back to his home, two girls laughing beside him as they swigged at the bottle they had hidden inside a plastic bag.

For the minutes that we three walked together I felt protective, guiding them through my territory. They followed, my friend's girl, me the boy, the man, who would bring them safely to where my friend would be waiting, grateful, our bond strengthened because I had brought his girl to him, she unharmed, me expecting nothing, gratitude unsaid, though the eyes of our gang seeing the signs of the man in me.

Then, beside the swings at the top of the playing field where – three years earlier – I had first watched my friends playing, Polly's girl collapsed onto the soft grass, and mocking laughter turned to derision then worry.

'Stupid tart.'

'Fucking pissed.'

Deena, the girl Polly had kissed at *Speakeasy* before his new girl had appeared in our town from her village across the fields, broke into the noise.

'Better get 'er 'ome. She's passed out. She's passed out. Yer so fuckin' stupid, you lot. Better get 'er 'ome. She's passed out. Can't yer see she's passed out? Standin' round ain't gonna 'elp her, is it?'

The girl vomited, and nobody wanted to pick her up.

Deena strode away then came back with Polly's dad. We watched, awkward, as he picked up the motionless, silent body in his muscular arms and walked away, propping up her head with his shoulder, Polly following, still swaggering slightly.

The freckled, unsmiling girl Polly had been urging me to go out with, appeared as we were sitting on our mound of earth later that afternoon. We were sombre, wondering if this was the real thing. Polly's girl had died, we were sure of it. We talked as if the gang were bereaved, the cruelty of the world now suddenly real to us. We might not survive. It would not be long before there was another victim, before our territory became the mean streets we imagined we must walk if we were to be initiated into the gangland we must stake out to live.

'Here's yer chick, Hube. Take 'er for a walk or summink. Ga'an. Show 'er yer goin' out with 'er.'

The girl – cold, plain – told us Polly's girl was not dead, but that she was being kept at home by her mum and dad at the pub they ran.

'Wanna go for a walk?' I timidly asked the girl. She said nothing, but followed. We went far out into the fields, beyond Dick's Pond and the slaughterhouse. We lay on a haystack in the hot sun and she fumbled with the button of my jeans, but I moved away in terror of being humiliated. After an hour we walked back to see who might still be out, treading in silence along the gravel track through the fields where roses were growing.

We said nothing when we reached our friends, and nobody asked what had or had not happened. The girl went away, back to her village, and Polly and Rick and I sat in the heat of Polly's room, smoking because in Polly's house boys were allowed to, the window open onto the summer afternoon. Rick played a new record on the turntable, the singer's voice crackling as his words took me on the first step towards giving my world a new voice…*I offered up my innocence and got repaid with scorn, Come in she said I'll give you shelter from the storm.*

'Right bleedin' row, this guy. Listen to that voice. Can't even sing,' Polly scoffed, the floor of his room strewn these days with images of Mick Jagger.

We left the room, me wondering who that singer was and where he came from, but as usual not wanting to ask in case it was something that I should already know.

*

On the street outside, the sun had baked the tarmac. The soft evening flowed in our long hair. More boys joined our gang during those weeks, coming from the estate where Polly's Uncle Gary lived, among them two Scottish brothers, dark-haired, one sharp-featured, his eyes never looking into mine, the other more friendly, his fringe always covering his eyes. With them were Alan, Frank, Mick and John. They lingered on the street outside Polly's house, where Deena was chattering about how Polly's girl had got so drunk she fell unconscious.

Polly's manner changed when he saw the Scottish boys and their mates. The tone became raw, the street a cage, the talk harsh. The unfamiliar faces were hostile, the laughter vicious. I listened in silence as the talk turned to fights, gangs and blood.

'Hube ain't 'ad a fight,' said Polly, and the harsh faces laughed and stared.

'Don't look as though he wants one either,' said Alan, tall, blond, older than all of us, his voice cutting the air.

'Who yer gonna fight, Hube?'

'Yer gotta fight.'

'Ain't nothing if you ain't 'ad a fight.'

'Ain't you never 'ad a fight, Hube?'

'Naa.'

'Why not?'

'Dunno. Just 'aven't.'

'Chicken, are yer?'

'Naa.'

'John'll fight yer,' Polly said, pointing at the smallest of the boys standing there. 'Ga'an, 'ave a fight with 'im.'

'Naa.'

'What?'

'I don' wanna 'ave a fight with 'im. Wha's 'e ever done to me?'

'Ain't the point. You gotta fight if yer wanna be…'

'I don' wanna fight either,' said the boy.

'Two fuckin' chickens. Both of yer, fuckin' chickens.'

The group started to drift away from the houses, towards the cricket pitch and the long alley that smelled of dog shit and passed between the neatly cut grass and the wall topped with shards of broken glass.

'You both gotta fight.'

'Ga'an chickens.'

'Hube, you gotta 'ave a fight. Yer just pretending, if yer don't have a fight, in yer DMs and yer jacket,' said Polly.

196

His words were like a knife to my throat, and the second after they had been uttered the boy suddenly lunged with a punch to the side of my head that flung me against the wall. My head crashed against the warm brick. The world went dark. All I could hear was the barking of dogs. Then I was alone, breathing hard, the alley empty ahead of me.

Days of silence followed.

I stayed at home and nobody called. I never knew what had happened, and was too frightened to tell my mum and my dad that I had been punched and had hit my head against a wall and that everything had gone dark. I only remember saying to my mum, as I sat in the calm brightness of our sitting room that evening: 'I don't think I want to see the boys from there anymore,' and remember her responding gently: 'No. Of course not darling,' without asking me why.

*

On 26 September 2013 20:59, Mark Huband < █ > wrote:
Dear Mark
Sorry if has been so long since I was last in touch. I hope all is well with you. It would be great to meet for lunch some time soon, as am in great need of our next conversation. Have just read all of Laurie Lee - your suggestion. What a dream of a writer.
How would it suit you to meet? Can't wait
V best
Mark

From: Mark P
Sent: Tuesday, 8 October 2013 20:25 PM

197

To: Mark Huband
Subject: Re: How are you
Hi Mark

Sorry to take so long to return your message. All is well with me. I'd love to meet up. As you know, Friday is the best day for me and I can pretty much make any week, so I'll leave it up to you - Any Friday you like. I hope all is well with you and yes - Laurie Lee is a dream of a writer.

See you soon - Mark.

On 28 October 2013 09:31, Mark Huband < ■ > wrote:
Dear Mark

Great to hear from you - sorry for my tardy for. How about lunch on Friday 8 November - next week? Really looking forward to it.

Best
Mark

On 31 October 2013 12:40, Mark P < ■■@gmail.com> wrote:
Hi Mark,

that sounds good to me. Shall we say one o'clock at the usual pub. Looking forward to it - See you then.
Mark

On 5 November 2013 12:11, Mark Huband < ■ > wrote:
Dear Mark

I am greatly looking forward to meeting up after these many months. However, I am really sorry but something has come up for this Friday, which I greatly regret. It would be great if instead we could meet a week this

Friday - 15 November; I am very sorry to mess you about. Would this be possible - I very much hope so.

Very best

Mark

From: Mark P [mailto:█@gmail.com]
Sent: 07 November 2013 10:43
To: Mark Huband
Subject: Re: How are you
Hi Mark,

again I apologize for not replying straight away. Friday - 15th will be fine with me. I look forward to it. By the way (and I can't think of anybody I know that I would end such a short email to with such a sentence but) I've just discovered Faulkner - Wow! - 'The Sound and the Fury'

On 12 November 2013 16:56, Mark Huband <█> wrote:

Dear Mark

Great. Really looking forward to meeting on Friday.

Faulkner, yes, wow. I started – and must continue with – As I Lay Dying; a masterpiece.

See you Friday.

M

From: Mark P [mailto:█@gmail.com]
Sent: 20 November 2013 22:03
To: Mark Huband
Subject: Re: How are you
Hi Mark,

so sorry, yet again, for taking a while to send this. I really enjoyed Friday afternoon - where does the time go when we are having a chin-wag? I hope everything is on for next Tuesday - Can't wait. See below for my mobile phone number. Let me know the plan etc. Cheers for now then Mark and I'll see you next week.

Kind regards - Mark

On 22 November 2013 16:52, Mark Huband <█> wrote:
Mark

Great to see you last week. Thanks for your phone number. Really looking forward to Bob at the Albert on Tuesday (26 Nov). Shall we meet at 6.45pm at the main entrance of the Albert Hall – the big portico on the main road?

Best

Mark

From: Mark P [mailto:█@gmail.com]
Sent: 28 November 2013 17:15
To: Mark Huband
Subject: Re: How are you
Dear Mark,

Thanks so much for an absolutely wonderful night out. I can't believe that I've actually seen the great man live after all these years, and at the Royal Albert Hall! Splendid. One thing we forgot to mention was the absence of the 'special guessed' – wonder what happened there? Thanks so much for the meal. Seafood Linguine wasn't it? Delicious. Champagne too – I say. Great conversation, as always. I must say though, I do feel like a plumb for leaving behind my program and forgetting to pay you for it. What a numbty.

I have spoken to T about visiting you over the holidays and we'd love too. Was it the 28th that you are busy? Let me know as soon as you can because we have to arrange dates to see our families over the Christmas period.

Thanks again for everything Mark.

See you soon - Mark

On 10 December 2013 19:52, Mark Huband <█> wrote:

10 December 2013

Dear Mark

Sorry for my tardy reply.

What a great evening! Wonderful. I shall remember it forever.

Yes, we are away on 28 December, so would you all be able to come down on 29 Dec and stay that night? That would be great. Will you be coming on the train? I will check trains over that period – not sure if they change the timetable for the holiday period.

Let me know.

Really looking forward to it.

Best

Mark

*

After Mum had locked the back door and we had cycled away from our house on a warm sunny morning a few days later, the open roads through the fields were all I saw as we headed towards the coast.

But even as the roads between high summer hedgerows bulged with blackberries and cow parsley, and drew us deeper into the tranquillity forged out of the distance beyond and behind us, I thought of my friends going to my house and finding it dark, and worried that they might never come back to see me. The freckled girl would laugh at me.

My long hair hid the bump on the back of my head from when I had hit the wall, and, when we pitched our tents under horse-chestnut trees in the field of a village school that had closed for the summer holiday, my brothers didn't know why it was I kept turning in my sleeping bag, as I tried to prevent myself lying on the painful bruise that stayed even as we left England on the Harwich ferry and arrived among the grand streets of the Hook of Holland.

I wondered what it was the people saw, as they looked and stared and observed an English family passing, their bicycles laden, the wind in their hair as they chatted and smiled and called to each other to turn right or left. My words were not really those they could hear. I assumed they could see who I really was, that they could see through my smile and read the signs in my manner. I was not the good traveller visiting their country. I couldn't hide the language of the gang I had left behind, nor the talk of the dark night alleys we strolled along in our dreams, nor hide the tough future we imagined for ourselves.

From one second to another I was torn.

A boy passed by on his bicycle with his brothers and his mum and his dad, stopping to read maps and examine road signs, and talking of perhaps one day competing in the *Tour de France.*

Then a word echoed out of nowhere, and there, by the roadside, from where the tulip fields swept red tides to the horizon, the trust and love – icons passed down through fragile times that were the treasure our family shared – lay tarnished by derision, by doubt cast on the meaning they had for me. In terror, I felt I had become an unbeliever, convinced that the roads we were following under the hot sun would take me nowhere. Nowhere.

Only when we arrived in Amsterdam, where I had heard the hippies lived, and women sat in alley shop windows selling sex, would my street talk find a voice to which my family would realise they must listen. Then they would acknowledge as real that world I seemed only to be imitating.

I wanted to buy my friends presents from Holland, but I had no money, and could not ask Mum and Dad for money to spend on kids I had said I didn't want to be with anymore. They would have understood that I felt ambiguous about my friends. But explanations had to be all or nothing. My defence of my friends would have to be total: loyal, aggressive, defiant. That was how things were and how the world was. Everybody was a part of a gang, and you were either with that gang or against it. There could be no half way. It was dangerous to be in doubt. My friends were the people of the street, the children of working men whose voices were authentic and whose lives were from out there in the real world. I was either a part of their world or I was not, and I talked of my friends as we travelled beside the canals in the shadow of poplars. I was their defender, justifying their lives because to do so justified mine. I would seem to be a part of their attitudes, talking of girls as if I had overcome my inhibitions long ago and was now a man of the world.

But all I wanted, really, was to be gently and wisely guided in some other direction. I was explaining away my childhood, as my talk drove a wedge between myself and my mum and my dad. Every word I uttered gouged an ever-greater chasm between us, as I sought to give myself an image that drew upon the lives I thought my friends and I were leading or might one day lead, while inside all I wanted was to feel comfortable in another place where I could live without imitation.

But that place did not exist, neither in the past nor the present, so I was an unbeliever, homeless, always hoping to be taken aside with kind words...*now, Mark, tell me how your life is going...* An unbeliever convinced of nothing, rootless in a world where politics was sometimes the voice we were all supposed to believe could explain, bring truth, demystify. Sometimes I would even try to believe it could. But such big ideas would always quickly float away into a sky we barely noticed. There were no big ideas. Our world was small – just a few streets, beyond which was the unknown.

From Amsterdam, where, by mistake, we found ourselves pushing our bicycles past the windows in which women sat in their underwear waiting for men to push through the door for sex, we went north. I wanted to travel on forever with my mum and my dad, through forests and across mountains to cities where we might decide to stay forever. There should be no end, no point of return.

Endless flatlands opened up, leading us towards the land of lakes that I hoped would reach the dark forest into which I once dreamed I would step. In the distance I would hear the howling of wolves, and would pass through the darkness to a warm hut beneath the forest cover, brave, a rifle slung across my shoulders, my life a pattern like the seasons of the year.

But we did not reach the forest.

At the lakes we turned west, back towards the North Sea coast and our journey home. Perhaps my friends would want to know how far we had travelled. I could tell them the story of my journey, of the places we had passed through, about the canals that bestrode the land, the huge barges, home to families, passing low in the water with their heavy cargoes bound for the heart of Europe. In Amsterdam there were women in the shop windows selling sex, and people in jeans, their hair long just like ours, sitting around smoking in Dam Square. I went there. I looked a bit like them perhaps, though I was pushing my bicycle and I was with my mum and my dad and my brothers.

I went to find my friends on the evening we got back, exhilarated, tanned by the sun of the hottest summer on record.

'What's your family's thing about bikes?'

'It's good.'

'What's wrong with going in a car? You' got a car, ain't yer?'

For a short while Polly listened to my description of what I had seen in Amsterdam, and even seemed to want to go there. We talked as if we would go together, mingle with the hippies in Dam Square, and become sweet boys who would be taken in for free by the women in the windows.

For a while it seemed to my friends that my holiday had not been about a family cycling together through Holland but about being part of the serious world of alleys and sex. I was the traveller who had seen a place that my friends had not seen, and for a while they listened and I was back among them. There was no memory of the time I had been knocked to the wall, as

205

the endless time of summer opened out in front of us and we strode further away from our familiar streets with the new boys in our gang, and swam in the river beneath the willow trees near a lock and an old mill now a hotel where I had once watched two men in a dimly-lit ballroom playing cards at a table. Sometimes, when old couples were chugging past in their river cruisers, we would strip naked and show them our bums, then leap through the sun-dappled surface of the water, screaming so they turned then looked away in disgust.

We shattered the tranquillity of the place.

The boys who appeared in our gang that summer smoked and drank cider that they brought in crates. Though they never told us, we – unsaid – knew that what they brought down to the river had been stolen. We were all too young to buy alcohol, and anyway nobody had the money to buy so many bottles of cider and packets of cigarettes.

Suspicion fed the feeling of danger. We were drunk kids smoking by the river, the summer sun burning our backs and shoulders, the days turning to warm evenings that, even then, as they happened, we thought perhaps might be perfect.

But always there was danger, usually in the friction that erupted between us, at the sound of a word or a tiny comment taken badly. It was a danger that we looked for, because moments in which nothing happened seemed wasted. Silence was embarrassing. We must always talk, and because all we knew was each other, we could only ever talk about ourselves, our latest music, a girl. Another boy, the eldest among us, said other things. I had never seen him with a girl. One day he told us how his mum never made a fuss when she had to change his bed sheets if he had had a wet dream.

'She doesn't say anything. She knows what's going on, when you get to my age. But she doesn't mind. She knows I'm a man now,' he said, then, only because he wanted to, he flipped down the front of his swimming trunks to show us his prick.

'Put it away.'

'Wha's tha' all abou'?'

The boy wasn't embarrassed, though he should have been, because nobody did that kind of thing. Polly and Mick sniggered, then we all became more reserved when the new boys in our gang turned up with cider and cigarettes and talked of other places we could go, further along the river, beyond the meadows where I had once slid on the ice when all the land was white with snow, and past the Bomb Dip where old men went for sex with young girls or to wank over porn magazines that were left torn in the mud and grass.

We were drunk by the time we reached the empty maltings which lay between the railway and the river at Sawbridgeworth. The building loomed darkly from the wasteland that surrounded it. Boats passed along the river, only their rooves visible above the reeds and bulrushes. Trains clattered by and we clambered up wooden steps to a door that opened onto a large empty room.

We sat in a dim cool room drinking the cider, the alcohol and the heat of the sun leaving our heads spinning. Boys went prowling through the labyrinth of rooms. There was the sound of glass breaking, then again, as if a window had shattered. There was yelling and laughter. The warm air outside was gone and I was cold.

The noise made me shiver. Another crash of glass, then banging in a room above, or perhaps below.

With Rick and Polly I wandered through the rooms, drunk for the first time, my throat raw from the cigarettes.

'Wha's 'e doin'?' Polly asked of one of the Scottish brothers.

Suddenly there were screams, and the Scot with the long fringe that covered his eyes came into the room in which we were standing, his arm gashed, blood dripping onto the floorboards. Ahead, where a balcony outside led to steps going to ground level, we could hear laughter, then the thud of what sounded like a hammer hitting the wall.

We followed the rooms through light and darkness until we reached the balcony. In each room the floors were strewn with smashed plaster and broken light fittings, every window broken. A trail of blood curled and dripped its route to the balcony. We slipped and clattered drunkenly down the wooden steps.

The Scottish boy was bleeding heavily and his brother had wrapped his shirt around the wound. The blood soon oozed through, and amid the laughter and the noise of the hammer smashing at glass and plaster, the brothers became aggressive as they panicked.

For a second I looked away at the boats passing on the river. Walkers on the tow-path were watching us. As I turned back to the boys, the brother of the injured Scot yelled:

'Rozzers.'

We ran. I caught sight of a white Mini, its blue light flashing on its roof as it sped across the dusty wasteland towards us.

A few of us hid inside an outhouse, which had a door made from planks that did not fit together. We watched as the police car skidded to a halt where the injured Scottish boy was standing. He was with somebody else, perhaps his brother, and was put inside the police car.

The police officers wandered around the waste ground and found two others hiding. They were taken to the car. We heard the engine revving then saw the car turn and leave.

The people watching had gone from the riverbank, but we stayed where we were hiding. How long to remain before emerging into the sunlight and running from there? We argued in whispers, for and against leaving where we were, until one – Shat, I remember – stepped out onto the waste ground. Others emerged from their hiding places, until there were perhaps ten of us standing there wondering if more police would come. We shared cigarettes and ambled across the waste-ground, trying to fake our innocence in the eyes of whoever we imagined might be watching, while keeping to the edge of the buildings so we could hide if we needed.

We walked to the station nearby, jumping the train, as there was no ticket seller there. Some lay in the baggage racks, and the mixture of ecstasy and anxiety erupted in gabbling talk and accusations. Would the boys who had been taken away reveal the names of the rest of us?

'Course they fuckin' will.'

'They won't keep their mouths shut. No fuckin' way.'

'Such a prat, cuttin' 'is arm. Fuckin' blood all over the shop.'

'Would all 'ave scarpered if 'e 'adn't cut hisself open.'

The train curled along the embankments on which I had watched it pass for years, through sun and snow. But this day I did not know the route. I knew nothing of the place. It was as if I was nowhere that was a part of me, the familiar land suddenly unknown because the day was unknown. We reached Harlow Mill, our station. I walked with Polly to his house then went home.

The police had not been.

Next morning I went to Polly's house and we walked down to the swings where I had first met him all those years ago. Michael, my brother, approached on his bike.

'Mum wants to see you,' he said, and cycled away.

Though unsaid, the urge to run away was strong in both of us, as Polly and I walked talking out across the fields beyond Dick's Pond and the slaughterhouse. It never occurred to us to ask ourselves what it was that we had done wrong. Neither of us had stolen or broken anything. We had followed. But perhaps we didn't want to admit that that was all we had done. We wanted to feel that we had been involved, that we had made a mark, that some folklore had been written and that our names would be a part of it.

We walked for miles across the fields, way beyond the haystack where I had lain with the freckle-faced girl I would never see again.

It would the last time Polly and I would be thrown together like that, sharing something. Neither of us wanted to make the last step, until there was no more track to follow and we knew that we must turn around, knowing we had been betrayed, sensing that talk of our gang, bikes, girls, music and Amsterdam, was fading into emptiness. And as we walked back towards our uncertain fate, the bond between us never seemed so strong. We sensed we had nobody else in the world. We were both helpless. Our talk had none of the street bravado that had forged our language until that day. Without risking any signs of affection, he asked me:

'You gonna be alright? What'll yer old man do? What'll yer old dear say?'

'Dunno. Dunno.'

At the corner of the playing field we parted. I went home without looking back at him, as he went to his house not knowing whether the police had already been there.

*

Only once, on my way home from school, did I dare knock on the door of Polly's house, though at the main door, not the one at the side. We talked on the doorstep, me in my school uniform carrying my school bag, as I leaned against my green racing bike.

He quietly closed the door behind him, to prevent his mum and dad from hearing us talk. We stood suspended between worlds, his dad having told him he was confined to home, though without telling him for how long.

I could not see those boys again, my dad told me, as we drove to the police station near the underpass that had marked the end of our fight with the cold wind that cast rocks at our faces as we edged slowly towards the town library where I always took out the same book – a story about two families who lived in windmills and only became friends after a storm.

Mum and Dad wouldn't want to hear that story now. I will tell them another story, to show them where the world of which we were now a part had started, and why it was that we were walking across the police station car park in the shadow of buildings that I had always thought were towers but which now seemed small and distant. I would tell them a new story, and they would know why we were sitting in a meeting room listening to a police officer explain what had happened on that warm day at the Sawbridgeworth maltings, how stupid and dangerous it had been, how much damage had been done, and what steps would be taken to compensate the owner of the building.

From the window I could see people cycling against the wind then disappearing into the underpass. Perhaps that was where it had started, with that fight against the stone wind. Or perhaps it had started at the aluminium door of the library as it had swung shut behind me and I had been poised to explain myself to the woman who wore her glasses at the end of a chain: I know I have taken this book out before, but, please, let me take it out again, the story about the two families who lived in the windmills. That was where it started, the story I would tell my mum and dad, with that feeling of not knowing whether I had the right to take my favourite book out of the library as often as I wanted, with that feeling of not knowing whether it was okay to be me.

Of course, I could never tell that story, because nobody told their stories, which is why I was waiting for somebody to ask me whether I had a story to tell, and was listening for that voice again: *Now Mark, tell me about your life…* Perhaps the police officer, as he looked out over us – at Shat, whose mum was wearing her auburn wig and her white knee-length shiny boots, at the Scottish brothers whose mum and dad I had never before seen, at Polly in the Afghan coat and flared jeans which had replaced the denim jackets we had once worn when we were together but which my mum and dad had said I should not wear that day, at Steve, Mick, the tall boy Alan, who would become Polly's closest friend after that time, and at the others I don't remember now – perhaps he, in the police uniform that proved he had the comfort of knowing he belonged somewhere, would ask: 'So, how are your lives going so far?'

But there was not much we would have been able to tell him. We had no more to say to him than we had to say to each other. We had no yesterdays we really wanted to share, I sensed, with a mixture of sadness and relief and loss, which lingered for weeks, and which is what had led to me knocking on Polly's door that evening.

'See yer,' he said, and shut the door through which I would never again pass, and I rolled on my bicycle down the gravel slope to the swings where I had first seen him and slowly edged my way home.

Mum would wake me in the mornings and, after a brief moment of distraction, I would remember. At breakfast I would eat their food, sitting in silence for fear of sounding like a boy without guilt.

I couldn't imagine my brothers wanting to cycle with me to school.

The people staring at me as I passed must know.

I must scream – could not scream. I must cry – could not cry. I must look nowhere – nobody must look back, speak, or smile at me. My teachers must know, though I never learned that they did.

In my school, in the corridors, I could barely look at my dad if I passed him. I was not a boy, nor a son. I was not a victim, nor a hero. I told nobody about that hot afternoon, about the friends I had been with, about the police officer, about the shame and the guilt.

I didn't understand the guilt, because it did not emerge as words.

There were no words.

The feeling was all – a combination of fear in the stomach that was like poison, of humiliation that glared from my eyes, of weakness in my arms and legs, my throat dry, my bed no longer a soft embrace.

But there were no words, as the fear and wretchedness infected my entire world.

I could tell nobody, and in school I wanted only to sit silently on the edge of the gangs, the class, the teams, the groups. I wanted to sit quiet, even disappear, hiding my guilt as it oozed through my veins, knotted my guts, burned me each time my dad passed me in the school corridor and each time my mum gave me food, because all that had once been dreamed would never again be trusted, even as a dream. Now we could see how the good times were ending. The journey south from Yorkshire was now endless, not definitive, as had once been dreamed. There would be no end, because the people, the children, the boys, this boy, would never allow the day – all the days, together – to reach that point beyond which the struggle would be over and the world would be won. Our happy years would never come.

Instead, the autumn came, and the world that I knew slipped into cold and darkness, dragging me with it.

214

In the evening the newsreaders of *PM AT FIVE PM* taunted in the kitchen, with news reports about big events that only happened in order to further imprison my world in its chains, telling me: 'You'll never be there. Listen and yearn. Listen and rot. Listen and drift further away from the imagined times, when the town was caught in the silver mirrored light of a rocket bound for the moon, when sunlight warmed the prairies of America.' A family had once driven south, on a day that may have been dry and warm. But then the weather turned cold. The journey ended on a stretch of waste-ground beside a cinema. There were stories, but some of the stories could never be told. The stories stopped being told, because the stories turned bad, and because there was nobody there to whom they could be told. Like all families, we were alone, within the dark red brick walls of our home. The storm never came that brought down the windmill and turned conflict into friendship. The storm never came, nor any of the moments that might end one era and mark the beginning of another. Each day's silence was followed by the same, and all that could be longed for was night and sleep.

Hate flowed naturally in the wake of the guilt, as memories of the crime receded.

I would look then, in the mirror, and ask myself my name, murmuring under my breath: 'Is that who you are? Is that who you are?'

I could never look for more than a few seconds, hating the face that looked back at me. I was frightened of it – frightened that it would always be a face eyed with suspicion.

Perhaps one day it would change. The wretched face would suddenly smile, the bad times having fallen away. The true face would emerge, and would look back at me with a smile, saying, in a kindly voice: 'Now Mark, tell me about your life. How is it going, so far?'

Then I would speak of a time when things might have gone very bad, but that somehow I was pulled back from the brink, from a dangerous time that could have led me into permanent darkness.

But then the voice would take on a different tone, telling me: 'Well, you know, everybody goes through bad times. They are a part of what happens to us. And then we emerge, richer in experience. So, don't let it worry you. You will move on. Don't dwell on it. Don't be haunted. Think about everything as some kind of a…journey. Tomorrow will be different, and something will happen to make you forget the bad things for a while. The bad, stupid things you did. Then you'll remember again, some time in the future. And you will have learned about what it is to take a risk, to know danger, to drift, but then to see what it is to pull back, to know when to run, so you can turn to yourself and say "Yes, that's who I am – *all* those things, *all* those things that happened. That's who I am. That's what I know about".'

Never.

Never, in the tightly-chained world of another wet evening did that voice speak to me. Room to room, each a cell. There was darkness on the stairs we had run down in the early morning when we knew there would be magic in the sitting room. The neighbours' homes were dark, the trees black, the long journey to the distant corner dark but for orange light pooling in the emptiness that droned with a last car home or the squawk of a bat flitting through the darkness.

I wanted the kitchen to be warm again. I wanted to make a wish in the bowl that oozed with rich fruit. But instead the hate of myself burned strong, always, to this day, returning in autumn when the dying months of 1976 are relived. Autumn's story will always be one of a year's end reached after a summer that never bore the promises that I still dream are made each spring. A summer lost, and autumn is the wake, its mourners journeying without end, the return of spring unimaginable.

I came to hate the hope in me that the autumn would ever end. Hope was a season many mountains away, and in my poisoned state I was too weak to climb, riddled as I was by guilt that oozed as I woke and which stared back at me in the mirror, when I gulped breathless, hating the face I saw: 'Don't look at me. Don't look at me.'

'Yer owe me a pudding.'

'I don't.'

'Fuckin' do.'

'No, I don't. I don't owe you a pudding. I don't owe you anything.'

'Wanna make sunnink of it?'

'No. But I don't owe you a pudding.'

'Fuckin' 'and it over.'

'No. I don't owe you anything.'

'Outside?'

'No. I don't you anything.'

Dennis' face was taut with rage. He stared like an animal about to tear me to pieces. But I didn't care. I didn't care if I lived or died. Kill me then, for a sponge pudding and custard. Kill me however you want, I don't care.

Nobody defied Dennis. But in my misery I was beyond fear. If the world came to an end I wouldn't care, the instinct of survival having slipped away from me. I was not defying Dennis. I was hoping he would kill me with one punch. One punch was all that was needed. Then I could die, and perhaps, many years later, somebody would ask: 'Was there a reason why that boy defied Dennis that day, when he knew he was risking his life?'

*

Dennis never threw a punch. A woman stepped in, seeing what might be about to happen. She told him to sit down and to leave me alone, then found me a seat at another table.

When the boy whose seat I had taken wanted it back I moved again, to a table of boys who sat under a poster of the Queen and Prince Philip that our new housemaster had pinned above the wooden hatches from where lunch was served.

They were boys I hardly knew, though we had been taught together for nearly three years. They were mostly from Tany's Dell, part of a different gang, a group that was good at football and was quietly dismissive of the loud street talk that boomed from Dennis and Neil's corner. They were more serious about their schoolwork, though they pretended not to be.

'I dunno why you ever sat with that lot,' the boy beside me, Richard, told me. I smiled, saying nothing, unable to explain that they were the only boys to have made way for me when I arrived at the school. I had become bound to them, though I never said it, because these other kids would have found that ridiculous.

I sensed that Richard had been watching, because some time later he told me: 'I never really liked that Tony that you were such mates with. Actually, I really couldn't stand him.' Again I said nothing, struck only by the realisation that there were people around me who watched and listened and had strong views, but who kept their views to themselves.

I didn't know how to respond to what Richard said about my friend who had by then been in South Africa for more than a year. He had been in the classroom that day when Tony had left, and had seen how sad I had been. He would not have cried. I shrugged and thought about Tony, and perhaps for the first time wondered whether I had liked him. He had been my friend, so I must have liked him. The risk would have been in defending him too much. But why would anybody dislike Tony? Some people had disliked his smile. Perhaps Richard had been one of them, and had perhaps been waiting for me all along, knowing that I was not really the kind of kid who swaggered along the corridors with kids who smelled of cigarette smoke or who talked with the hairspray and high-shoed gum-chewing loud-cackling girls Lorraine and Beverley.

Had these new kids known all along that that was not really me? Why hadn't they told me? I could have been saved early on. Then the heat and the steam and the tensions, the illegal runs out across the park to the distant trees, the misery of a cough I had had for the wet months of one endless autumn and into winter, would have been eased. We might have been thriving as we headed towards youth, kids at play, boys sharing their secrets.

219

These new kids did not seem ever to have been part of the landscape of my classes, though they had been there all along – Richard, Jeremy, Lee, Alan – kids whose homes were on streets that I could cycle along without feeling I was entering hostile territory but instead crossing a land on which we could grow up together. Now, in the corridors, we talked of getting to classes on time, slinging our sports bags over our backs, book-filled as we discussed homework and what it was we had learned in our lessons. Where once knowledge had been stone, now we competed to show what we had learned. One boy, Martin, who had appeared on a television quiz show for brainy kids, was not afraid to throw signs of knowledge into conversation. Perhaps our town was, after all, a part of the world, its image caught faintly in the mirror of a rocket bound for the moon as its sheen stole a faint glance at our once-new streets.

Some of our teachers had even waited for us to emerge from the animal bodies we had worn when we had arrived there nearly three years earlier as the children of the golden decade, who had become the cracked pieces that the new world must now pick up.

But we never were picked up – not by the currents that flowed, nor by the breeze that blew us towards the spring of 1977. In our strange state of childhood we could do nothing but learn to compete, to win the most merit marks from the teachers who had waited for us. They kept their grudges quiet. Perhaps they had no grudges, and after all were only there to teach us about the Rift Valley, long division, Boyle's Law, and the French future tense I was thrilled when I realised I had mastered.

Now, at day's end, I stopped running from there. The smell of polish no longer oozed like poison in the air from which I must flee into the cold freedom of the evening light. I had a busy schedule. My team would win against the other schools, as we pulled on our red silk shorts and strode out onto the basketball court. Of course we would win. It was the only thing that mattered. Then, afterwards, a fine victory taken in our stride, I would stroll with my new friends to the safety of their territory, and perhaps drink tea at Richard's house, where his kindly mum smiled and chatted with me as if I had known her forever.

My evening ride home would be smooth and swift. The wind didn't cast rocks anymore, because I was stronger. Now I could look back at the people I sped past. There was nothing they could see that would make them wonder whether I was good or bad. There were no signs. I was just a boy cycling home, his bag full of books, school closed now, the basketball court silent and dark, the smell of sweat lingering long after the game had brought me the applause of the sports teachers who looked at us as heroes and whose praise tightened the bonds of our team.

Our imaginations ebbed as the days passed and our bodies changed. Glances lingered on the smiling faces of girls, cold stares softening. Friends waited for each other in doorways, after classes, at notice boards. After school, on the warming pavements of early spring, boys and girls, patient with each other, waited for the risk, waited for the given sign of a gentle secret that might hold the promise of a shared moment. We all dreamed in secret. But who would be the first to tell?

'What do you really think of her?' Richard would ask me quite often when we were talking of a girl in our school. 'And don't tell me you don't know. You always say you don't know. And this time I really want you to say what you think of her,' he would stress. He would smile and laugh in ways that made me happy because I sensed that my opinions mattered to him.

'I don't know,' I would reply, never wanting to give anything away.

'You can't say that,' he would exclaim, exasperated by my evasiveness, unable to comprehend why I could possibly want to evade the question.

We became friends, trusting each other, growing up together.

'You can at least say something. Just some hint.' But I would only smile, as if any sign I might give would lead in a direction I might regret, or might lead to somebody saying something, or to somebody asking me to admit to something or to state some truth in which I had no confidence. I would not speak until I knew what it was I really felt. I feared being mocked if I gave an opinion or if I revealed too much of myself. Better stay silent, then nobody could know about the man that would one day emerge. Keep secret now, then nobody would be able to say: 'He didn't used to be like that. I knew him before he was like that.'

'But you must have something to say about her,' Richard persisted.

'No. Nothing.'

Sometimes I knew I was guarding something that did not exist. It was a secret that I did not really have – a belief I would not let anybody see, because it was not there at all. But even though it did not exist, there was a secret. There was something that must be guarded. Everything had been risked, and now I was a protector; I had lived for many years, and now its survival depended on me.

But I could never explain what it was that had fallen into my hands.

Only now do I realise that it was my own future I was protecting.

My instinct was to remain uncommitted, and to wrap myself in words that would leave the kids of my class wondering what was going on inside my head, as we talked about girls, some hinting vaguely that they had secrets that they would not share for fear that they would be derided as cheap – if it was cheap, it wouldn't count, that first time with a girl, whereas if you did it with a girl who wasn't cheap, you could be reinvented.

There was a couple who were a few years older than us, who sat each break-time on the same old, knife-scarred table beneath the photo of the Queen and Prince Philip. They were always there, their lips thick and red, sucking hard at each other's faces, kids all around them too afraid to watch but too mesmerised to take their eyes off them. They were cheap, that couple. After kissing, the boy would stare at the kids who were too close and order them away, as if the table was a private place. His girl would walk away with small steps, the only girl among her friends to have a deep-voiced boy who kissed like that in the common room.

There's became *the* kiss. Were there other kisses? Should kisses be there, on the knife-scarred corner table?

It was never explained why there was an old table in our school, where the furniture was new and broken. Perhaps the old table had been there when the couple

223

arrived, and had been claimed by them years before we younger kids had entered the school. We had interrupted their private times, stealing glances at the kiss which we might one day have to do just like them.

I didn't tell my new friends that I knew about kissing because I had seen it during times whose traces were disappearing, at night when kids had danced at *Speakeasy*, and had smoked outside in the rainy dark, sharing spliffs while kids on the dance floor kissed to the music that had borne us into our decade. Perhaps I didn't look like a boy who knew, or who had seen it before in that other world whose traces had faded ever since that trouble we had had.

My new friends went back years together, to a time before my time. But they seemed now to be forming new stories. They were not like the friends I had once had, who I now sometimes saw from a distance, as I cycled home or shopped for apples on our High Street. Those friends had had stories into which I could never have been written, out of which old characters were melting away without explanation, while minor characters took on new roles, Rick's long denim coat swaying from side to side as he strolled one March evening along my road towards his house around the corner.

I called out to him, though had no idea what I would say if he stopped and turned. He waited for me to speak.

'You playing your guitar still?' I asked.

'Yup.'

'With the others?' I asked, he having briefly played guitar in a band with Polly and others from their school. I wanted news of the friends who had gone, though without wanting to reveal that I no longer went to see them.

'No. Not much.'

'On your own?'

'Mostly.'

'What are you playing?'

'This guy Dylan. Heard him?'

'No. Dunno. Maybe.'

'Easy guitar.'

'Right.'

'Bit different.'

'Got any of his records?'

'Yeah. Come round and listen if you want.'

'Alright.'

'Not now though. Some time.'

'Right. Thanks.'

He strolled away, leaving me wondering if he meant for me to follow later that day, or at some time in the future.

I didn't really know Rick, and found him strange. It would be odd seeing him outside our gang. Really there was no gang. Nobody had ever said there was, except Polly, when he had imagined life as an outcast, sometimes a hippy, sometimes a Hell's Angel, sometimes a skinhead on the stadium terraces.

But all that was over now, Rick strolling away, others seen from a distance on their way home or to their work.

*

At The Stow, an arcade of shops to where Richard and I would sometimes make forbidden lunchtime runs from school for no reason other than that it was against the school rules, two painters were stroking brushes of green paint onto a hut. There was an alley up from the road, and from there I saw that one of the painters was the boy I had collided with on my bike, years ago. He saw me and smiled and nodded.

'Painter and decorator, me, now. But I'm gonna train to be a cabinet maker.'

Our friends would all have left school – or be about to – at around Easter that year. But to have asked him about them would have turned our story into the past in a way that I could not bear to do, so I said goodbye and walked on with Richard, who didn't ask me who the boy was and why I knew him, as the traces between my worlds disappeared still further and I wondered if I could open the door wide and let my new friend see beyond my home and out into the past that was the private land of our family secrets that I hoped one day I could share.

Mist still hugged the land as we set off into the bright coolness of the morning – two kids on bikes, Richard on one belonging to one of my brothers, bags on the back filled with food and clothes and maps. Ahead of us, the road glittering in the morning, soon dry and warm in the Easter sunshine.

We skimmed across the soft, warm surface of the world.

Our world was a land of great trees that shaded narrow English lanes. It was a world of fields that had been ploughed and planted and which were now rich with fresh shoots. We sped along the roads that lured us into an England we felt we had long-known but never seen. Our journey was north, from Essex into Hertfordshire and beyond, far beyond the routes that on Sunday

226

afternoons a family had once cycled along in a row beneath soaring chestnut trees, returning home before dark as evening's fall paced the minutes to morning and last waves at school gates.

'Bye bye. Have a lovely time. And do take care. Stay off the main roads...much nicer to go on the country lanes...have you got the maps?' then last waves from Mum and Dad, and gone, out into the morning, whose tranquillity brushed our cheeks as we floated upon the humming and the buzzing and the sun warmed our backs.

I had long-imagined the journey. We would travel further than ever before, on a road rising above fields that rolled down to the railway and passed thickets that hid a place where a bomb had fallen during the war, or that's what the kids used to say. It was a dark place now, hidden. Maybe there were old men there, with girls. But we were only passing, cycling fast, going much further, leaving them behind along Lower Sheering Road, the back lane past farms, then freewheeling among houses, and on down to the railway near the river where cruisers slid among the reeds and bulrushes and the dark empty windows of the Sawbridgeworth maltings cast an unblinking gaze at me as we travelled on and on, fast, until we had gone further than ever before.

The web of past times drifted away on the breeze as we cycled deeper into the warm spring countryside. People could stare at two kids on their journey. They could look into our eyes and see only good things, as we chatted and called ahead with directions at country crossroads, at junctions beside village greens. We had no time to waste if we were to reach my grandparent's home before dark.

227

They were ahead of us, waiting, I imagined, in the house to which they had moved when they had retired to a corner of rural England near a country church in Cambridgeshire. They would want to hear the story of our journey, our fine time cycling through the English countryside – countryside that was unchanged, thanks to the sacrifices of the generations that had gone before us and to whom we owed so much, as we planned our future as successful professionals who would look back to the time when we went on a long ride through England, past fields where the wind turned the crops to sea and a boy laughed ecstatically as he balanced on the crossbar of his dad's bicycle for the length of a long straight road between the woods and a village where a German Shepherd barked outside a pub.

We passed the gibbet at Caxton, where once the highwaymen had been hanged. Our car had slowed so many times there, at the junction that later became a roundabout. Then we had passed among the dour homes of the Papworths, approached the turn among the woods on the left, and glided across the fields of summer corn or winter frost towards the cluster of homes in that corner of England my grandparents had made their own.

As we approached, I panicked. They could not want me there, I was sure of it. They had no reason to open their door to me and my friend. I hoped they would not ask me why I was there.

'So lovely to see you, dear,' my grandmother said. 'Now, you must be Richard.'

'Ahh. You have done quite well,' said my grandfather.

We sat at the dining table, and I wished my mum and dad had been there. Then there would have been the right kind of words spoken. I would not have had to try and create a whole new world of stories.

'We left at 8 o'clock and mostly used the country lanes, and only took a couple of wrong turns.'

'Oh, so you took some wrong turns.'

'Well, only once or twice.'

'Yes. Well, that wasn't very clever.' My grandfather laughed, his gold tooth glittering. 'And you read your maps properly, did you.'

'Well, yes.'

'Mmm.'

'You've both done very well. Quite an adventure, I should think,' my grandmother enthused meekly.

My grandfather switched on a radio that stood beside his place at the head of the dining table. We listened to the news.

'Really, this government is the end. You follow politics, I assume. What a mess this government is in. No leadership. Though I suppose you support them, just like your dad.'

'I agree with you,' Richard told my grandfather, while I hoped the subject would change, because this was not why we had made our journey. I was afraid of politics, afraid that it would force me to pretend I had answers to questions that were too big for anybody to answer.

'Thank-you Pat,' my grandfather told the newsreader, his joke, as if the radio voice was that of an old friend. We smiled, as the radio was switched off.

Then silence hung in the room, in the house, in our minds, and out across the darkening fields. The trees were silent beyond the closed glass doors that gave on to the veranda, and my mind raced as I imagined creating a new beginning. It was almost in my grasp, the chance to

229

forge something out of nothing. New words. I would be new. My grandparents would listen for a moment, and then slowly feel their way around the new sounds being uttered. I would talk of the world I saw before me, and perhaps one of them would say: 'What a world you are seeing. Let me tell you how I think I can help you learn to cope with it. Let me share my experience. Let me tell you what it was like when I was beginning to make my way in the world, just like you are.'

Their language would not have been strange to me, because I could imagine the perfect time against which they compared everything that followed those long-ago days after men, crippled and haunted, stumbled home to tranquil villages, blind, mad, wondering why anybody had ever tried to convince the imperial British that it would 'be over by Christmas.' My grandfather had been born in 1916, and if I travelled far enough along the roads and lanes that were his corner of England and on whose every village green were the stone monuments to what had been lost in the Great War, I imagined I would catch a glimpse of the summer and the peace – the perfect time before the fighting started – that he was told by his family had been lost.

But he assumed I knew nothing, and that I did not care, and that I could have no idea where his imagination had its root and where his memories started. That was why he assumed I supported the Labour government of Mr Callaghan, because Labour was all about the new, while the Conservative party was the real guardian of the sacrifices that the crippled and the blind had made.

Even so, I almost reached the point where I would tell him that my life was a continuation of his own.

But if I had spoken he would have said: 'How can you possibly know what life was like before 1914? You can't possibly know what kind of sacrifices men have made for you young people.'

We left early next morning.

*

Richard's parents had grown up in Rushden. Rushden was his Bentham, his Indonesia, the Algeria, the Rogny-Les-Sept-Ecluses of his family. Now we were the vital link, leaving my grandparent's house with the last wave at the corner, my grandparents examining their shrubbery, their door a little open in case we perhaps had a reason to remember something left behind. Then the door closed and we two were gone, winding through the village beneath the great trees that traced the road to the last house then arched the open country onto which we rode fast as we travelled towards Northamptonshire.

I wanted to tell Richard of my grandparents, of how my grandfather had been, how it was they haunted our conversations at home, how they dulled the joy at Christmas, and that they had refused to attend my parents' wedding.

'Nice house. Not going to be like that in Rushden. Nothing like that. I hope you're not expecting anything like that,' he said, as we coasted along.

'No. I don't know. I've not thought about it,' I said, wishing there was no talk like this, as the sun rose and we cycled past the baking hot glare of a country brick works.

Our words were all that broke the silence.

231

'They're not quite as they might seem, my grandparents.'

'I liked them. Nice house. It'd be alright to end up living somewhere like that.'

'Yes, I suppose so.'

'Everything you could want. You've got to admit. Everything you could want. I mean, what more could you want?'

'Quite a lot else.'

'Like what?' he laughed, exasperated.

'Dunno.'

'C'mon. Like what? Nice house in a little village. That's what it's all about, isn't it?'

'I suppose so.'

'Course it is. What more could you ask for?'

'I suppose ending up like that might be okay.'

'Course it's okay. Sometimes I really don't get you. Can't you see? It's really obvious. You do it deliberately, just to be different, don't you?'

'No.'

'Well, what's wrong with saying that living in a house like that, in a nice little village, is what you want?'

'Nothing. I agree. There's nothing wrong with it.'

'Right then.'

'But it depends who you are there with.'

'Course. Wife, kids. Perfect.'

'Maybe.'

'There you go again.'

'I'm not just trying to be different.'

'Why can't you just admit it then? That's handsome that house. It's all you could ever want.'

'Not me.'

'There you go again,' he said, smiling but exasperated, the conversation tinged with friction as his incredulity rose. 'You are just saying that to be different.'

'I don't. I'm not,' I said, really meaning what I said.

'You are. Just admit it.'

But I could admit nothing, because I didn't know why it was that my hope of finding a place in the lives of my grandparents had been so strong. Nor did I understand why I had deluded myself into believing that the fear I had of my grandfather was something I had grown out of. He remained that debilitating presence, even when out of sight, as we sat at our dinner table at home wondering what it was he might be thinking of us. I wished that my feelings had been something as simple as a difference of opinion about politics. But I couldn't explain to Richard that my grandparent's house was as haunted as the other homes of theirs in which I had visited them over the years. To have tried to explain would have meant delving deeper into the past than I was able to do. It would have meant pretending I could grasp what a family is, and giving the false impression that lives that were hidden behind closed doors could be shared and discussed and even analysed. I couldn't do any of those things, because I had no idea of the truth of the story. Who had been good? Who had been bad? My instincts provided some clues, but in our family we viewed our instincts with suspicion.

We stayed two nights in Rushden, went on a day trip to Bedford with Richard's uncle and aunt, and left just as another bright morning was unfolding across the fields.

I dreaded going back to spend another night at my grandparent's house on the way home, now that Richard had a sense of my doubts about them. Perhaps now my grandfather would be full of praise, because we had reached our destination and were returning with the story of our journey.

'Rushden. Never been there. Leicestershire is it?'

'Northamptonshire.'

'Knew a man in Kettering, from the Lodge. Didn't know him well.'

'You must be tired after your long journey.'

'Quite tired,' I told my grandmother, not wanting to seem too tired in case my grandfather would think of me as weak.

'Early start tomorrow, I expect,' he said, an excuse for us to go to bed soon after supper, then be up early next morning, and gone before the mist had cleared from the fields.

*

I could hear Rick in his room, singing as he played his guitar when I went around the corner of our road to his house the day after getting back from my journey with Richard.

I stood outside his bedroom door to listen, wondering what it was I should say when I went inside. He would not want to hear about bicycle rides. I wouldn't talk about what it was like to have travelled across a land that seemed unchanged since some time before the wars we knew about because there were old men still around who had fought in them. He might ask why I didn't see

Polly any more, and I would be confused about how to respond.

I wondered how Rick had been seen by Polly's family, with his reserved manner and rock star clothes, which set him apart. Nobody laughed at him, even when he strolled down our High Street among the shoppers and the school kids. I passed him once, unnoticed, on Charing Cross Road, perhaps ten years later, long after drugs and music had split us apart and he had seen me as too young to try and seduce, after he had made it known to us all that he was gay. The person I saw in the London street crowd stood out as much as he had always done, his hair and coat just the same. He strolled just as he had done when he walked down my road to his house, when everybody could see the role he had given himself. Nobody laughed at him because nobody could be sure that he was playing. He seemed to know where it was he would end up. Perhaps he became famous, as it seemed obvious he would, and that the person I saw on Charing Cross Road had become his dream.

It would have been good if it could have been like that. Then his room overlooking his parent's garden really would have been the kind of room from where rock stars took their first steps on the road to fame. We could believe it might be us, whose fame would begin in small rooms on backwater roads. We had to believe it, because we had nowhere else from where to start, though of course it was a bit of a joke that it could indeed be one of us who would one day stride onto the stage at Hammersmith Odeon. It would always be other people, though Rick might be one of them.

He kept singing when I stepped into his room, unselfconscious in a way that was unimaginable to me. He nodded for me to sit on his bed, while he stood strumming and singing with a quiet, soft voice.

The song was a long ballad about a boxer who had been blamed for a murder in a bar in New Jersey. Rick had learned all the words and had deciphered the guitar chords from a record that was spinning silently on a turntable.

He stopped strumming.

'Listen to this,' he said, switching on the record.

The low, mesmerising strumming of a guitar filled the room, then the long, haunting notes of a violin.

Then the story started.

There was anger and defiance. There was the heat of the night, the fury of darkness, the spilling of blood. Images appeared and disappeared, creating a world of a kind I had never before heard in a song. There was the sound of the street captured in the words of the outsider who watched and listened from the shadows in the corner. There was power in the sound of the violin, guitar and drums, which twisted around words that combined all the languages I had ever learned – street talk, politics, romance, violence – and which together swooped and glided until the tale was told. The song was its own universe – passionate, uncompromising, shining a piercing light into a tiny corner of the world and transforming it into the only place that mattered. The story was the whole world, and Dylan's was the only voice that could tell of it.

I was overwhelmed. I had heard the voice that perhaps I had been waiting for. It could say anything, sing any song, and could speak of a world that I could take or leave. I envied him, being able to talk like that. He dragged me into the sounds and the streets as if they were

236

my own. He wanted to share them as if they were my story too.

But his was a voice that didn't care about me – one that would always be thousands of miles away, a voice so powerful and fluent that I could never imagine myself speaking back to it. I could never answer it. Dylan's words cowed me into silence, as if there was nothing left to be said. They were the words of an actor whose drama was real. The stories were real, the cops, the gangsters, the children playing on the beach, the woman lost to him, the hot chilli peppers in the blistering sun, the man in the corner who approached him for a match, all were real – or imagined – it did not matter, because a new, half-real, half-imagined world was opening up.

But it would be a long time before I could give anything back, and only then when I learned that all I could give was my own voice – a voice that in the early months of 1977 had no sound, no words, nothing to say, nothing that was distinct from anybody else's, because that was not the way we were, whatever went on in inside our heads. All I could do was make my voice appear as though it might be different, by having people look at me in a way that made it obvious that deep down I was not the same. I would give some clues about what might be going on inside, though not too much. So, I hid beneath a leather hat, inside the long Afghan coat like Polly's, which I had bought from Mick, the boy who took his mum's Jack Russell to get laid by the pedigree dogs at the slaughterhouse. On my feet I wore a pair of cowboy boots that were too tight, until the day my brother Michael wore them and they stretched and became too big.

The hat was my best disguise. My mum had brought it back for me from America, where she went on a long holiday with Uncle Mark. They had flown to Canada to see Mum's old school-friend, then taken a train all the way down America, to San Diego, where one of their half-brothers lived with his wife who came from Costa Rica, and who swept into our house in Harlow one summer with her sister, and who must have thought me strange because I asked them all about America, and told them that was where my leather hat came from. But they were from another America, and didn't know Bob Dylan. They wore flowing trouser suits and had a Hollywood style that glittered, while I hid inside my clothes and wondered if they thought I was happy with what I seemed to be, and wished they could see that I wasn't, even though I could seem to be happy with imagining myself as belonging to a land to which I had never been.

And that strange fascination with a place across the sea became stranger on the day our neighbour's daughter came into our house and gave me the book I had heard that people had to read.

*

It was mysterious to me, that anybody in our town could have heard of *On The Road*.

On Saturdays my dad worked in our garden. But I didn't want to help make our garden bloom. It was not like other people's gardens. It was never going to be perfect. It would always be makeshift, while our neighbour Howard had a garden with a straight gravel path, a greenhouse and a conservatory. So when I was a kid, I went to help Howard with his garden, because his seemed more professional. He didn't use old stakes and wire for his rose trellis, but proper wooden frames. He had a garden like those that appeared in magazines.

In the mid-morning we would stop our work and Dora, his wife, would bring us refreshments. We would lean on our shovels, take off our gloves, pocket our secateurs, and talk about the bright blooms that grew in their garden. Howard grew the same flowers every year – big yellow and red and purple chrysanthemums – that he picked for Dora, who put them in a vase in their perfect house.

We had first been inside there a few days after we had walked in wonder into our new home in the freezing winter of 1969, and had all dismissed the possibility that we could have heard a knock at our front door, until Mum opened it and found a short-haired, greying man wearing glasses and a rain coat standing on the doorstep in the twilight, who said: 'Hello. My name's Hughes, from next door. My wife and I wonder if you would like to come round for a drink.'

There's was the only home along our stretch of the road whose house we could go into. When my dad turned 70 years old, in 2008, Dora, more than 90 by then and nearly blind, telephoned to wish him a happy birthday, from the house in which she still lived with Howard, on the corner beside our home, until she died a year later, during the cold of winter.

'They were the best times of our lives, when you were all living next door,' she told my dad.

Sometimes we would go there for lunch on Sundays, and would sit in their dining room, which was formal and cold and unlike them because they were all warm and kind and liked to laugh and joke. Sometimes

239

their two daughters were there, both of them older than my brothers and me, women really, both born in the 1950s. They were very pretty, serene, sophisticated, both with long dark hair and soft voices. They could have been film stars. A local photographer had taken formal portraits of them as they had grown up, and which hung in their hallway.

Howard and Dora traced our lives from that cold December evening when we had heard the knock at our front door.

My brother Paul went often to their house to sit with Dora, who was always kind to him. They were friends, he six or seven years old, she in her sixties. Sometimes I would see them walking to the church together, where Paul sang in the choir, or going from house to house on our road collecting money for the NSPCC or the Lifeboats. They would stroll from house to house as if it was normal to go and knock on the front doors of the homes where the smart, serious people lived. That was one of the ways Paul got to know the people in our road, and how he got to know Dora's daughter Patsy, who would sometimes take him out, even to London, while I dug their garden with her dad and we talked about chrysanthemums.

But when I was ten or eleven I stopped going there, because I had new friends, who Howard and Dora sometimes saw me with when we were swaggering in our gang down our High Street.

They looked at me differently when I was with my friends, because people knew what my friends were like. But when we went to their house for lunch or for a drink at Christmas I still had the feeling that a part of their garden was mine, because I had dug the soil there when I had been a kid. I wondered if it was remembered, or whether too much time had passed and too much had happened that people wanted to forget. Perhaps they would want to be free of us, because we might confine them to the past. But it did not seem like that, as we traced each other's lives, and we three boys became teenagers, and listened in awe as we were told that Patsy had once gone to a pop festival in Lincoln and had taken a bin liner to sleep in.

On an autumn night long after the times when I had worked in their garden, two men with long hair and beards knocked at our front door. They said they were friends of Patsy's, that nobody was at home next door, and could they use our bathroom. I watched them, sure they were on their way from a field in Lincoln, wandering the land, playing music and making their way to another strange and beautiful place.

Mum let them in and, separately, they went to the bathroom and we listened as they vomited loudly. They both said they were sorry, then went away, and I was sure that all of Patsy's friends must be hippies, like I wanted to be, wandering the streets, like I wanted to do. It stayed in my mind for years that she had been among people like them when we had moved there, long before she married an air force pilot and talked about life in the military.

She recognised the signs in me – my clothes, my hair – as we ate mince pies and drank sherry in their house one Christmas.

'You've probably read *On The Road*,' she said.

'No. Don't know that one,' I pretended, my instinct to conceal my interest and knowledge part-rooted in the need to hide, part-inspired by the possibility that I might be disappointed by the book, or not understand it but would hate to have to admit it.

'I have it somewhere. I'll find it for you.'

Sometimes, in the early evening, as we were eating our dinner, we would hear the back door to the kitchen being opened. It was a sign that we belonged, that the door would be opened, a voice call out, and we would think it normal that somebody we couldn't see was stepping into our house. Usually it was Dora.

'Oooh oooh,' she would call out. We would all mimic her: 'Oooh oooh,' and would laugh, and she would laugh too.

But this time it was Patsy who walked into our sunny hallway holding the book.

'Here it is, the book. I don't need it anymore,' she told me.

*

In our house books, like the words in them, like *The Guardian* newspaper, like the voices on *PM AT 5 PM*, were part of the towers and castles of a world that I would never scale. I would never understand the stories in them. The great minds of the world – the dead authors, the people whose names appeared in the newspaper – had written or spoken all that needed to be expressed. The books had been studied, conclusions drawn, theories devised, and the thoughts of great minds shared between the people who could understand and who must always be in charge.

I could say nothing more than the great men in Whitehall and Oxbridge, who had already said what was important.

I could barely open a book, a novel, a famous work, without the assumption that of course I did not understand, because such understanding was the preserve of those whose minds had been formed in a different, richer, better world than mine. Books were trophies, their completion a challenge I could not meet. Discussion about books, with the teachers who came to see us in our house, was torture. All I really wanted to tell of was the story I was making of myself. But that was not a story that would have any value in the telling. The only stories of value were those that had been carefully bound within the musty red and green cloth-bound hardbacks that towered over me in our sitting room. *That* was writing. That was all that could be written: Shakespeare, Milton, Defoe, Brontë, Austin, Dickens, Fielding, James, Lawrence, Eliot. All else was cheap, and possibly corrupting. The greats, whose work was like the face of a doctor who had once lived across the road from us and whose every stare was proof of his importance, were the only men and women with a story to tell, their awesome power made even greater by their deaths.

I feared and resented the writers whose works heightened my sense of ignorance and which I could not bring myself to venture into, and felt embarrassed when Patsy handed me her well-worn copy of *On The Road*, my face betraying my self-consciousness, as I knew that I would not be able to explain why I wanted to read it, and felt disappointed that she had given it to me because she did not 'need it anymore'.

I had imagined Kerouac and Dylan must be friends who drank together, travelled, and wrote poems and songs and books in the wild places of America. I envisaged them sitting together in New York bars reading their work out loud to beautiful women who smoked and watched them with big, dark eyes.

Then I learned from the book that Kerouac was dead, and his story became even more precious to me, but one that I could talk about to no one in case they thought me strange for following the life of a man who had always been on the run, writing and writing, until he drunk himself to death.

I knew nothing about death, and never thought about it. But he was dead like the writers on our bookshelves, and we would never meet. To be like him, would I have to die? The question disturbed me. Then, secretly, he became a ghost of my imagined past, the feeling he created being one that I could reach out and touch in his story – a story that seemed always to happen as evening fell, when the hope of the day lay silent against the darkening sky, when the gathered moments of the day could be seen for the emptiness that they were.

Sometimes there seemed no point to Jack's days – particularly those days when he was not moving from place to place. By contrast, Dylan made days of his own. His songs were about days I could imagine were happening to me, because they happened to everybody and nobody. Jack's days were longer and quieter. His days were real, while Dylan's were fiction. Jack's days could run one into the next, entire weeks and months being lost. Then he would move, and the days with him. And as he moved, travelling across the land, all the moments of past and present flooded the landscapes through which passed. He travelled always with his entire world in mind, always carrying with him the memories of every day through which he had passed, of days as tranquil as the purring of his cat, days haunted by the name of the brother he had lost, of tales told in the strange language of his mother-tongue, of the euphoria of football stardom, with always the Catholic spirits lingering in the space between light and dark.

But Dylan made his days work for him. He had the power to inspire and mesmerise, while Jack struggled to find the ride that would take him to that secret place where the land would speak his mother-tongue and the evening-time be filled with the hope that tomorrow he would wake to a new and perfect America.

When I had finished the book I wondered what it was I had become and what I was supposed to do next. My room seemed small. Perhaps the evening outside was just like those evenings at the heart of nowhere that was everywhere about which the mind could dream – New York, San Francisco, and the vast land between them, out of which the voices I was hearing had been born. The voices were somewhere just beyond the darkening shape of the great tree in our garden, from which the knotted ropes now hung motionless. I would soon be among them, the people of those places, those kinds of people, because they were perhaps all around me, in my town, which was just like the hometowns of Jack and Dylan. Their towns had made them, even when they had left them forever. Those towns were where their hearts lay and where they began to tell their stories. They perhaps been strangers in their towns, just like me, but had turned their towns into stories and songs, just like I would do.

*

She might have been the first of those stories, the girl whose face I had once known and who I took awkward moments to recognise when she reappeared in the early summer.

Hers was the familiar face of a stranger. She was from the time between the class of the teacher who had arranged the roses from our garden and placed them in a small blue vase on her desk, and the later years spent in the shadow of the stubble chinned man who rasped smoking in the store room and cracked the air with a stick on cold wet mornings.

Her appearance one day in 1977 resurrected a time that had been almost forgotten, because nothing had happened to keep it in mind. Other things had taken its place. My past with her had been an interlude without consequence, until now, when the chance came to see what had endured and what was no more, as we both sought carefully to discern how it was we had been remembered.

She had been there one day in the spring five years earlier, when a trainee teacher at our primary school had taken our class for a month. We had been asked to read *The Last Battle* by C.S.Lewis. Each day we read a few pages, somebody in the class being asked to read out loud, then all of us having to read in silence to ourselves.

It was a book I loathed. The story was fake. I could never believe a story like that. The children could not exist, even in a fantasy. It was a story that pretended to take me on a journey of imagination into a world of good and evil. But it took me nowhere. The book was a trick, and the fake land of Narnia a place that was no more than a haven in which kids like the smart ones who lived on my road could pretend they were kings and princes. I would never go there, and there was no point in me imagining it, nor any point in pretending I might one day reach that fantasy land.

When the young teacher told our class to continue reading the story on our own, I took another book from inside my desk – *The Goalkeeper's Revenge* by Bill Naughton – and slipped rapidly into the story of Bill's friend Spit Nolan, a boy who was a bit like some of the boys I had met that summer of 1972, who lived in the houses I could see through the windows of my classroom.

A girl sitting next to me saw that I was reading about Spit. Her hand went up.

'Miss. Miss. Mark's not reading the right book.'

'Why not?'

'I hate that story.'

'I asked…told you to read it.'

'I don't want to. I hate that story.'

'Put that book away, and do as you're told.'

'No. I won't.'

'You will.'

'I can't. I just can't. I hate *The Last Battle*. It's a waste of time.'

By then the teacher was standing over me. She grabbed Bill Naughton from my hands, slammed my desk lid down on top of him, and thrust C.S.Lewis back at me.

'I won't read it. It's a stupid story. I'm not going to read it.'

The teacher fumed. But she didn't know what to do. If only she had asked me why I hated the story. But there was no discussion.

The girl who had betrayed me now sat beside me with a smile on her face. But I did not remind her of it, when we met again in 1977, by when the reasons I had

247

reacted so strongly to *The Last Battle* had become a part of me in ways that I assumed she ought to have been able to see, if only she had remembered the time when I had – for the first time in my life – stood alone in public and refused.

'Do you remember us on the school field, when we danced?' she asked. 'You danced well,' she said, both of us wondering how much we should remind the other of the past.

Where it was we met again I cannot remember, though we had lived all this time only the length of one long street away from each other. The years that had passed were as many miles as the street had become. The distances were vast, the minutes between our homes now long years. We had not once passed on the street with a nod of recognition, nor noticed a familiar stare in the greengrocer's shop. Neither of us had been noticed, our tiny world too vast for the possibility of a chance meeting years later.

'I liked the dancing,' I told her.

'And you were good in the sword-dance team, and in the play. You made people laugh. Do you still make people laugh?'

'I've not done a play for a while. I...I stopped enjoying it.'

'That's a shame,' she said.

'I'll do it again,' I said and, for the first time in our lives, a time that seemed like ours alone had passed. The days we spoke of were years behind us. But they were ours, and the sense – the recognition – that we no longer did the things that we had once done was proof that we could be different, be free to change and grow, and that there was now somebody there to know and to notice. I had never felt that before, and didn't know how much I should make clear that I was different, and how much would anyway be obvious to her.

But from the beginning it was there, the feeling – unsaid, of course – that what I had become was not what she wanted or needed.

She was not beautiful, though to think so would have been cruel. She was taller than me, a woman almost, though sometimes the childish times recalled of the past reminded us that we were only a few years ahead of those days when we had danced on the school field to the tune of an accordion, held hands, flown timelessly through the air of a summer afternoon knowing all the dance steps that made us the real and fine people we would remain as we grew older. We laughed a little when we reminded each other of those times. But we did not want to laugh at each other, and instead wanted to see what it was we could become next, in our new bodies.

It was never clear why it was me that she had found, those years later. There must have been other boys who lived closer to her large house, where she lived with her brother, sisters and parents. Their house was one through which people came and went – from concerts, church, the theatre, to and from distant places where they studied or worked. They were confident, leading their lives purposefully.

The first time she took me there we sat around a large dining table, her family all talking, seeming to have ideas about where they were going, while I sat quietly, hidden beneath my leather hat, inside my Afghan coat, the hope in me that something was about to happen twisting uncomfortably with the feeling prowling through my veins that I could never be what she wanted or needed, once I realised that I was there to be a part of the show she was trying to put together for the elder sister who obsessed her but who for most of the time was away.

'Would you like to hear my song?' she asked me, as we sat in her room that first time I went to her house.

It was a mysterious room, dark, quite medieval, with long posters of Arthurian women by Alphonse Mucha hanging from the walls. It was like a room high up in a dark castle, where a lonely aristocrat awaited the return of a confidante whose arrival would transform the day and night into rich deep times that would seem never to end and would always be talked about.

She plucked gently at the strings of a guitar.

She sang as she had done when we had last seen each other, at our primary school behind the dark fir trees. There had been a choir, and at a concert when we were nine or ten years-old she had been the only singer who had learned the words to the song we were to sing in front of all the parents. Her voice had rung out loudly across the school hall, and the music teacher had applauded her because she alone had been good.

Her voice was the same, there, in her room, though now she sang in pain about the sister who was her obsession:

> *With a friend like you*
> *Life would never fail me.*
> *People tell me*
> *I'm not your kind of friend*
> *But I know better than all of them*
> *So let me let me*
> *Be your friend today.*

She did not say that she had sung the song to the sister who had done all the things that she could not do.

250

She risked being seen only as an imitator, if she took the drugs and went with the men she told me had horrified and terrified their Catholic parents. But her sister was all that my friend wanted to be – bohemian, worldly, a malcontent, brave, aloof, obscure in what she read and listened to. Her sister's world was a whirlwind of people talked of in awe, people who lived on the edge, people who rarely spoke, who turned up unexpectedly, out of the darkness, hoping for a bed for the night.

One evening her sister appeared, having travelled across country, carrying a suitcase. She was hunched inside a big fur coat, her gaze never settling, her manner that of a celebrity rebel, her talk reserved, her long hair falling over eyes that never caught your gaze. At the dining table, where all the family gathered, she sat at one end, perched sideways on the edge of her chair, her back almost turned to the people there. She barely spoke, her awkwardness silencing me as I watched her.

I saw in her something of myself a year or so earlier, as I sat at Mum and Dad's table, guilt threading through my veins as I fumbled with the languages that I wanted to have speak for me. The boy criminal could speak. An accordion played as children danced. In an alley beside a nightclub boys shared their spliffs. At daybreak my mum watched, helpless as I slipped away into the mist to deliver newspapers, unable to protect her child, people watching their children slip away, like the child my friend's parents saw in their silent, distant daughter.

'It would be nice if you would speak with us,' my friend's mother told the sister. She spoke nervously, with pain and kindliness and a faint hint of resentment in her voice, but so full of hope that she would not provoke the daughter she had lost long ago, and who now sat in silence, slowly eating as if every mouthful was a compromise or concession to the parents whose role in her life she so despised.

'I'm going back tomorrow,' the daughter replied.

'So soon? You've only just arrived. Can't you stay until the weekend?'

'I have a few things to do in Oxford.'

'Are you working?' asked the eldest of my friend's three sisters. She was a music teacher, about whom everything clashed with the girl sitting a distance away at the end of the table. Her hair was short, her glasses serious, her clothes plain, her manner pleasant.

'There's a job that might come up.'

'Doing what?'

'Oh, in administration.'

'Not another one.'

'It's about all I'm qualified for,' the sister mumbled, turning further away.

Their brother tried to shift attention away from her, by talking of motorbikes.

'It would be nice if you could stay until the weekend,' their mother repeated, nodding slightly.

My friend, three or more years younger than the sister about whom she had written her song, sat opposite the girl she wanted to be like. Her ambiguity collided with her confusion. She smiled to impress her sister, to seem carefree. Then she fell silent, as their mother's pain froze the air we breathed. Then my friend stopped smiling and uttered no more of her short laughs. The sister gave no signs that she cared what my friend thought of her. There seemed no secret alliance. In the sister's eyes, my friend seemed as ludicrous as the rest of the family from which she struggled to distance herself and from whom she would try soon to escape back to the dark, cold room in Oxford that she had made her own.

None of them could explain how she had become like that. Her discontent, the tension, the awkwardness, had not emerged from the world they had shared as children. She had created it for herself, and would be leaving next day. We would be standing still. It did not matter where it was she was going. It did not matter that it was to a cold room in Oxford, in which nothing more happened than was happening elsewhere. Even so, she was going away, to where life might seem really to be taking place. That was how she made it seem.

'Tell us some more about the job,' said their mother.

'It really won't be that interesting.'

'Well, a job, nevertheless.'

'I don't think Mark is finding this conversation very interesting,' the sister said, casting a glance at me. 'I like your hat,' she added, pointing to my friend, who had been wearing it.

'It's Mark's hat.'

'A man of taste,' she told my friend, who laughed, blushing. 'Are you two lovers?' she asked, unsmiling, looking at each of us in turn.

'No,' my friend replied, too quickly.

I smiled, wanting to run while calling back: 'Nobody knows me. Remember that. Nobody knows me. Nobody ever will, because that's the way I want it.' But I said nothing, because I didn't know the answer to her question, and the story I perhaps for a moment had in mind to tell her – about the boy I had been a while back – was lost.

'What do you think of her?' my friend asked me, perhaps that day, or some time later.

'I can see why you like her.'

'Some people think we are quite similar.'

'Maybe. In some ways.'

'Which ways?'

'I don't know.'

'There must be some things that are obvious.'

'No. I think you are very different.'

'You're not supposed to say that.'

'Well, you are different.'

'Yes. I suppose so.'

'But that's okay.'

'But I want to be like her.'

'Yes. I know.'

'Is that strange?'

'No.'

'Why not?'

'Because she seems to be free to do whatever she wants.'

'And tomorrow I'll be in my uniform, on the bus to school.'

'Yes.'

'Is that all you can say? Don't you want more from life than that?'

'It's not going to be like that forever,' I replied, the need in me to have us cast an eye on the future being strong.

Thus, we edged around each other, neither quite knowing how to give the unambiguous sign that we were no longer children.

The weeks passed, and sometimes we kissed. But it was not beautiful. I had wanted my first kiss to be beautiful. Raw instinct danced with sacred memory. We must be all we had once been, then more. That was what we must be, the voice in me was saying. We had danced hand in hand on the school field, to the tune of an accordion. We had not thought to kiss, during those past times when she was a girl not a woman and we had danced hand in hand. We should dance still, and remain what we had once been. Then there would be no lie, no pretence that I saw in her the beauty about which I dreamed.

But on Sundays, when I knew she would pass by after singing and playing her guitar at the small church near our house where the priest must still remember the kids who had long ago gone there in the hope of being handed pineapple sweets after mass, I would lie in my bed long into the morning waiting for her. I daydreamed of her stepping into my room unnoticed as I slept, and she slipping her hand in among the sheets. Perhaps then I would have seen her beauty.

But only once did my door open and she stand there as I lay in my bed, the voices of my family all around in the house. I was embarrassed, not excited, and felt childish, not virile. She would go away thinking I was a kid. She had intruded. I didn't want her there, her body too much, her voice so soft it was like that of a caring aunt rather than a lover.

'Still in bed?' she said, slightly embarrassed. 'Rather lazy.'

The idea was immediately lost that she could have imagined what it was I had been dreaming. 'I've been dreaming,' I could have told her.

But really I didn't want to share my dream with her. I would have had to lie about beauty. I would not have been able to hide it, the truth. We were not together, not like a friend I had once had who had been together with the girl he kissed in the dim light of the club where I used to go with other kids on Tuesday evenings. We were not together like them. We were different from those kids. We had big houses to go to, where we could close the doors and be left alone in rooms that may have been in far off places. It was other kinds of kids who held each other tight in the music and coloured lights of dance floors, then went home to their mums and dads and baby brothers and sisters. They kissed like that, because that's what used to happen at *Speakeasy*, or on wet weekends near the public toilet opposite the Post Office. They were the kids who, when the warm weather came, spent days down by the river drinking cider and smoking cigarettes, laughing when a boy flipped down the front of his swimming trunks and said that his mum didn't mind if his sheets were soiled when he woke up in the morning.

Perhaps the things that had happened since the last time she and I had met, when we had been kids in a classroom, did not make a story. I would have told her that the cops no longer came to my house, that things were different now, that I didn't care who won the F.A. cup final. The words I used were different. These days nobody hung around on the street at night in wet alleys, sharing spliffs with kids whose names were unknown and who might not make it home tonight. Nobody I knew had ever stayed in that strange hotel where men played cards in a ballroom, beside the river where we used to spend our summer days flashing our arses at the people passing on the cruisers.

My silence meant that she could imagine my past, but only if she wanted to. I told her nothing, perhaps for fear of losing her. She didn't fit into that story of the past, because she could not imagine I had friends like Polly and Shat and the two Scottish brothers. I knew she could not imagine it, so the story was left untold, and her world remained safe, while mine that had once been shaken to its roots by uncertainty remained the secret I wanted to tell. She would have wanted it told, but it was the wrong time, because when we met again she wanted to take the risks that her sister had taken, while all I wanted was somebody with whom I could feel safe. So for a while I pretended to her that she had understood me well. But I would have to wait before I could turn my town into stories, like Kerouac and Dylan, whose words were the secret language I would never use with her, even as we strode together along the street between our two homes, almost at ease as we passed into the cool of my home, long into the autumn of that year.

My brother Paul was alone in the house, playing the piano in the sitting room below my bedroom.

There were footsteps on the stairs beyond the door I had locked behind us.

'Mark, would you two come out of there please,' said my dad's voice, stern as he knocked on the door. 'Come out of there please,' the voice ordered, a moment turning to ashes, my timidity with her turned to humiliation, as if I was bad. As if I was bad, when all I had felt was fear.

Four: *Wandering*

Warm gold light oozed through the shutter slits into the sudden silence of waking.

Must move.

Sleep.

Hide for a few minutes more. Nobody is waiting. Silence is all, broken only by the oozing stealth of the morning light, of tomorrow, after the falling of the night stars that had lit our way across the valley.

A convoy of tank carriers, the massive bulk of their loads hunching beneath canvas as they roared north towards the war, had forced us off the road some time long after midnight. From a dry ditch we had watched as the silhouette turrets and cannon passed in the silver light.

There was laughter. Our spirits had been high, there, beneath the stars, even as the farm tractor pulling the trailer we clung to in the cool night breeze had left the ground and at any moment seemed poised to spin and twist into the ditch. Then its engine clattered confidently, chattering with the valley sides as the convoy lights faded from view and we rattled into the darkness that now lifted its eyes onto the gold blue light of the next day.

Must move.

One moment more, there, to capture again what has been lost. Must get up before the others stir, before the first sound marks the start of the day. Wake, and become the new day.

A moment more to recall where it started, then I will know how it should end.

'Yes. Alright. Won't be a minute,' I called back to my dad.

'Hurry up please.'

'Yes.'

She had quickly dressed, stood, we both avoiding the other's gaze.

'We were only talking,' I had told my dad as we stepped out onto the landing.

I was dirty, of course. That was the phrase people used in those days.

'I don't like you locking your door,' he had said, looking with sympathy at the girl, pitying her for what I may have tried to force her to do.

She said hello, goodbye, and was gone from my house. Alone for longer in my room she might have drawn my fantasies out of me. Perhaps I would have seen beauty in her. But we were not like that, our kind of people. She wouldn't have asked me: 'You gottit in yer?' as a girl had once done, on a street, where a gang of kids heard me say 'no' and the girl had cackled and mocked.

But she mocked in her own way. I didn't want it. I didn't know why. She was right. I was not a man. I was a dirty kid. A weird virgin. Actually I was honest. I was kind to her. She didn't know it. Nobody would ever know it. So, I was bad.

I saw my badness fixed in my grandfather's eyes when he arrived that Christmas, with presents in small brown envelopes and plastic bags.

My humiliation had become hers, though we still saw each other sometimes, in her house or mine, as winter drew in and we walked through cold dark evenings past closed shops. Reaching her home or mine, along streets we strode in our boots and coats and hats, our parents eyed us amused, a gentle mocking tone ever-present, revealed in smiles that nevertheless erred towards contentment that she and I had at least found each other. I was lured by the safety of their attitudes, and played along, hoping only that when the person arrived who would see the hidden side of me, that it would be at a time when I could speak unhindered. Until then I was bad, though seeming to try to be good, when she stepped in through our kitchen door on her way home from church that Christmas morning.

My grandparents had already arrived, and looked at her suspiciously as she said hello.

'So, you're the girl we have heard all about,' my grandfather said.

'Oh. Well. I don't know about that,' she said, blushing, her tired eyes darting from him to me.

She and I went to sit in our dining room. I played her a record I had bought, one she had told me about, whose fragile sound belonged only to us. I wanted the two of us to escape, as Neil Young sang, and she perched on the arm of the chair on which I was sitting, put her arms around me and kissed me just as my grandfather opened the door and stepped into the room. He glared at us disgusted, grunted, then walked out. I was bad. I was dirty, and was later told how embarrassed my grandfather had been, finding us like that. I should apologise because I had been an embarrassment, and had probably tried to force the girl to do something she did not want to do.

Her face, smiling, passed across in front of me.

What might she think I was doing now? I probably never cross her mind, except perhaps when she sees her sister, the one about whom she had written her song.

I would like to be remembered when she sees her sister. That would be the closest I would ever get to her sister. I remembered that song, and sung it under my breath in that hot room where I had woken. She had known all the words when we had sung in the school choir. Hers was the only voice we could hear. She must have been strong, to have sung like that, and to have sung to me about her sister. I should send her a postcard, to tell her where I am and what I have been doing in the years since – since then. I could write, out of the blue. That would surprise her, intrigue her even. She would like it if I told her that I had thought about her as the sun was rising over the valley where I had lived from early spring and into the summer of 1982 among the sad and broken people of Israel.

I began to frame the note I would write her. Every word would be a conclusion. This is how it ended. We – I – reached this point, in the end. Look at me now. I moved away and changed. You would see me differently now, if we met again. If we met again, and I told you about all that had happened since. You would forget what had been, and think only about what happened later, when I became the one I wanted to tell you about.

Soon after that Christmas we had taken a coach to Oxford, to stay with her sister.

We walked across a frozen water meadow lined by lifeless poplars that paraded along the riverbank.

My friend had been waiting in her castle room, and now the waiting was over and the one she had awaited was there with her, the two of them like tapestry figures lost among the folds of their wraps and cloaks as they strode across the frozen meadow, perhaps imagining there would be a rugged bard or troubadour awaiting them on the other side. They would disappear into the mist then emerge into a world of their own.

I dreamed their dream for them, but saw no part for myself. I was the one from whom they must disappear. There were no words for what I was imagining for them, in her sister's cold room where we smoked spliffs beside the dying glow in the grate.

'You two can have the bed,' her sister said, she wrapping herself in coats in front of the embers with a man who had appeared out of the mist hoping for a bed for the night.

The sheets were cold. I made to hold her and she pushed me away, in a silent way that her sister would not hear. Now the silence was hers – resentful, angry, almost hate, as I became repellent and longed to be repelled and to be far away from there.

'I don't want to see you anymore,' she told me over the telephone on the evening after our return, words that were cruel and pathetic, words that could have been funny if I had known that one day I would be looking back.

I was uncertain what I would write to her on a postcard.

Still there was silence, the Sabbath always quite there, in the Holy Land.

I had dreamed only for seconds, thoughts of her flitting into mind like the single toll of a bell. She would have thought I needed her, so many years later, if one summer morning in her large house near Mr Collins' bicycle shop, where we took our bikes to be looked over by Mr White in preparation for our family cycling holidays in Holland, along the street from the house of a boy from our primary school whose mum's Pekinese dog had bitten my face when I had gone there, if among the letters strewn in their long hallway was a card telling her about what I did next. It would seem as if I wanted to make amends, to excuse myself, to re-live, to apologise for something. But I didn't want to do any of those things. I was gone away. She did not know why. I wondered if she would say: 'I knew he would go away. He was always the one who would go away.' Then, a card from me would have drawn a smile, a nod, perhaps a feeling of completeness. But more likely was that it would have reminded her of what might seem best-forgotten, of the half-lived half hoped-for times, talk of which, even four years after we had walked through the freeze of an Oxford night, would have left our past a passing time, not the time whose consequences that were lived everyday.

I would not write to her. It was better that silence should keep our time alive than that words should turn it into history.

I had walked quietly out of my house when her telephone call ended. I was free of her, but rejection and loneliness were the strangest feelings. A door had closed that would never reopen.

In my school there were kids who asked about her. My friend Richard had seen her a few times, and had told me I could do better than be with her. She was not beautiful. I didn't ask him who it was he thought was beautiful. He and I were close, despite rarely agreeing on anything. I would have liked to explain to him that she had been right for me, because there had been the chance to see how it was people changed – kids becoming something else – without pretending. I had known her once, as a child. Then I knew her again, and I had lost nothing in the meantime. We had just talked.

'You didn't do anything with her?'

'No.'

'You mean, you spent the might in bed with her, and you didn't do anything?'

'She didn't want to.'

'I don't believe that. I don't believe it.'

'She wouldn't let me.'

'What did you try?'

'Her sister was sleeping in the same room, with some bloke.'

'Right waste of time going there then, weren't it?'

'Yeah, I suppose so.'

'Anyway, I really don't know how you could fancy her.'

'I know. I suppose I didn't fancy her.'

'You could always do better than that, if you ask me.'

'Who's better?'

'Dunno. But you can do better.'

'But with who?'

He wouldn't say. He had no idea that everything I might want would be unattainable. That was the way things were. I assumed I would have nothing, and that nobody could want me, because I would never trust the girl who made the promise I was looking for. Every

267

promise was false, because nobody had the power to keep them.

*

Rick hovered on our doorstep. He was never quite sure whether to step inside. It was never clear to him what the reason would be for saying hello to my family, while all the time he was thinking of other things.

He was wearing a large white fedora with a black band. He had placed it carefully on his head so as not flatten the blond hair that now flowed in permed curls down to his shoulders. He had a new long denim coat, hanging open despite the February cold.

'There's a girl wants to see me.'

'Who?'

'Some girl.'

'Right.'

'D'jer wanna…she's got a friend. You could meet her.'

'When yer seeing her?'

'Tonight. Yer doing anything?'

'No.'

'Right. D'jer wanna come now then?'

'Alright.'

We walked in silence to his house, me in my army surplus jacket, jeans, and trainers, hardly dressed for an evening with a girl, beside Rick as he strode on his high heeled shoes beneath his hat. In his room he played a new record…*In the year of the scavenger, the season of the bitch*… and on, into the nightmarish world of David Bowie.

'Bowie's where it's at.'

'Right.'

'Dylan's too serious. Look at Bowie. Master of disguise.' He showed me a photograph of Bowie wearing a big white fedora with a black band around it. For me, there was no point in even thinking about being like Bowie. I was still trying to see how I could turn my world into stories, as Dylan and Jack had done, stories that grew out of the life and the earth and the buildings all around me. But Bowie's world was a nightmare. His was an escape, a world hidden behind closed curtains when I wanted to be out in the sun. His was the world of night, in the deep of the big city. It was not Harlow. I had to capture what was real, in daylight, not escape into the anonymity of night and cities.

But Rick wanted the escape.

We strolled passed the closed doors of homes we used to go into, leaving unsaid the names of the kids who lived there, and walked out onto First Avenue then turned onto a road that wormed among houses in a part of town I had never before been to.

He knocked on the door of a flat in a low-rise block. A girl stepped out into the fading light, so quickly that she must have been waiting behind the door.

'Bye Mum,' she said. There was a television on inside, and a woman's voice called out.

'Where yer going?'

'Out.'

'Out where?'

'Just out.'

'Don't want yer back late.'

'No.'

The door was slammed, rattling the frosted glass.

'Brought my mate,' Rick told her, gesturing towards me.

"'ello,' the girl said, wondering why I was there.

'Don't you have a friend?' Rick asked her.

'She couldn't come.'

We walked down the echoing hollow of the stairwell, me following as they led in silence.

They lingered at the bottom step beside the dustbins. Cars passed but the street was empty of people. I stepped out onto the street and lingered on the path that led up to the block, hearing them talk then hearing the silence, glancing back to see their closed eyes as they kissed. They talked again, then there was silence. They went further into the shadow of the stairwell, and I ambled slowly across the trimly cut grass that led to the pavement, then walked quickly away.

'Where yer going?' Rick's voice called after me.

'I'm in the way.'

'Don't just fucking run off like that.'

'Sorry.'

'She's not really meant for me anyway,' he said as he caught up.

'No.'

My awkwardness fell away, and everything instead seemed stupid and pointless. What were we doing, hanging around near the dustbins in the stairwell of a tower block waiting for thrills from a plain girl whose mum was watching telly upstairs? I had followed him to that place to see a girl he hoped would like him for his fedora hat and permed hair and high-heeled shoes. But no girl was going to go for that. I didn't know what he had hoped for and didn't know him well enough to ask. We both wanted to escape, but to completely different places, though far away from the girl in the stairwell.

*

'You will be there, won't you,' a short girl with long frizzy hair and arty clothes asked me, as I passed her in the school corridor, which back in the early 1970s had been decorated with psychedelic paintings. The paintings, which the school painters had never had the heart to paint over, reminded us that our style and manner and attitude were a copy of what had gone before.

'Yes,' I told her.

'I won't go if you won't be there.'

'I'll be going.'

I had seen her for a long time, but never imagined that she was the one who could see inside me. She was not the one I had in mind, though sometimes I was tempted to let her be the one, to give her the chance. I liked her style. But her desperation was terrifying. I worried that she would think I was going with her to the party a girl was having at the weekend. But really I was going with my mates, boys from my school, who I met up with in the afternoon at a café beside the market square where families ate spaghetti and drank mugs of tea. We had a party to go to, as we drank Coke and laughed, kids in jeans and checked shirts, some still kids, others growing faster, me shifting between all their worlds, older, younger, kid, youth, hoping all the time that nobody would ask me who it was I intended to be with at the party.

It was early evening when we left the café. The market square was all empty crates and papers that once wrapped apples and now rolled in a cool wind round the bronze statue of men shouldering a hog on a pole near the place where a friend of mine had once had a job selling greetings cards.

We strolled passed a stretch of waste-ground beside the cinema, where people used to park their cars when they had a meeting at the council office.

It was good to be late.

The parents of the girl who was having the party were watching television downstairs.

'She's upstairs,' her dad said.

'We'll leave you all alone,' said her mum, as we filed up the stairs and into a dark bedroom.

The girl who had told me she would only go to the party if I did, smiled and moved close. She was a child, her body barely formed though her face seeming older.

'Hello,' she said, excited, suggestive, as if she had spent the hours waiting for the door to open and for me to step through. 'I'm glad you're here. What have you been doing with those other boys? Are they really your friends?'

'Yes.'

'They're not like you at all.'

'Why not?'

'They all seem so…normal. Aren't they boring?'

'No.'

'But you play the guitar, and listen to Bob Dylan and go to concerts. They're not like that.'

'I don't mind.'

'Shall we sit?'

'Okay,' and we sat on the edge of a bed.

'You're much more interesting than them.'

'Oh. Right.'

The room, now full of kids, fell dark.

'I want you,' she said, leaning heavily on me so we fell onto the bed.

I must stop this. I don't want you. But I was blind in the darkness. Nobody would see. There were no witnesses to my lie. We lay, as she unzipped my trousers and pushed a hand inside.

'I've wanted you for so long. Have you ever noticed?' she murmured.

I said nothing. The light will be switched on and I will never again be able to hide. Only in darkness, lost among voices, 'Roxanne' playing, no kids seeing, except the childish ones alone in the corners with drinks, only in the darkness could I lie with her. I despised her fingers. Her words were all lies. There was nothing about me she could know that she wanted, because I had told her nothing.

'Let's go to another room,' she said, and I followed.

In an empty room she undressed. Unashamed I did the same. Nothing to hide. The feeling of being wanted was powerful. I wanted her to see that she could have everything of me but my secrets. That first time must not be cheap. That first time must be holy, sacred, a kind of sacrifice, an offering. But if we made love, if we fucked, she would own me. I would never be owned. That was my secret. I would never sell myself cheap, whatever the pleasure. The moment later was what I feared. Then the next day, the aftermath of averted looks and eyes, comments ignored, unmade promises broken in the crisis sweat of embarrassment. Her body would never be one I could pretend to love, not for a night nor an hour in a well-lit room next to a room where The Jam blasted out...*going underground, going underground*...and she

273

waited for me to enter her tiny, fragile, childish body and to pretend that she was what I had been waiting for.

She said nothing. I longed for darkness, as her big dark eyes stared hard at me, waiting. I waited for her to speak, to calm my fear, to tell me that I was not her whore, not just a cheap cock. But there were no words. I needed for her to speak, to prove we were not animal. Silence still, for long minutes, until we dressed, and wondered why what was meant to happen had not.

*

Nobody would believe that the boy they had known no longer existed. But I would never tell my story to those girls. They would be women now, and me a man, changed, sexual. I would never tell, because really I was just the same. My virginity had been precious to me. But nobody would have said that in those days. Get fucked. Fuck. Then fuck again. Fuck whoever you can. I could pretend I was like that, except to the girl who was naked at the party. Most kids really were like that. They didn't care about the aftermath. For me, the aftermath was all that mattered.

On that hot morning on the side of the parched valley, sun slicing through the shutters, I carried it with me.

Nearly 6am now. Mum and Dad would still be sleeping, though Mum always woke early. The springtime would be playing in the garden at home. I thought about my brother Paul, and wondered how much of my story I could tell him.

I dressed, quickly packed my rucksack, made the bed that a kind lady had given me for the night, and stepped out into the heat that drowsed among the shadows beneath the eucalyptus.

As I stepped away from the room, out of the shadows and into the hot fresh gold and blue of the early morning sun, the consequences slipped away. Not since a hot afternoon on the deserted street of a Normandy village had I been loosed freely like this into a quiet space, free of watching eyes, alone with my footsteps. But this time, in the early summer of 1982, on the side of a valley somewhere between the West Bank and the Mediterranean Sea, I alone had to find a way to create the day and bring it to a close.

The place where I had spent the night fell away behind me. The dream world I had half-lived over the years opened out in front of me. I recalled being mocked and deserted and lured and tempted, and though I could not tell anybody my story I began to see what it was that had happened on the first page of a time which, there on the valley side as the sun rose and the solitude rang in my ears, was moving towards its end.

'So, did you do it to her or not?' Richard had asked, after the party in the girl's bedroom.

'No.'

'What is wrong with you? If you don't mind me saying, there's definitely something wrong with you. You're both stark naked in a bedroom, and yer don't fuck her. Couldn't you get a hard on?'

'Course I had a hard on.'

'What was stopping yer then?'

'Dunno. Something.'

'What. I sometimes wonder...are you a poof or something?'

'No. Course not.'

'What's stopping yer then?'

'She might have got pregnant.'

'True. But you can always take it out before you come.'

'Yeah.'

'Did you come?'

'Yeah.'

'Where did yer come?'

'What d'jer mean?'

'Where did yer come? Did yer come on 'er?'

'Yeah.'

'Where?'

'On her.'

'But where did yer come?'

'On her.'

That night we had had to walk for miles, having missed the last bus from St Peter Port to the hamlet a few miles along the Guernsey coast where his uncle and aunt grew tomatoes a short distance inland from the beach. It was the last night of our week-long holiday on the island in the summer of 1978. We had talked until late into the night and then into the morning, at the height of a summer that had begun as we were walking along a corridor past the coat pegs where kids used to hide when they were dealing the cigarettes they would smoke beyond the fence near the school farm.

'Look, either you ask her out, or I'm gonna,' he had told me. I didn't, and by the time we were on our holiday in Guernsey he was with the girl he told me would just as likely have said yes to me as to him.

I was glad she had yes to Richard. It meant I didn't have to try and find her a place in my world. All she seemed to do was smile, her slightly buck teeth slipping out from between thin pale lips. Now, instead of fixing our gaze on each other in classes and corridors and conjuring up a mirage of gestures and signs from which could emerge a momentary feeling of expectation, I had the role of the one cast aside, the boy whose presence could make her think only of what might have been. I thrived in that role, tempting her, giving her clues as to what she could have had if only she had chosen me, amazing her on a Monday morning in May when I told her of how I had spent Saturday night sleeping on a London street queuing for tickets for Bob Dylan's first London concert since 1966.

'But where did you sleep?'

'On the pavement.'

'But wasn't it dangerous?'

'Very.'

'Were you alone?'

'I was with a friend.'

'What did your mum and dad say?'

'They were fine. They understood.'

'All night?'

'And all day Sunday.'

I imagined Richard wished she had been there with him on Guernsey, rather than me. The sun shone every day, and we cycled all over the island, swam, picked tomatoes, laughed, and drank beer in pubs where the landlords didn't ask us our age. But I knew he wished his new girlfriend had been there, though he didn't say it.

It would be the end of my friendship with him when we got back to school, because from then on he would go with her to his house where we had gone every lunchtime to listen to his records of Queen and the Electric Light Orchestra and had drunk chicory flavoured coffee before racing each other in sprints through the alleys to get back to school before the bell rang. In the autumn months I would watch the two of them walk calmly out of the school gate, kids in uniform, unnoticeable and unnoticed except by me, as they strode out of sight and on to his house where I could no longer go, because that was where they went upstairs to make love, though he only told me so a long time later, years after they had split up and married other people.

*

It was during that summer, after Richard and I had returned from Guernsey and my mum and dad and brothers and I were on holiday together in Scotland, that I stopped waiting for the one who would take me aside and ask to know how my life was going.

I was looking down from a hillside high above a loch in the Highlands. We had talked for years of going to Scotland, where our friends Philip and Carla went most summers.

Until then our holidays had often been part of the times that had long-gone, revisiting places on the map Mum and Dad had drawn.

One summer we drove to the south of France along roads lined by plane trees that Michael and Paul and I counted mesmerised from the back seat of our black Wolseley, Mum telling us as we drove that back in the war she had had to escape through France with our uncles, aunt and the grandmother we had never known, and that the plane trees had been planted by Napoleon to guide his troops as they marched through the countryside.

The old man Uncle Mark lived with had died while we were in France that year. Mum cried but didn't really want to tell us why, so we stayed out of the way and hunted for lizards under hot stones in the garden of the house we had been leant by a French woman who years earlier had taught at my dad's school. Some days we threw ourselves into the waves at Biarritz, skimming across the water on polystyrene boards, and staring out to sea.

Another summer, we sailed across the North Sea in a yacht, crashing through huge waves that I would dream about every night during the springtime which ended when I left Harlow behind and went on the journey that would take me out into that bright morning that was so tranquil the only voice was my footsteps pacing the warming earth of the Middle East.

I watched Mum and Dad moving silently, far below me, beyond where the bracken I had walked through gave way to heather and moss as the slope fell to the dark water of Loch Rannoch. The ripples poured diamonds in the sun, the slopes hunched in shadows, morning light sucking at purple, gold, brown, deep green, fingering the curtains that swung draped across stark worlds that drifted in and out of light and mist and cloud.

My first lines were written as Mum and Dad stopped, peered up the hill, and waved at me. I waved back, and they watched me for a while. I wanted to be seen, a blank sheet of paper resting folded on my legs.

I watched them as they took our camping equipment from inside the Mirror dinghy we towed behind our car. I was as much of a mystery to them as I was to myself, perhaps even more so to them, the words I needed to tell them remaining unsaid, as they waited, patient and kind, assuming that something was in the making. They would wait years, perhaps forever, as I filled sheets of paper with words I would never show to anybody, the fear always the same – that the words were not my own, that I was just imitating, that they would read like poor imitations of the greats, of the writers who lined the walls of our home, who had already written all that was needed and done all the things that could be done.

But I had my own private world of stories, like the one I had taken from the town library years ago, the story of two families who lived in windmills. The storm that brought them together had died down. The people lost the reason to be suspicious of each other. They had found what they were looking for. Neither family had been right. Neither family had won. They had both survived a time of trouble. The family that emerged stronger had no reason to feel stronger. All they could do was learn why it was the other family had not been friendly.

In the end it was the gloomy family that had shown itself to be stronger, because when it needed help it had had the strength to ask for it. That had taken courage. It had had the courage to admit it was weak. It took strength to do that. Always, the weak were the closest to being the truth about people. The strong could pretend. But behind the veneer they were weak. They were just better at hiding it.

I would go looking for the weakness in people. That's where I would find the truth. The land – mountains, lakes, forests – would sort the weak from the strong. I would climb mountains. I would wander across lands that would be my test. I would return stronger, after surviving times that nobody could imagine for me. Then my mum and dad would understand why I could not rest until I had seen what lay on the other side of the hill whose peak rose above me. Strength would come from that, because one day I would look out across the other side and be able to tell my story. Then everything would make sense.

I waved again at Mum and Dad and they waved back.

Now the page was full.

It would of course not be a good poem. I was almost fifteen years old. It could not be a good poem. It could only be a poem about a boy of fifteen – screwed-up, angst-ridden. But I didn't really feel those things. I felt only the need to speak the words that the land was speaking to me. I would be a part of that place, feeling the pulse in its veins, watching the look on its face, sensing its strength, and would speak of how it created lives deep in a forest, inside a warm hut where there was the scent of woodsmoke, a thread twisting from a chimney and rising along a valley side where a boy trudged homeward, a bag slung over his shoulder heavy with the weight of a catch whose silver skins caught the evening sun.

Mum and Dad alone would understand, though I folded the poem and slipped it into my pocket, then turned towards the summit and walked, occasionally looking back to see if anybody was following.

*

A fresh breeze clattered the leaves of fig trees that sprawled wildly at the roadside in the morning heat of the valley floor. Dry fields gave way to lush orchards on the opposite slope, surrounding the cluster of huts and bungalows that had been my home for months.

I stared up the slope from the crossroads. I was as torn as the road signs. Northwards was the road to Lebanon, which passed the long track ending among familiar faces that I must leave and perhaps never see again. She would be there, anxious that the man who still wanted her would curse and rampage through that cruel and violent land in search of revenge against me for what had happened between the three of us. South was the road to Afula and onwards to the coast. If I took it I sensed I would be returning from a journey whose destination I had not yet reached. It was July 1982. I had been away for four months. I wondered if that was long enough to have changed, and if life would be different now.

Four years earlier I had looked out from a hilltop in the Scottish Highlands, and seen Mum and Dad far below me and the brow of the hill above. There had been no voice telling me which way to go, and I had reached the peak and stood in wonder at the sight of what lay on the other side. Today, I must leave. I had left a room and stepped out into the warm fresh light before the people had stirred, and was now walking down the open road and out across the plains of the Holy Land. Tonight I must be nowhere I had been before, among strangers who would not know my name.

I turned south and was gone from there, no sound, only memory following in my footsteps.

I hitched a ride to Afula, morning sounds humming, moving with the freedom of a stranger, my own needs hidden as the pace quickened. I must move, just like before, during the months and years when I had travelled all over England and beyond, wrapped in my coat against the wind and the rain, Jack's travels sometimes in my mind, but always my own hope and purpose telling me why it was that my story would never be like anybody else's. I was free of imitation and knew what it was I had slowly become, the spirit that had been there all along now breathing the dust that poured through an open window as the roaring bus broke into the Sabbath silence and the route to the coast meandered out of the small town on the hot valley floor.

It was eight o'clock in the morning. I had slipped away unnoticed, and nobody in the world knew where I was or where I was going.

*

Mist curled among the high branches of the woodland. We had driven west and had never before known the solitude that we found on Ardnamurchan.

A forest reached down to the water's edge. Rain-clouds crawled across the slopes on the far side of the grey water, which spun and creased in the wind. We pitched our tents in a clearing on the banks of Loch Sunart. Paths wound through the forest. From our map we could see that it was the Isle of Mull that rose up on the other side, sometimes gold and purple in the sunlight, sometimes lurking black and grey behind the mist and clouds that sailed across its slopes.

We must reach the opposite shore.

For a day we looked out at the water, which flew, ripped by a wind that swirled in from the sea. We were nowhere our family had been before, but I wanted Mum and Dad to know that this was a place I had long-imagined. I had been here before, alone. We could set out across the water, in our boat with its bright red sails. I would explain to Mum and Dad that I had been here before, though they might not remember, or know. But I wouldn't tell them anything, really, just suggest that it was a place with which I was familiar, because I had imagined it. We could reach the far shore, through the waves, and drag our boat onto the shingle and make our way through the forest. I looked for signs of a warm hut, its thread of smoke twisting from a chimney. But the forest was dark and empty.

Dad and I stowed the oars and bags and turned the prow to face the wind which grabbed gusting at the sails. Our forest camp was warm and safe, but we had to reach the far shore, the wind billowing the jib and mainsail as we leapt in among the slap of waves on the ply that skimmed us out across the dark emptiness of the water.

A perfect wind tore us away. We feared the wind, feared that it would overwhelm us. It had happened once before, on the Suffolk coast, when we heard the distant roar of the sea beyond the river mouth and felt the tide and wind hauling us towards the noise. Fear had silenced us, and it was the silence that had drawn us back behind Orfordness, back into the tranquility of what we knew, as the grip of the turning tide loosened, the force that had terrified drawing us back, our powerlessness confirmed by its power to protect.

We still feared the wind and the tide, while knowing we must reach the farther shore, which seemed to recede as we skimmed deeper across the darkness of the splintered water. But we were determined. Dad was determined. We would ride the waves. We would master the roaring gusts that spiralled in from the sea. Our sails would fill and we would not be afraid. Our mast would pierce the sky, our sails laugh, the sheets thrum, the halyards screech as the taut ligaments of our journey.

Seals peered at our passing, their silken bodies sliding beneath the prowling current. Spray scattered the ply and we laughed and gasped and sensed the euphoria of speed as the slopes on the far shore loomed above us. Nothing before had been like this, the energy, power, water and air all seeming to be ours, my dad gripping the tiller as our full sails hummed happily. We breathed deep and were one with the place and with each other, walking again on a festival eve among the bright lights and voices of a market square, leaping the last gate of a summertime slope where, from the summit, the whole world opened up before us. We laughed and swooped and twisted in the wind. We were not frightened. Our sails would take us across to the other side. The power of the land would not harm us there where, between wild water, sky churning silver-grey, slopes massive, the wind our power, the water our path, I was gliding with my dad across the world.

*

'Three days on the deck – it's not too bad at this time of the year.'

I handed over most of my few remaining shekels to the heavily made-up woman in the water-front travel agency. A fan hummed but did not cool the stifling room. There were large colourful posters of places that had not been like that when I had gone to see them. She had not reassured me that I would find a space on the deck. 'Just turn up at around five in the evening. Just turn up. Sure, you'll get on.'

She folded my ticket with her bright red fingernails and adjusted her large, elaborate glasses, which hung from a gold chain around her neck, like those of a woman who had stared at me over a library desk when I was a kid.

I asked her for directions to the ship, and for its name.

'Just go down to the port and find it,' she told me, exasperated, determined to be unhelpful, and I stepped back onto the near-deserted streets of Haifa.

It was good, the feeling of not having the need to tell anybody what it was that was happening to me. The woman in the travel agency did not look up at me as I passed by her window. It was good, being nobody, just a figure on the street, ambling through Haifa with hours to kill. I had once been in a castle beside a river in France. It was from there that I had first seen this place – honey stone, warm light, the desert beyond, dreams, life among believers.

I wandered along a shaded street waiting for my ship to cast off into the warm Mediterranean night, alone on the edge of the sea with most of my money gone, mountains and cities and thousands of miles between me and my home.

It was good, knowing there was nobody in the world who could watch my story unfold. Things had happened. It was not the moment to explain, though I wondered if she would mind that I had disappeared, leaving her behind with the man who would not give her up but who she knew she must leave. I had no idea how I could explain my disappearance to her, as my thoughts

286

drifted across the times when I had first dreamed of beauty. I laughed at myself for thinking like that, then fell silent as I felt the distance between the street I was walking, my dreams of such places, and the far-off land where I would be home. It would take more confidence than I had ever had, to feel at ease.

I wandered around the hills of Haifa until mid-afternoon, everything closed, no money for food, then walked under the hot sun to the port. I found the ship easily – a gleaming white Greek ferry – and climbed steps and stairs to the highest deck, eased my rucksack off my back, lit a cigarette, delayed as long as I could the long gaze out across the sea to the horizon I would cross beneath the stars, and murmured in an ecstatic rush: 'I am real. This is me. I am real. I am for real, and nobody knows anything about me. This is my story.'

*

My world was different after our days and nights in the Scottish Highlands. The land had a new voice, because I had shared it with Mum and Dad and we could even sometimes hear it together, among the day and night-time sounds as the autumn of 1978 gathered in the Harlow sky. Do you remember the time we sailed across Loch Sunart? Do you remember Ardnamurchan? We all remembered the time spent among the mountains, remembered the haunted look Mum alone saw on Paul's face as we drove through the dark silence of Glencoe, and remembered Michael's rare expression of anxiety as he awaited the results of exams he had taken earlier in the summer. We all heard the voices, though they told us different things.

My brothers and I became different in each other's eyes that summer. We were no longer just 'the boys', but three very different boys, childish conflict no longer the force defining us, the spaces in which we lived seeming to have been staked out without us realising that it was so.

I had my space – my empty pages, soon filled with words. I had my route – the sick-sweet factory road to school, which was smooth, easier now as I grew. One winter I had coughed all the way, retching, terrified I would vomit among the twigs of dead cow parsley or in the wet deserted playground at lunchtime. Now, I glided through the cooling air of early autumn, just arrived from the Highlands, poetry the new voice in which I could tell the tale of the landscape, the story of *Tess of the D'Urbervilles* – the summer holiday reading given us by our teacher – my new treasure, its secrets celebrated by me alone as it became the first book by one of the greats who lined the walls, which spoke to me and showed me that I could read and follow and sense as real the language that I might one day speak or write, perhaps because her story was from our world, from the time when Mum had taken us back to her earliest times among the soft gentle colours of Dorset where we might once have noticed a country parson trotting by on horseback, and where we might have heard a village band playing for dancers gathered among tall grass and poppies in a field at the golden end of a summer day that was just as I remembered them.

Tess's story tore at me. Sometimes I would want only to remember the times she spent in happiness; then all I could feel was anger. She had done nothing to deserve her fate. She was an innocent who had lacked the strength to take hold of her life. She had been murdered by judges who could never understand – nor care to understand – what it is to be fragile. She had done nothing wrong, I was sure of it. If she was wrong, then everything was wrong. The whole world could be wrong. I could not believe that the world was still as cruel as during the times when women were hanged though they had done nothing wrong. Things must have changed. It was only a story. I should not be so moved by it. I should not be angry, because it was only a story.

'Right boring story,' a voice declared, the autumn rain galloping across the roof of the wood and plasterboard hut on the edge of the playing field, which was our English classroom.

'Boring?'

'If she didn't like Alec, she shouldn't have gone to back to see him.'

'Did she have a choice?'

'Course she did.'

'Wasn't she under pressure from her family, who needed the money?'

'I blame Parson Tringham.'

'Why blame him?'

'He was a troublemaker.'

'But he didn't know what it was he had started.'

'I blame Angel Clare. He really let her down.'

But I blamed nobody, remaining silent, as my class levelled blame at the characters. All that mattered was to blame. Nobody would say that none of them were to blame. The story was about what people were like: innocent, cruel, naïve, ridiculous, virtuous, selfish. Where were Good and Bad? It was too easy to say that Angel was good and that Alec was bad. They were both weak, while for me it was the punishment that was cruel, perhaps because it was easier to blame the society – the state, England – for hanging women who could not be blamed. The characters were just symbols, so they could never be blamed. They were not real. That was why it was just a story. All that lasted beyond the end of the story was the society that had created it, and which had hanged a woman, a child almost, whose innocence was, I knew, an innocence that was in all of us, but which nobody could see.

I could not explain it to my class without revealing more of myself than I wanted. People were essentially troubled, but the country must be just and protective. That's what I would have said, and everybody would have sighed and raised their eyebrows, because I would have been making it difficult for them to blame the parson, the aristocrat, the vicar's son, or the poor family that needed the money. The country would be fine if the police were all like Ozzie, the constable who wheeled his bike along our road and nodded to everybody and said 'good morning' with a smile, like policemen were supposed to do.

'So, do you like protest music or basketball? You can't like both,' the argument spilled out of a classroom and into the corridor.

'Yes I can.'

'How can you like both? You can't go and see Bob Dylan one week, and do sport. They don't fit. Hippy types and sport don't mix.'

'Why not?'

'It's obvious. They're too different.'

'I know they're different.'

'How can you smoke and do sport?'

'I don't smoke much.'

'But you can't do both. I don't get it, how you can be a fast runner, and you smoke, and you can swim, and you talk all the time about Bob Dylan. I don't get you. Are you a rebel, or what?'

'No.'

'Come off it. Course you are.'

'I like different things.'

'But you can't like them all.'

'Why not?'

'You've gotta make some choices.'

'No. Not yet. I'd like to. But I can't yet.'

'You're a right mess sometimes, you are.'

'Maybe. Not my fault.'

'Not blaming you.'

'I know.'

'You've gotta decide.'

'I know.'

'Well, do it then.'

'It's alright for you to say.'

'Me?'

'Yeah.'

'Why?'

'Just is.'

'You'll be alright.'

'Maybe.'

'You will.'

'Hope so.'

'Course.'

'Hope so,' I said, watching my friend edge his way towards the school gate with the girl who could have been mine, while I sped along my route home, where the same people passed by. We had passed each other for years. Perhaps one day we would exchange nods of recognition:

been passing here for years now, as the days grew from one into the other, we the strange witnesses to each other's passing.

*

On 13 January 2014 18:39, Mark Huband <██> wrote:
Dear Mark
Happy new year. I hope you had a good Christmas.
Can I find you on this:
<http://www.harlowbandsarchive.co.uk/>
It would be great to see what your rocking days looked like. It's a great website - I am beginning to see what my school friends did after I left Harlow. They had good times.
See you very soon
Mark

From: Mark P [mailto:██@gmail.com]
Sent: 15 January 2014 11:24
To: Mark Huband
Subject: Re: How are you
H Mark,
Yea, happy new year to you and you family and I hope you had a good Christmas too. Sorry we couldn't make it to yours during the hols.
My old band do appear on the 'Harlow Band Archive' though there is only one photo. I think they're in alphabetical order and you'll find us under the squeamishly outdated name of 'Midnight Panic' - Very trendy at the time, but like things that are very trendy, they date very quickly. You'll recognize Alan on the left. He played a wonderful fretless bass with that slide and

slap technique that was really cool at the time. Between him and me is Andy, whom I am still good friends with who now lives in Exeter. He played funky rhythm guitar. Then there's me with my slicked back, bleached, Bowie haircut. Ray, our sax player who now lives in Brussels is next to me and, next to him is a young guy who played percussion. On the write is our drummer, John, who was great at harmonizing on the backing vocal. He now live is Canada. He was from Old Harlow so, you may remember him. Soon after this we got a trumpet player in. Having a brass section was almost unheard of in Harlow bands of the time. The photo was taken in the Essex Skipper in the Stow and appeared in the Harlow Star. We were about to play at Benny's night club for the first round of the Harlow Rock & Pop contest which we reached the final of only to come third, almost causing a riot in the disgruntled crowd. At the time most of the bands were heavy metal or punk, where as we were funky which, was unusual in Harlow. Funk, generally, needs more discipline and skill and less ego, with each musician leaving space for others to be heard.

Anyway Mark, will have to get together soon.

Mark

On 16/01/2014, Mark Huband <█> wrote:

Mark

Fantastic photograph. It's the kind of picture which has an entire history behind it.

Take a look at this: https://myspacc.com/theosamasisters/video/bagno-di-romagna-1/103139069

Do you recognise the guy at the back - wearing the hat!

Mark

On 22 January 2014 20:50, Mark P <█@gmail.com>
wrote:
He Mark,

 Wow! Who IS that dude in the Panama hat?
Can't quite make up my mind about the shorts though.
Seem like a good band Mark. Anything reggae-based is
deceptively simple. Easy to listen to – hard to play. Well
done.
Mark

*

Before us, others had done the same. I traced their time
back along the route of the oldest lives I knew –
sometimes as far back to the last summer of peace, which
was as long ago as I had learned to remember and which I
assumed must be the mysterious time where we could
find an explanation for what we had become.

 That was where my imagination started, and
where it came alive when a teacher asked us to write a
story she titled 'The Retreat'.

 My characters retreated through a silent village,
through long grass between a railtrack and a river, and
then crossed a narrow road where cow parsley swayed in
a breeze near to deserted factories. It was wartime. They
thought they had escaped the fighting, having left behind
the rat-infested trenches that were far away in the
distance. They lay down on the soft grass of a garden that
surrounded a country house. They thought they were safe.
Then the air exploded with gunfire, and the soft colours

of the summer turned to red. The sky bled from blue to black. The last summer was over.

I assumed I had imagined that place. But really I saw it whenever the light was right. I saw it along the route I took to school, which had remained unchanged since 1914.

And that place of imaginary beginnings appeared most vividly when we opened 'Strange Meeting' and...*It seemed that out of battle I escaped*...and our class was struck silent by Wilfred Owen's rage and despair, all in a voice that I could hear beside me. It was not so long ago, and now I could read the words that lined the walls, because others had seen what I had seen: *War broke, and now the winter of the world, With perishing great darkness closes in*...he told us in '1914'. But he had not lived beyond the last winter of the war, and never knew that after his time winter would remain in our lives forever, and that we would be reading his words as winter clung to us, as if the season had never changed. His voice, carefully crafted in the trenches, was powerful because we were being taught about him in our classroom, which made his rage respectable. Memory, emotion, ideas, politics – Owen was the strongest proof I had ever heard that they were all one and that they could all be one, whether they came from a singer or a troubadour or a soldier. Poets could write to be heard not just studied in the cosy rooms of far-off colleges. Owen's words were raw. They blazed and cut and screamed, and were there with us in our classroom, and among the trees along the route that I took home.

I raged like him, in my mind, when the cruelty and the horror and the injustice and the 'old lie' poured off the pages. But part of his power lay in his not being a rebel. He was no freak. He was a soldier. His hair was short. He spoke truth. His was the first angry, raging voice I had heard that was not that of an outsider. I didn't want to be an outsider. I wondered how to be angry without being an outsider. These days you were both or neither – you supported Mrs Thatcher's new government, or you were an angry outsider. There was no middle ground in 1979. You either loved or you hated. Wilfred Owen had done both. But he was dead, and there was nobody to show me how to exist between worlds, their distinctions anyway beginning to fade when the summer exams brought an end to all those years, and our class looked alone and in secret for the poetry of losing what it must sometimes have believed would last forever.

There were no goodbyes, some kids staying on in school while others disappeared off to distant parts of our town with no reason to speak again to me or each other, as if there was no bond, nothing shared, and that we had never really passed time together. There was no story. There never would be, nor ever was. Do you remember? Do you remember? Nobody was around to ask. It was gone, that time ending with banality on the day when you wore your school tie for the last time. Then you were free – free to step out unrecognised into the world. Nobody would think of you as a school kid now, because you had taken off your tie and rammed it into your pocket, or thrown it into one of the roadside hedges where the red berries grew all year round and where the leaves smelled of piss when it rained.

*

On 25 April 2014 15:50, Mark Huband <█> wrote:
Mark

296

How are you? I am in need of some good conversation - what say we have lunch some time soon?

Best

Mark

On 28 April 2014 21:01, Mark P <███@gmail.com> wrote:

Hi Mark,

sorry took take a few days to get back to you. I had a busy weekend. Yes - it is about time we met up. I can't make this coming Friday, but apart from that I'm flexible. Let me know when is convenient for you. See you soon ...

Mark

On 7 May 2014 23:10, Mark Huband <██> wrote:

Dear Mark

So sorry not to have responded before now - been a bit frantic!

I know it's a bit late notice, but how does this coming Friday - 9 May - look for you? If it is okay for you, could we meet at say 3.30? Really hope we can meet up.

Very best

Mark

On 8 May 2014, at 20:05, Mark P <███@gmail.com> wrote:

Dear Mark,

I've only just read your message. 3.30 is fine for me. I hope I haven't left it too late. Shall we say - in the usual place? Drop me another line tonight to confirm.

Cheers

Mark

On 8 May 2014 20:16, Mark Huband <█> wrote:

Dear Mark

That's great. Looking forward to seeing you tomorrow.

Mark

On 14 May 2014 12:00, Mark Huband <█> wrote:

Mark

It was great to meet up last week; so much to talk about.

As I mentioned, it would be great if you, T and L could come down to see us; how does the weekend of Saturday 14-Sunday 15 June look for you? I really hope you can make it.

Looking forward to hearing from you.

Best

Mark

On 16 May 2014, at 21:42, Mark P <█@gmail.com> wrote:

Hi Mark,

sorry, as always, to take two days to reply. Yes, I really did enjoy the drink last Friday. I think the atmosphere in the new pub was better for a summers day. Mark, I don't know if it is coincidence but, the date that you have suggested for us to visit is the same date as your party last year. And, yes, you've guest, T's Grandma is having another (between you and I, bloody) birthday party - 91st. I know that I said that we are free except for the last two weeks in July, but it wasn't until I spoke to T that I realized. So, basically, any weekend, except those listed above will be fine, but we can't come on the weekend of 14-15 of June. Sorry to be a pain.

I've been reading your amazing book, by the way - Wow! I'm up to your second day in captivity and am truly gripped. Have a thousand questions, so not enough time for now.

As I say Mark, any date but those above will be great and we'd love to come.

Speak soon - Bye for know ...
Mark.

*

But by the time the autumn came and I returned to my classes in the jeans and checked shirts that sixth formers wore, I was well away in my own world, the drawers of my desk at home bursting with words on paper, a world taking shape in poems and in songs composed on the guitar that Mum and Dad bought for me in a shop in Bishop's Stortford.

Dad and I went there with Bob Gale, a quiet, ponderous, guitar-playing teacher whose long beard stained with nicotine and whose smiling eyes and big face lined from smoking, might have been the signs of a mentor. He and his wife Sue, who taught music at my school, lived the life of music and politics and songs of which I sometimes dared to think I might one day be a part, if I could become somebody completely different. They were sure of things. They were in the Communist Party. They could sing any folk song that Bob Dylan and Peggy Seeger and Leon Rosselson and Nic Jones might know.

Bob could pick up a guitar and make it sing, his voice as soft as the Dorset hills from which he came. He was short, and had limped from the time he was a boy, from the time he had been cycling through a tunnel beneath a railway and in the sudden darkness had not seen a car in the tunnel and had been knocked to the ground. In hospital he had had one of his legs amputated below the knee, so he turned to playing the guitar, and years later pointed up at one in the shop in Bishops Stortford and said it would suit me.

But instead of being inspired when he sang, I was intimidated. Instead of asking him 'please show me how to play that song' I would listen and think it impossible. He would have taught me. But I was unable to ask. I wanted to learn 'The Little Musgrave', 'This Land Is Your Land', and all the songs of Woodie Guthrie that my dad played on his record player, and all the songs Joan Baez played on the record that for years was the only one Mum had when we lived in a cottage on the Yorkshire moors and which she told me she listened to as she watched the land change colour and her children grow.

But those were not my songs. I would never manage to play them as well as the singers on the records. I had better give up dreaming – that was the best way.

But Bob Gale was not like that.

'Let's just play. The guitar is going well now, is it? What have you managed to pick up?' he would ask.

'Well, I've just listened to, umm, some records of my dad's, and some other things.'

'So, play us something then,' he would say gently, his eyes smiling, a grin emerging from his beard, as we sat in his kitchen one Saturday morning before taking the train to London together, for a meeting of the Workers' Music Association. But I had not been able to learn anything as well as him, and told him it would be best if I did some more practice, as the lines of the songs I had

300

written passed through my mind, as if testing how they might have sounded if I sung them in that room.

We sat around a large table in a wood-panelled room at Caxton Hall, musicians and other artistes talking about their projects, and I felt like a fake, because I had nothing to say.

A smart man in a blazer gesticulated with a stump where his hand had been, talking passionately about the ideas and writings of Sydney and Beatrice Webb.

He was interrupted by a man with no teeth who called for the WMA to do more to promote the work of the poets who had written from the trenches during World War One. Tentatively I approached him when the attendees went to a pub for lunch. I told him all about Wilfred Owen.

'No,' he railed. 'The one who has been forgotten is Isaac Rosenberg. It's a name you should not forget. Isaac Rosenberg. Will you remember it? Isaac Rosenberg,' he repeated, as he pulled indigestible fatty skin from his toothless mouth while chewing with his gums at a ham sandwich.

He was the kind of man I had seen through the steam of the car windows when we were kids on our way with Dad through London to the Young Vic theatre. Now, there I was with him, a character once safely seen from a distance who was now a part of my world, in a pub with musicians and thinkers and people of the street who were waiting for me to pick up a guitar and sing like Bob Dylan, everybody listening to the passion and beauty of the ballads I scribbled down in the secrecy of my room but which I would never dare play to anybody in case I was asked why I was singing about a world I could not possibly have seen. It was the world of my mind that I

301

wrote about. Bob Gale, who had taken me to London to open my eyes, wouldn't want to hear about what was going on in my mind. He would want to hear songs about ideas and life and work. I tried once to tell him how confusing everything was for me. I told him I didn't know what it was that I should believe or care about or fight for.

'I just don't know,' I told him. 'I just don't know.'

'That's all very difficult to understand,' he said, sympathetically, as we were driving to a festival at Alexandra Palace one Saturday afternoon, where he introduced me to singers and activists.

'And this is Mark.' He told some people from Ireland.

A woman nodded carefully, eyeing me closely. 'Well hello there Mark. I see you're in good hands,' she said, nodding at Bob. Then they laughed and chatted, and as we walked away I asked him who they were, because the signs above their stall were in a language I had never seen.

'They're Sinn Féin,' he told me. 'The Irish republicans. They have their doubts about communists like me, but we get along alright.'

'What are they hoping for?'

'To get us lot out of Ireland.'

'We should be out of Ireland.'

'Why?'

'It's they're country. Not ours.'

'Good lad. I'll bet you never tell that to many people.'

'No.'

'Where did you hear that opinion?'

'I never heard it.'

302

'But you believe it?'

'Yes. I think I do,' my doubts setting in, as I remembered that there must be something that I should know about the Communist Party's opinions on Ireland. 'Do you think it – that it's they're country?'

'Of course it's theirs. But don't tell your mum and dad I said so.'

'Okay,' I told him, confused about my own opinion, which he seemed to doubt, perhaps because he knew my mum and dad, and assumed they had certain views and that I could not possibly differ from what I must have learned from them. My views could perhaps be a little different, but not so much as to make me an outsider. Outsiders couldn't make any difference, because they were eccentric, and could sometimes be dangerous. In England, people could be eccentric – even outsiders – as long as they didn't expect to make any difference. Eccentrics were people like Barbara Moore, 'That Crazy Woman', whose life had been made into a television play that I stumbled on by chance and which I have remembered ever since. Barbara Moore lived between the worlds of truth and imagination, proving that people could be free if they were strong and determined. She had created something of the times into which I had been born, but was dead by the time I had heard about her. I felt a bond with her, because when she was living in defiance of the pressure to buy and consume, I was being born. For a while we had walked the earth together. People remembered her, and watched the story of her life on television.

But 'That Crazy Woman' could make no difference, because what she said required imagination, so she was categorized as an eccentric and allowed to live like that only as long as she did not expect to make a difference.

I had to make a difference, and to make my world rich with ideas and beauty and songs. Then there would be no politics – only truth. Politics should be about truth. Everything should be about truth. I wondered if that was eccentric, and remembered an Irishman who had burst out of a van on a long ago summer afternoon, who had hit me on the head and threatened to beat me with his belt if I called him a 'Paddy' again.

*

Autumn drifted towards winter, and for a while I wanted to see the one who would look into the dark place that I assumed must be my soul, and have them ask me how it was all going so far, my life.

But then, as the words poured out of me, the need for that character to appear on the landscape ebbed, as it had done in the Highlands. The voice that wrote itself onto the pages which today lie stored away in boxes in my home, was far more precise than any conversation I might have had at that time. I can hear that voice now, in the poems I wrote as the autumn of 1979 became a time of blinding, excruciating darkness. I was terrified – still am – by the lines I wrote then, the world of my mind seeming always to be drowning, marked by scars and wounds. It was a place of war, a desolate place stalked by fear and the loss of hope. My poetic world was a nightmare, lived each evening as the sun was setting over our garden and the sky turning blood red, as the sounds in our house – the radio voices at *5PM* – became terrifying for being so sure and confident and all-knowing. In every line I wrote, beautiful things were threatened. Day was suffocated by night, blackness flooded the colours of the world, people were weak and at war with life.

But sometimes I dreamed in rhymes of warm lands and of classical times about which I happily fantasised, because they were fixed in childish images of Greeks and Trojans. They had once been real – real legends – in which I believed and must believe, or at least not dismiss, until the feeling diminished and the walls rose around me and I was again crippled by ghastly visions that I scratched onto paper late at night in the desperate hope that the effort would end with me being thrown into the deepest dreamless sleep. Often it happened like that, the flow of words numbing to a halt as the last lines were written. Then I would strip and swim into the soft arms of my bed, masturbating in the hope of ending my waking hours with my body drifting on the same calm sea on which my mind had been cast by the last line I had written.

Then, waking was the worst time.

Day would cast a harsh light on the lines that night had left behind on my desk like the foul trail of an animal…*Your cries pierce the undergrowth, while from under shelter the stones cry hush…Ears pricked, the black giant snorted, eyes ablaze with curiosity, as the old tree above bent its branches to a cool wind…I felt my hatred raise its fist towards your lovers, though to you and them it's all the same…* I was screaming at myself, and nobody knew or could know, because I alone could see the world of which I wrote. There was no form to my thoughts, just the rush of words that could never be explained on our streets or in the homes I sometimes went to, nor in school, nor in the cosy world of pubs I found I could drink in without being asked my age.

I went with Rick at first, and stood beside him at fruit machines, as he lost the money he earned at the electronics factory where his dad had got him a job. He hardly talked, but there were others there who slowly got used to me being among them, men who talked about work and holidays and home improvements. They bought me pints as we leaned against the bars at the Green Man or the Queen's Head. They were regulars, some with their own pewter tankards that were kept for them behind the bar. They always knew their tankards would be there, and that the barmen would know it and would fill them with the same beer without the need to ask whether anything other than 'the usual' was required. That was belonging, where they were at home.

The Green Man filled.

Rick sauntered in with somebody familiar but who I took a long moment to recognise.

'Alright?' said a voice I knew, and then saw Polly in the slightly ageing look that had crept across a face I had once seen every day, and which I had once expected to see forever. Now he was eighteen, a man, with a hairy mole on his cheek, a lean, tanned look, and still the same slightly hooded eyes, in whose stare I had once seen sympathy but which now drew down a veil. His look was one of ice, as if a gaze from a distance, a look back across a shoulder as he disappeared from view. The worst thing I could do would be to pretend we had once more than vaguely known each other.

'Yeah. Not bad,' I replied. 'You?'

'Yeah. Alright.'

'You working?'

Yeah. Same as me old man. You?'

'No. stayed on at school.'

'Oh. Right. A-levels then?'

'Yeah.' I told him, not wanting to sound as if it had been obvious all along that that was what I would do. I wanted him to ask me about what I had done, after he had shut the door to his house and I had rolled down the gravel slope past the swings.

'Should've done that misself,' he said.

'You still could.'

'Naa. Too late. Got money in mi pocket now. Couldn't do without that.'

'Money in your pocket. Sounds like you can buy me a drink then,' said a tall, thin figure who had sidled up to where we stood and had lingered there unnoticed.

'Fuck off Tet,' said Polly.

The stranger smiled. 'Well, it looks as though I'll just have to buy my own then,' he said, a grin of humiliation forcing his stubbly chin to stick out. He ordered himself a short and paid with a ten pound note. 'Sorry Bernard, I don't have any change.'

He turned to me.

'You're Mark,' he said.

'Yer know Tet?' Polly said to me.

'No. Hello.'

'Dunno Tet?'

'No.'

In that small map of streets there was no reason not to have met him before. He and Polly and Rick had all been in the same year at school, and were all now working. But their jobs hardly mattered. Sometimes, in other places, there were people who would ask 'what do you do?' Discussion about jobs would be long and

307

detailed. If Polly and I had married two girls who were best friends, if our lives were like his Uncle Gary's, then we would have been able to talk. But I couldn't tell him about my songs or my poems, the things that were the growing up I was doing on my own but which once I might have shared with him. He still saw me as a kid. Rick was the one he had invited to his parent's anniversary party. Now Rick stood at the bar, his hair down his back and a pink badge with the words 'Gays Against The Nazis' pinned to a cardigan that sagged from his hunched shoulders. Nobody commented on his badge, or what it might mean. He had not actually told us he was gay, and was now leaving us to assume it. Years ago he had gone out with Joan, a quiet girl who lived in Chippingfield, so there was always the assumption that he wanted to have sex with women. The girl I had gone to see him with in the tower block never came into his life, and no others followed. He turned to Polly.

'Do you wanna come back to my house?' he asked him.

Polly blushed. 'No. What for?' he asked.

There was an awkward silence, of a kind that never happened when we had been kids together, when there was never silence, always noise. Rick shuffled, fidgeting with a cigarette, gulping at a glass of white wine.

'Gotta go,' said Polly, and strode out of the pub, subdued, shocked even, without turning again to anybody in case he was asked why it was to him that Rick had made his pass even though Polly had for years never been without a girl.

*

On 25 May 2014 14:17, Mark Huband <■> wrote:

Dear Mark

My turn to apologise for late reply.

Of course, 15 June is not good for you - I should have remembered. Please come the following weekend - 21-22 June. Shall we make that firm?

Best

Mark

On 29 May 2014 19:34, Mark P <■@gmail.com> wrote:

Dear Mark,

I'm so sorry to have to say, but having had a chat to T, we are actually going to a friend's birthday party that weekend. Having told you that we are free on any weekend except 15 June, I feel terrible. I feel that I am messing you about and am truly sorry. Is there another weekend that that is convenient for you and your family? As I say, I'm truly sorry about this.

PS - Your book is amazingly good.

Kind regards -

Mark

On 2 June 2014 12:37, Mark Huband <■> wrote:

Dear Mark

That really is absolutely no problem at all. How does August look for you - will you be away on holiday? July is a bit full for me so August looks a bit better; I have something on the weekend of 23/24 August, but other than that am fine.

Do let me know what suits

Very best

Mark

On 3 June 2014 22:19, Mark P <█@gmail.com> wrote:
Dear Mark,

We are on holiday for most of the first week of August. How about the second or the forth weekend of the month? That is Saturday 14th or Saturday 28th? Either of those would be great for us. Am looking forward to it. Please let me know which suits and we 'll book train tickets. Speak soon ...

Cheers Mark

Mark

On 10 June 2014 13:42, Mark Huband <█> wrote:
Dear Mark

Great, let's organise for August; the weekends seem in fact to be the 16/17 and 23/24. If it suits you, the weekend of 16/17 would be good. How does that sound?

Best

Mark

On 13 June 2014 22:16, Mark P <█@gmail.com> wrote:
Dear Mark

I'm glad we have finely settled on a date - the weekend of 16/17 is perfect for us, as it give us some time after our holiday in Devon. Can't wait. I'll speak to you before, of course.

Cheers Mark

On 16 June 2014 07:06, Mark Huband <█> wrote:
Dear Mark

That's great; I am really looking forward to it. Yes, let's speak before then.

Best

Mark

On 30 June 2014 22:12, Mark P <█@gmail.com> wrote:
Hi Mark,

we are about to book tickets to Stroud for the 16th/17th and have found that the best deal is to leave at 1 pm on Saturday. If we were to get the 8.30 pm back to London on the Sunday, would this be convenient for you? If not, we could book an earlier train. Please let us know so that we can book tickets asap.

Hope all is well with you and your family.

Speak soon - Mark

On 11 August 2014 17:29, Mark Huband <█> wrote:
Dear Mark

I hope all is well with you, and that your holiday in Devon wasn't a wash out.

I am really looking forward to you all coming at the weekend; what time will you train arrive?

Best

Mark

On 12 August 2014 20:20, Mark P <█@gmail.com> wrote:
Hi Mark,

as it happens, we were lucky with the weather in Devon. It was sunny nearly every day except one, which we spent in the city roaming the thrift stores and second hand book shops, which was always a part of the plan anyway. We are looking forward to the weekend very much. Our train arrives at 2.43 pm.

See you Saturday - Can't wait.

Mark

*

'Well. That wasn't very successful,' Rick said, his lack of awkwardness almost unimaginable. He laughed, his composure regained, as if his breaking of childhood's greatest taboo meant nothing. 'See yer.' he said, and was gone, leaving me with Tet.

'There are some people…friends of mine…getting together,' said Tet, in a secretive, muttering voice. 'Perhaps you'd like to join us?' he asked me, the hint of formality in his choice of words both sinister and intriguing. I asked him where they were meeting and he mentioned a flat in a large red-brick house close to the pub.

We stepped out into the November night and walked up the gravel drive of a house that I had passed hundreds of times over the years but never entered. Inside was a long, dimly-lit corridor. We ascended a wide staircase that rose up into darkness, and he knocked on the door of a flat.

A young blond man opened the door. He knew Tet, though not well, and did not seem happy to see him, though let us in even so. Inside, the room was full of people sitting in gloomy half-light, the smell of marijuana intense. Everybody was smoking, and on a cushion though half-lying on the floor was the girl I knew from my primary school, the one who had been in my room, who had sung the song about her sister.

'Hello Mark,' she said. 'Do you want some?' She handed me a tightly rolled spliff. I drew heavily. My head span and the room flowed like the sea. It had never been like that before. The strangers in the room were silent. The girl smiled. I sat close to her. She spoke, stoned and drowsy, and we shared the spliff. Her sister. Where was her sister? Don't ask questions. 'More?' she asked, and I drew heavily as the spliff began to burn. But I was away, her smile the last thing I saw before I slipped gently away into oblivion. 'Get up. It's past midnight,' a voice, hers, told me. And I was on the ice of the silent street, stepping through the kitchen door, Mum sipping tea.

'You had me so worried. You look awful. What have you been doing?'

'I'm fine. Just a bit too much to drink. Goodnight.'

For a few weeks I saw Tet often. Then he started going out with the girl who had once been there in my room. I didn't like seeing them together. He was thin and dressed like a spiv. She could have been artistic, even theatrical, lonely and romantic as she waited in her castle tower. Now she was with him, perhaps from desperation. She would never show Tet to her sister, because he would seem to be all the things that her sister despised. He was thin, the girl tall and broad. They were ugly together. But at least neither of them could expect anything of me. I could move in and out of their lives as I wanted, walking in the late winter afternoons to his house beyond the church where my brother Paul sang in the choir.

Tet's mum was sometimes there, seeing her two sons before leaving for the home she had somewhere else. When she was not there his dad would arrive for a few hours, cook his sons some food, then leave. His parents never saw each other, and the house was mostly left for Tet and his brother to use as they wanted.

As the sun was setting, 'Wish You Were Here' playing loud, Tet would roll strong spliffs and we would

313

be stoned until waking into the evening darkness, his dad banging on his bedroom door.

'Open this bleedin' door,' he screamed. Tet opened it cautiously.

'What do you want?'

'Get down those stairs and tidy this house, you waster. That's what you are – a waste of space.'

'Who do you think you are, talking to me like that?' Tet retorted indignantly.

Their hatred of each other rooted me to the floor between them. I was sure they would fight and that I would be too weak to separate them.

'You can just get out of this house. And take your friend with you. And what have you been smoking in there?'

'He does have a name.'

'See if I care.'

'His name is Mark.'

'Hello Mark,' his dad murmured, as embarrassed and confused as he was angry.

'Sorry. I'm in the way. I'll go,' I said.

'No. Stay,' said Tet.

'It would be good if you could…sort things out,' I told them both.

'Too late for that,' said his dad. 'He's a waste of space, and he's gone too far. What are you two, anyway? A couple of junkies?'

'Don't get involved, Mark,' said Tet.

'Why shouldn't he?' said his dad.

'I think I should go,' I said.

'No. Stay,' said his dad. 'I'm leaving anyway.'

'Well I'm glad to hear it,' said Tet, in a voice more angry and bitter than I had ever heard.

His dad picked up his coat, slammed the front door behind him and drove away, the two of us following him out into the night, smoking a spliff along Mill Lane, the cold air as brittle as the mesh of words and aimless streets that were the good times we were supposed to be having or which we might be able to invent, as we stepped in among the hearty gents and smooth professionals holding court at the bar of the Queen's Head, where old world evenings of village England took shape around us as the end of the 1970s approached.

'You're Mark. I've known who you are for years,' said one of the group standing at the bar in the frantic clamour of that New Year's Eve.

He was tall and blond. I felt timid and slightly suspicious. It was strange to me that I had not seen him before. I had been spied on, I thought, and wondered what I might have been doing as he passed unnoticed. He knew the people who were drinking there, people whose world I occasionally thought of myself as being a part, and wondered where he had been while that world had been forming.

'Where have you seen me?' I asked.

'On your bike, with your family, going on your holidays. And with all those kids you used to hang around with from Chippingfield...I heard there was some trouble over at the maltings in Sawbridgeworth, and your dad stopped you from seeing them, which must have been hard for you. But then you went out with that girl from the top of the High Street. The one who's going out with Tet.'

'You know a lot of things.'

'I know that you wanted to be an actor, and that you know the words to all of Bob Dylan's songs, and that you write poetry.'

'What's your name?'

'Peter.'

'Yes, I write poetry.'

'Can I read some of it?'

'Maybe. I suppose so,' I said, warily, wondering what his aim was in asking, then regretting that I had not said no. I could not read my words to a stranger. They were my words. I felt possessive. I assumed he would forget as soon as the midnight bell tolled. But instead he kept talking, about writers I had not read – Ernest Hemingway, Alberto Moravia, the Marquis de Sade, Henry Miller. The talk was like a competition, though he did not see for a while that I was not taking part. I wanted to tell him that until only months earlier I had been frightened of books, as he told me about the novels and poetry that filled his shelves at home, a home that I imagined was probably large and grand, in keeping with the dinner jacket and blue silk neckerchief he was wearing, and the confident manner he conveyed.

'Can I read your poetry later? I know where you live,' he said.

'Yes. If you'd like to.'

'I'm here with my brother and sister. Can they come too?'

'Okay.'

'We'll go from here then.'

'Yes. I don't understand why we haven't met before.'

'Well, you always kept yourself a bit aloof.'

'Did I?'

'You must know that.'

'No. I never knew that anybody thought that about me.'

'What would you like to drink?'

'Oh. Thanks. Wine please. Red.'

'So, happy new year.'

'Yes. Thanks. Happy new year,' I repeated, the words seeming to mean more than they usually did, and still resonating hours later when drunk and exuberant we ambled out into the new decade, where a robe of thick fog cloaked us as we were drawn along what became our own secret way through the darkness, opened to us alone by the conjuring of mystery and wonder that only the voices and hopes and imaginings of new friendship can bring.

*

On 25 Oct 2014, at 18:51, Mark P <█@gmail.com> wrote:

Dear Mark,

We are looking forward to your poetry night and have confirmed that we will be attending. I hope all is well with you and your family. See you there.

Please excuse this very brief email.

All the best – Mark

On 25 October 2014 19:14, Mark Huband <█> wrote:

Mark

Wonderful that you can come along. Really looking forward to seeing you both.

Mark

On 11 Nov 2014, at 20:14, Mark P <██@gmail.com> wrote:

Mark,

we have been let down by a child minder and I am wondering if the event is appropriate for seven year olds. If not, that is fine, it'll just mean that I'll probably have to come along alone. Could you let me know? Looking forward to seeing you ...

Mark

On 11 November 2014 22:29, Mark Huband <█> wrote:

Dear Mark

Yes, please do bring the 7 year old - it will be great to see her and you.

Greatly looking forward to seeing you

Mark

From: Mark P [mailto:█@gmail.com]
Sent: 18 November 2014 20:36
To: Mark Huband
Subject: Re: How are you

Dear Mark,

we had a great time last Wednesday. It was an excellent event to be a part of and I thank you. Having your poems read by professionals made it much easier to 'get' them and it really was an enjoyment to witness. It was nice seeing your family again, as well as Phil, Bear, and Nell.

Speak soon -

Mark

On 20 November 2014 at 11:41, Mark Huband <██> wrote:

Dear Mark

I reckon the most poetic part of the evening was that you and T were there to hear it.

I'm participating in a poetry reading in Victoria on Friday 28 Nov – starts around 7.30; would you be able to come along? We can booze and plan when you might be able to come and stay during the Christmas holidays.

V best

Mark

On 24 Nov 2014, at 21:05, Mark P <███@gmail.com> wrote:

Hi Mark,

sorry to take so long to reply - We've had a rather busy few days. I'm afraid to say I can't make the poetry reading; we've got a Birthday dinner party that's rather binding. Thanks for thinking of me. We'll definitely have a drink soon.

 Thanks again Mark,

Mark

On 24 November 2014 at 21:32, Mark Huband <███> wrote:

I was just thinking of you as your email pinged onto the screen - just passing through Harlow on the train to Stansted airport.

No problem about the Friday reading. How about lunch on Friday 12 December?

Best

Mark

On 26 Nov 2014, at 14:35, Mark P <███@gmail.com> wrote:

Hi Mark,

Friday 12th is good for me. Where do you fancy meeting. I rather liked the last pub we went to called the Barley Mow, which is on Curtain Road. Let me know what you think. I'm open to other ideas.

Speak soon ...

Mark

On 2 December 2014 at 22:07, Mark P <█@gmail.com> wrote:

Okay Mark,

See you there...

Mark

From: Mark Huband <█>
Date: 11 December 2014 at 21:01
Subject: Re: How are you
To: Mark P <█@gmail.com>

Mark

Yes, looking forward to seeing you at 1.30 Friday.

Best

Mark

On 11 Dec 2014, at 19:45, Mark P <█@gmail.com> wrote:

Hi Mark,

Just checking on tomorrow – 1.30 at the Barley Mow. Also Mark, I was chatting to T last night and I am afraid that we cannot find a window during the holidays for us to pay you a visit. I'm truly sorry.

Because my sister has left this year we are going to stay with my Mum from the 24th to the 27th and are staying with T's parents from the 28th to the 29th. We have a New Years Eve party that we always attend and T still has to find some space to visit L's cousins. Because L isn't going to get much of chance to play with many other children over the hols, T is determined to take her to see her cousins before the holidays are over.

We would love to come to see you soon into the new year. Anyway Mark, truly sorry about that.

I just wanted to give you the bad news before we meet tomorrow. In other words – I took the coward's way out. Mark

*

Dawn was always creeping across the sky by the time those winter nights of talk edged drowsily to a close, our sitting room thick with cigarette smoke and the smell of Dad's homemade beer, the silence seeming to let in the cold. We wanted our talk never to end, Peter hinting, comparing, contrasting and sometimes suggesting that our lives might even be like the characters he had read about. The sex lives, the radicalism and the iconoclasm of his heroic literary mavericks, were what drove him, his enthusiasm stoked by the conviction that one day he would be ranked among them, his own appeal as a character strengthened by the melancholy that emerged with the hint that of course the world would conspire to deny him the chance.

The conflict was always there – that first evening that ended long after sunrise, and all the evenings and nights that followed through the spring and into summer – between the hope, then the hope dashed, the innocent becoming the victim of conspiracy, the cruel world poisoning the dream world of the romantic who sought only to love, be loved, and give pleasure to women who would never forget their seduction by the tall blond youth who inevitably moved blamelessly on to his next conquest, all in the manner of Miller or Moravia – misunderstood men who meant women no harm and wanted only to maximise their pleasure.

I listened, wondering often why it was to me that Peter was telling this. As far as most of my small world knew, I had barely started to break through my childish shell. I had rejected two women who had wanted my virginity. I should be embarrassed. In my town, I was weird. My friend Richard had told me so. This new person would be no different, particularly if I ventured to match his poetics by daring to reveal that whatever I said about my American heroes, the voice that truly spoke for me now was one that would have been crushed underfoot by any of those virile dwellers of his literary pantheon, as the line that echoed around and around that winter…*St Agnes' Eve, Ah bitter chill it was*…became all the evenings and nights through which I had ever passed on my way, as I dreamed of the time when it would be me who melted into her dream…*like the rose blendeth its odour with the violet, solution sweet.*

These new sounds were a revelation that would have been the petals of a flower to Peter's muscular literary rampage. Keats's was a man's voice speaking, but one that was delicate, fragile and sensitive. I had been hiding his words for my entire life, and awaited the time when I would become a woman's dream, as the first hint of dawn gathered around the great tree with the rope swings in our garden, and Peter gathered up the books he had brought with him and over which we had poured in a

322

voracious search for the perfect line that would speak for us. Then he crept across the creaking floorboards of our hallway and stepped out into the January mist, as I drifted to my bed, unable to know if I wanted to be John Keats himself, or one of his characters.

Whichever it was, I had always to pretend it was the other when we read his poems in our class. To voice an affinity with Keats would be like standing naked in public. The girl I had followed into a bedroom and lain with naked at a party was in that class. My imagination was hidden from her. But in the classroom, exploring Keats's mind, the risk grew that she would unearth the secrets I had kept from her. I could not look into her eyes, as I explained why it could never be me…*who could burst joy's grape against his palate fine*…because after joy there was only sadness, and I was afraid to admit to the sadness.

But I wanted to speak of it out loud.

I wanted to say it because I wanted my dad to hear me say it – that joy was just the first sign of the sadness that would follow, which was why…*in the very temple of delight, veiled melancholy has her sovran shrine*…I wanted my dad to hear it, but could not say it because to have sounded as though I believed it would have said too much to him, as he sat there – my class teacher, my dad, who had smiled and laughed, 'well done, well done' as we walked together from Corfe Castle along Nine Barrow Down, with whom I strode across a market square on the festival eve, and who had laughed and whooped in the thrall of a furious wind that we had captured in our sails. If there was only sadness in the joy, then I was still the unbeliever he had known as we cycled along beside the Dutch canals and I had wanted only to be away from there and with my friends before…*youth grows pale and spectre-thin and dies*…though I could not tell him that that was what I thought, nor that all his kindness and encouragement and love and patience had been in vain.

'Mark, what do you think Keats is saying here?' he asked me.

'He's saying that unhappiness – melancholy – is an integral part of happiness. That one follows – naturally – from the other.'

'And is that an experience that many of you have had?'

'It's pretty pessimistic,' said Alex.

'Yes,' said Dad. 'But Keats was young at the time. Do you think perhaps it's an emotion that came of his age?'

'Well, I don't feel it,' said Alex.

'I'm glad to hear it,' said Dad.

'I think it's a boy thing,' said Kerry. 'Not a girl thing at all,' she added, with a wry smile.

'Girls don't feel melancholy. Is that what you're saying?' Dad asked, always amused by her comments.

'Well, I do when somebody's just chucked me, or when I've got my period. But I certainly don't get all grisly like John Keats. Secretly I think he quite enjoys wallowing in it a bit,' she said, with gentle mockery but without derision, a combination that was clever.

It was a relief for me that we all laughed and she became the focus of attention and everybody forgot what I had said about the 'Ode on Melancholy', which had been such a struggle to speak about. I needed a camouflage for my words – to throw them out into the world without anybody thinking to ask me where they came from. So, as the night approached when the lights would go down and the faces would hold still, when the eyes and mouths and ears would listen, I learned my lines immaculately, and became the character I never was during those times. This time, as the lights transformed the world and I became the confident young lover, there would be no horrible moments when the words would not come, when the audience would watch me stumble and stutter. Instead, I would make them laugh. They would wonder whether it was me, there in the rose light of the faery world that had been conjured up by Shakespeare for me alone. My lines were a gift from him, as he took me with him on his journey into the wonderland of *A Midsummer Night's Dream*.

Nobody doubted that I was indeed Lysander. Nobody could say that I was not the lover I had never been. Nobody knew that I had never been a lover. But as our school hall became Oberon's domain, Titania mocking his love for an Arab boy and Puck going…*with broom before, to sweep the dust behind the door*…I was living among the Athenian kings and queens in the shadow of the faery folk, in a place I hoped I would never have to leave. Inside the mind of my character, I built a kind of trust. Only Shakespeare could do that for me. I looked to him for a complete, believable fictional world. His people were perfect. Their weakness, their foolishness, their laughter and fun and seriousness, were all part of the perfectly imagined world he had created. I must stay there forever, with the writer who was the master of his universe, where there were realities inside fictions inside fantasies, which transfixed the corridor kids and their mums and dads and the teachers who must listen to me now.

But then it was over.

The applause of the last night went quiet and the stage was dismantled. It was unbearable, the destruction of the world we actors had made.

I read and re-read the play, its pages worn, my scribbled notes seeming dead, the cast now dispersed to lessons, the words all spoken, the audience back at work. I hated the finality of the last curtain that was the wall between the two worlds of which I was a part. The imagined must become the real, and must be there tomorrow when I woke. It wasn't just for fun that Keats and Shakespeare imagined the worlds about which they wrote. The imagination envisioned a place that must be reached, where the end would be and where everything would make sense, I convinced myself, as I wandered out along the open road one weekday morning in late winter when I had no classes to attend.

*

The sun glittered through dark fir trees clustered in the garden of the primary school my teachers had left years ago, or so I had been told. I heard children shouting in the playground, but couldn't see them from the road outside, where I walked beside a small wood to which a girl called Helen used to take boys to be kissed.

Away from the trees and streets was the open road where nobody walked.

Cars passed, and trucks, and I walked out into the unknown. A driver stopped and took me to the motorway, then drove on, out east onto the flat lands of Essex, and I stood beside the slip-road hoping I would not see anybody I knew, waiting for a ride north, hoping I could be silent with whoever it was that stopped. The truckers waved, 'Sorry mate', they couldn't give rides. The car drivers looked closely, slowed, then changed their minds. Some stopped then sped off as I approached.

But soon I was speeding along the motorway, cutting through the fields where my friends and I used to take our bikes, smoke, and sometimes drink whatever somebody had been able to steal. Then, those lands were gone, and the vast open plains of Cambridgeshire opened out before me, swept by the sunlight.

'Where are you going? Where are you coming from?' I was asked, and I told of a family that was from all over the world, that was quite international, and that my parents were away and that I travelled a lot on my own, though sometimes with friends, who were older than me, but usually on my own, because I liked it that way, and I was going to see a friend who lived on the river in Ely, on a narrow boat he had built himself, and we might go travelling together, perhaps abroad, or all over England.

'Thanks for the ride.'

'Have a good journey, wherever you might be going,' a driver said, an hour or so along the motorway, and I could hear in the tone that I had only been half-believed, myself barely convinced of my own strange tale of a life of journeys to the timeless space I imagined lay somewhere further along a country road, past signposts to the ports and the big towns of the east. That place might lie ahead of me, beyond where the country road crossed the dark earth of the Fens, through villages I came to know by name but have forgotten now. There, the voice in me was silenced, as I moved through places where nobody knew me. The silence was always there. It was a part of the landscape, where I became a figure on the roadside.

Ahead, in a haze of winter sun, the vast mass of the cathedral towers were my castle. I came upon this place from across the fields. I was the traveller, young, perhaps a poet, perhaps a mystery, drifting in from the still horizon of the Fenland, slipping unknown through the streets and down to the cold steel of the river. A name called, a surprise, then a welcome, some resentment that I had arrived without warning, and I stepped into the fragile life my friend Theo had made among the river folk, the countrymen, the cathedral schoolboys, the riverside pub owners, the travellers and the daughters of the town gentry he longed for, but who followed him confused as to whether he was their sort or not.

He still had that damaged lip, and since he had left Harlow he had come to speak like a country boy. I had tracked him down the previous year, and he had come to stay in my house, and I had gone to stay with him, travelling by train across the dark wetlands in the winter. Now, his parents had a fine house on the riverfront. He and his brothers had all left school as soon as they could, to find work and money, and he had built a narrow boat, moored there among the cruisers that were shuttered for winter on a stretch of river fenced on the far side by the stark strands of leafless poplars.

Theo thought freedom was mine, when I arrived out of nowhere, a knapsack on my back, smoking a cigarette, a book in my bag for him – all my poems, each written by hand on a new, clean page, with titles and careful spacing, the cover white, the writing my neatest. Freedom was what I had, he thought. He had the need and the capacity to say it, which was not an easy thing in those days. That wasn't what people said and not the way people talked in 1980. Freedom was what he told me he saw when I walked in from across the fields and called out his name beside the river, while all I wanted to be was the one he thought I was – the traveller, seeing and hearing the world, appearing from nowhere, disappearing unnoticed for weeks or months, before returning with a tale to tell.

But I had no tales to tell. Neither of us had. Though now I see that we did. Everything that was happening was a part of the long story. But like every boy then, we had no idea how to live our lives, only how to look at other people's and wonder how well we could imitate, while making the imitation impossible to detect. So, he looked on at the fantasy of my life, and I wondered why he never seemed to want to fill his boat with wine and marijuana, meet a girl in one of the riverside pubs, walk back there with her as the stars fell into the ripples of the river, make love with her in the wooded scent of the cabin and, while the town slept, just before the dawn, quietly untie the mooring ropes and stand watching the naked girl sleeping softly as he steered the boat out into the midstream and be gone.

There was no girl to take along. There were young kids who hung around on the quayside hoping for rides on the boats. They talked to my friend as if they knew him well, and I could see he wished they wouldn't. They were just kids. We had other things on our minds – the wide world, the endless world. How to get there, that was all we didn't know. So, when he talked to the young kids who remembered him from his school and who knew his younger brothers, he had it in his mind to force a distance. They were the cold light of day.

'Why d'ya go nowhere on yer boat, Theo?'

'Ahh yer can fuck off. I'll go when I want.'

'But yer never go anywhere. What yer gotta boat for?'

'Look, just piss off will yer. Who asked yer for yer opinion, anyway?'

Then the boys would move on somewhere else.

'Maybe we should go somewhere,' I would say. More than once I said it, and only once, one hot summer afternoon, we loosed the mooring ropes and guided the boat out into the midstream. There were no girls around to ask, but I didn't really care, as all I wanted to do was drink and smoke and read out my poems, as the silent meadows of the Fenland opened out in front of us. That summer day was when my friend's melancholy set in, as we moored under trees, drank and ate, smoked and sat under the sun, he wishing we were not there alone, me sad, maybe angry, that we were not composing the sweet and furious lines brought on by the drunken summer place which was ours. Always there was another place. I never learned whether he knew what it looked like, as my head ached under the sun and I stripped and dived into the green smoky flow and felt the brush of reeds, and swam through the darkness hoping that when I rose to the surface I would be in a different place and that my friend would be gone.

But on that winter's day, after sunset, the cold whipped across the river of steel. He looked for long silent moments at the book of my poems I had given him, and I wondered if our talk would change, and whether it might one day flow with rich words that would make our dream-lives real. Perhaps I had made it real, giving him the poems I had written down for him. Maybe that was something real, there in his hands. But where would it take us, in the darkening, after the sunset that was the end of everything, while all that lay ahead was empty night? To step out of the soft warmth of the narrow boat where we had talked of poetry and dreams and of the troubles which to write down here would be to betray his trust in me, and then to wonder which way we should turn along the river bank as we stepped out into the cold, was to be forced to make choices we could not bear to make. But we couldn't stay forever beside the small iron stove that soothed the cabin. We reached dead ends as we explored our teenage minds, perhaps because we had no tales to tell, only dreams of what might be, of what we might become, our minds set on being nothing less than pure.

So we stepped into the cold, and walked through the shadows of the silent town.

He would say: 'I don't know, I just don't know.' He would say that a lot, until it irritated me, as if nothing we had talked of was ever meant to make any sense. Talking seemed pointless. But it was all I had – talking and writing, and the belief that they were real even if we talked alone, until we stepped inside a small café where we sat with a woman and her teenage son who were Theo's friends.

The son seemed drunk, but he wasn't. He gabbled, thrashing around in a muddle of slang and kid's talk, though he was older than he sounded. After we had eaten, the four of us walked through the night streets to the cold terraced cottage where the woman lived with her son.

The cottage was cold and damp. The woman called my friend to her room, and he grinned as he went to her and closed the door behind him.

In the kitchen her son ranted and mumbled. He clattered up the stairs and came back down wearing a swastika armband and a denim jacket over a leather waistcoat that was emblazoned with a skull and wings woven in torn thread. His heavy boots clattered on the floor. The room was so cold we could see our breath. The room beyond the closed door was quiet. The son filled the silence, spluttering a laugh, adjusting his swastika as he railed, then scraping a chair across the stone floor.

He went to the closed door of his mother's room. She laughed back at him and told him to leave her in peace.

'Fucking whore,' he yelled back. He clattered up the cold hollow well of the stairs, and came down wearing a Stormtrooper helmet.

My friend was silent beyond the closed door of the woman's dark room.

I remembered his mother's dark, brittle hair. It tumbled down across her face. It was always falling across her face. I thought of his brothers, as the silence rang in my ears. Outside it was cold. The son growled agitated, snarling. My friend was fucking his mother, and the thought of it was turning him mad. Her hair had fallen across Theo's mum's face, so many worlds of summers ago, when metal-blue dragonflies had skimmed the green swirling river and the gentle brush of wind had rippled the shallows where perch lingered motionless in the shadows beneath brambles that hung from the riverbanks. Sun had fumbled the drift of the leaves across the gentle flow of hues that glided like sails through light and shade. In the shadows the dark shore fell damp from the parched grass to the shingle shallows. A rat broke into the light. A moorhen slipped into the midstream. A swan drifted at the head of a flotilla of perfect ripples that carried its young. The light breeze was silk to our faces, as soft as the coolness and the sudden warmth, as soft as the rhythm of a pigeon's call and the distant clatter of a train passing between the fields to the town and on to London, the city a thousand years away.

After an hour he stepped out of the darkness and into the cold of the kitchen.

We walked in the biting freeze of the black winter street. I felt the night like a river of ice. The empty street was as bright as day against the darkness. Could he see what I saw? I never could ask, and in the cold morning, mist draped the silent river. I had dreamed of being in a place lost in mist – of passing through the mist, into a secret place that would be lost when I stepped back into the clear day.

The morning silence was of the beginning of time, as we both wondered if summer would return. While I could make my journeys, my friend had no choice but to stand still, imprisoned by the mist on the river.

I left him on the quayside, where the river barges moored for winter, and walked up past the tower of the great cathedral where my grandfather said he sometimes came to pray. I walked across the dewy grass then stepped out of the town along a deserted road. From across the fields I looked back at the cathedral, its towers lingering in the mist. Always, there was the feeling that this would be the last time I would stand on the cold desolation of the Fens and look back at Ely as it slipped away from view. Each time I had been there seemed the last. Something in me wanted it to be that way, to say goodbye to my friend and his town for the last time.

A car engine hummed in the distance, hidden by the hedgerows until it edged into view. It slowed and stopped and I asked for a ride south.

The car was cold inside, and the driver alone. He wore a blue raincoat buttoned up to his chin. He apologised, sorry that the heating was not working. We talked. He told me where he worked. I told him about my uncle, who had worked there too. He said he knew my uncle.

'Your poor uncle. Poor man. Poor man.'

He repeated the words.

'Poor man.'

Then he smiled and laughed momentarily, and asked me what my uncle was doing now.

My uncle was spitting the pips of a watermelon onto the floor of a railway carriage as it wound across the Spanish plains. He was moving from one passenger to another to ask for food, which he then carried back to his mother, his brother and sisters where they waited in the last carriage of the train. He had reached England, though for days everyone had assumed the family had drowned along with hundreds of others, when the ship they were supposed to have been on was hit by a torpedo. He was serving a delicious dinner to us on an evening after we had been to the theatre at Christmastime. He was arriving at our house in his smart French car, cradling the tiny black cat he gave me for my birthday. He was striding into the summer garden of our home, carrying generous gifts for my mum, my dad, and we the nephews he intended would be nothing less than perfect boys.

'Poor man.' The driver chuckled. 'And where did you say he lives now?'

His flat in the house behind the rhododendrons on a smart North London corner had always been warm. It had had soft settees and glass tables, a bubble lamp, a colour television that had a door to close it, and in the hallway a drinks bar where bottles on shelves glittered in bright red and green and golden brown. When we had stepped into the golden light of his home and had shut the world out behind long curtains, the laughter and the warmth and the generosity had overflowed, as we ate and drank and talked of the years from which he and Mum had arrived. Those years were just around the corner, as we drove north through London one wet summer Sunday afternoon, after I had had an evening with a stolen bottle of whisky and had drunk it with a friend in the Town Park. I was sick all the way to London that day, driven there to see some paintings at the Royal Academy. As we walked down Piccadilly I vomited onto the street, and Mum looked at me with the fear in her eyes that we could all be dragged into a time of wretchedness and uncertainty, as we walked past a place where a bronze horseman would one day stand outside a café, where the first line of this story would one day be written.

When we reached my uncle's flat that evening he laughed and chatted and handed me a drink of fizz, voicing sympathy and understanding, and I stopped wanting to vomit, and the day was swept into the evening, around a table loaded with food and laughter.

'And where does he live now?' the driver asked after my long silence, his cold words pumping steam from his smirking mouth.

'He moved to Manchester.'

The morning sun had barely pierced the Fenland mist by the time he slowed on the roadside and drove off into the haze. I was at a junction. The motorway went south. Roads led to the market towns of East Anglia. The dour college gateways of Cambridge lay some way across the frozen fields, and I wanted the certainty of a road that I knew, one I had travelled long before the delicate web of childhood had become the fragments of youth.

A car took me a few miles along the motorway then left me standing in the cold as I waited at a silent crossroads for farm traffic that would take me west towards Bedfordshire. The world was vast in the mist. Three rides got me as far as the gibbet at Caxton, where the highwaymen had once been hanged. A woman in a caravan sold tea and bacon sandwiches, but I had no money. I walked through the Papworths – silent deserted winter villages where nothing moved, which we had passed through in our family car to visit my grandparents after they had left the north-west and settled into their new life in the Cambridgeshire countryside.

The dips in the roads, the trees, gates – I knew them all. The mist cleared and the sun was bright. I walked the last miles along the narrow road Mum and Dad had driven as we had pieced together the map of the lives we had tried to build. The road rose towards the empty sky, and I thought I should find a callbox from which to telephone my grandparents to say I happened to be passing and would like to pay them a visit. They would have accepted the operator call, but might think it strange that I should be passing their remote bend in the road, turning up there without Mum and Dad for the first time since I had cycled there years ago on a hot summer day with a friend of mine. Where could I have been going, to be passing their house? I decided not to call them, as they might have said something to discourage me – that they were going out: 'Do not take the trouble.' I had simply to appear from nowhere for no reason, and trace those last few deep dips in the twisting lane that hid their corner of England, that passed the sedate homes and the fine trees that dappled the old walls marking the entrance to the hidden glade where they had staked a claim to the world they had made.

From the corner, where the road turned sharply, where the chestnut trees rose stark against the harsh blue of the winter sky, I saw them sitting in their warm living room chatting with visitors whose cars filled the gravel of their driveway. And I walked past, never slowing my step, remembering the time my parents by chance had met some of their friends during a visit to a hospital where my grandmother was being treated.

'We had no idea that she had children,' my grandparents' friends had told Mum. 'And are there grandchildren?' Mum had been asked. 'How strange that we have never heard of you,' the people had said. 'After all, we have known your in-laws for more than ten years. They never talked about you.'

Mum's retelling of the story flashed across my mind as I walked on without stopping, out of the village, unnoticed, onto the open road between the frozen fields and the endless sky, not knowing where to go nor knowing where I had come from.

*

'So, where yer from?'

The question had become a kind of password. Throughout the spring and into the summer the travellers had sought the tale of each other's journeys. Where you

337

were from was one of the poles that held the imagination. The journey had been long from there, perhaps via Bali and India, or across the Arabian Sea, or from Tangier or Istanbul or Zanzibar. But then, as if by chance, or by some vague coincidence that might even be experience, we had found ourselves drifting in the same direction, under the sunset that turned the Mediterranean red-gold beyond the white railings of the ship I had boarded at Haifa.

Everybody was drifting like that, in the summer of 1982, or so it seemed to me. A generation was on the move. Perhaps I was a part of that movement. I was one of the kids who had drifted from somewhere in Europe, south to the Mediterranean and beyond, to Arabia maybe, or to the islands of Africa, to Madagascar. Couples – young, wizened, sick from malaria or dysentery – pitched up at youth hostels, at the Joc in the Old City of Jerusalem, with no idea of what was going on in the world, vaguely aware that the years of the opium route to Afghanistan were long gone, that gurus were not the answer anymore, and anyway India was getting expensive. Borders were closed. Iran is hard now, since the Revolution. Which revolution? Yeah, they had a revolution. Are they communist now then? No, they're all religious. The Shah was bad though. Turkey's hard too. They arrest people. They don't like travellers. How did you find the Israelis? Where did you say you were from?

'England.'

'London?'

'Near.'

'When did you start travelling?'

The two Canadians sat, fresh-faced, smart, skinny, cross-legged on the upper deck beside the ship's swimming pool. They looked like twins, but were boy and girlfriend, neat in their matching khaki shorts and clean shirts. I imagined they had plenty of money and travellers' cheques and credit cards in the money belts that were strapped at their waists, from which they paid their way around the world – Sydney, and Bangkok by plane, then fruit-picking on a kibbutz, this ship to Athens, then Paris, and home.

Peggy spoke more than Grant.

'You shouldn't smoke,' she told me.

'No. You're right.'

'So, what's your story?' Grant asked. His voice – courteous, tired, going through the motions of communication – turned the question into the familiar mantra rather than the sign of curiosity that would have got me talking to two complete strangers on the deck of a ship that was steaming from the harbour at Haifa and out into the white spray and warm breeze that night after night during the weeks before that journey had begun in the spring, I had dreamed I would be sailing through.

'Umm. Well. I don't really know where to begin.'

But really I did know. It had begun with a boy who imagined himself travelling alone through airports. He had been smart and confident, and had carried a suitcase emblazoned with his initials. Sometimes he travelled with his parents. Other times he was alone, though he didn't mind, and his parents had complete confidence in him, because he knew about how to get through airports and what to do at railway stations.

Then, one cold bright morning he had walked out of a village along a road between ploughed fields which rose steadily towards the stark blue emptiness of the sky. That time he hadn't known which way to go anymore, and the smart boy with the suitcase disappeared into the distance ahead of him. At a crossroads sign that bore names along journeys to old days in a family car on distant Sundays that were silent now, the entire empty world was the scrape of a shoe on the gravel at the roadside.

Where to go? Where to go now? North?

There was nowhere to go but home.

*

'That's a good book,' said a voice beside me in *The Bookstack*, the bookshop on our High Street.

The owner of the shop had a way of conveying suspicion at the books I chose, as my library expanded in ways she could not see as permissible for the boy I was. I bought *The Age of Reason* and *Iron in the Soul*, and she looked longer at the titles than at the price, before dropping them into their paper bags. I imagined she would think they would be wasted on a boy wearing ill-fitting jeans and a corduroy jacket of deep red. Then I bought *Brave New World*, *After Many A Summer*, *Bonjour Tristesse* and *The Outsider*, and her look was as I imagined a woman in the town library might have adopted years beforehand.

'You should get that one,' said Peter, and I turned, exhilarated that what I might like to read had been noticed.

'Okay. Thanks. I'll buy that one then,' I said. I handed it to the bookshop owner, who eyed it with a mixture of pity and resignation as she took my money then handed the book to me across a counter cluttered with miniature volumes of poetry and showcases full of fountain pens from which I might one day dare to choose, when I had the courage to show her that I was a writer and that I needed a good pen.

She sold sheet music in her shop. Once I asked her if she had the music and words for 'Farewell Angelina', which I wanted to learn and play for Mum, so she could be reminded of the times when she had played her record of that song in Yorkshire.

'No. We don't have it. It can be ordered.'

'Well, I would like to order it.'

'Well, can't you just listen to the song on the record, and pick up the music by listening to it?' she barked at me.

'I think I'd rather order it.'

'Well, it'll take weeks.'

She wrote my order on a piece of paper and handed me a copy. But the music never arrived. Sometimes I would ask if it had. 'You'll just have to learn it from the record,' the shop keeper told me. But I could never tell her that I didn't know how to do that.

I walked home wondering if Mum and Dad had heard of the book I had bought.

'Oh yes, *Le Grand Meaulnes*. Yes, it's very well known. It must be nearly forty years since I read it. Lovely story.'

I didn't say that Peter had recommended it, because then there might have been questions about why he had known that I might want to read it. Or perhaps there would just have been silence, as I was watched to see which world I might seem to be sinking into now.

But Meaulnes' world was one I was already in. Not as him, of course. As his classmate, the teacher's son. I wanted to be Meaulnes. But in my world I would only

341

ever be the one who watched, and who followed when he was called. It was Peter who would be Meaulnes. He would throw himself into love, and I would be the one to whom he would tell the story in which I could never play a part. It was when I read *Le Grand Meaulnes* that I knew I could never become the story. Life would never be a story like that – the story of a life that began in a year that had no number, and which passed through the seasons in a hidden land where in the winter the rose light oozed from the farmsteads. My mum had been there. We could never go there, because our family had moved away from there long ago. Once, we had had the run of the fields. I would join a troupe of players, travelling in a wagon between village squares. I would make people laugh. A woman would await my return.

I read it quickly, and then read it again.

It had a magic that I could not believe would never be real.

In the summer a girl who never kissed, and who behaved more like a mother than a girl, went with me to see the film of *Le Grand Meaulnes* by Jean-Gabriel Albicocco. It had been showing at a small cinema on Oxford Street that has long-since closed. We took the train to London, and in the darkness I was gently carried into a place where all that I imagined was as true as all that I saw around me. A woman in the row in front of us cried for most of the film. The girl I was with laughed quietly at the woman's tears. Meaulnes cried. His tears were all that could ever be sacred. One day I would be able to cry like Meaulnes. Then the lights came up and I saw the face of the woman who had cried. She was young and beautiful, and a young man was holding her in his arms. The girl I was with smiled, because all she ever did was smile. I wanted her to cry, so I could hold her in my arms.

'How touching,' she said, with a hint of sarcasm, not clear whether she was referring to the film or the tearful woman. Either way, I wanted to be away from her before I stopped being able to hide my disappointment that she didn't even want to be like Yvonne de Galais. She knew I could not be Meaulnes. Really, that was what I wanted to be away from – a woman who could only ever tell me of the spirit I could never be. It unnerved me, the thought that I could only ever become Meaulnes' friend. But then I thought it would be okay to be him – the one who had written the story; the writer. Really it was he who had the story. Meaulnes would never write it down. Neal Cassidy didn't write the story. He just lived it – like Meaulnes.

But secretly I didn't want to be like Meaulnes at all. Secretly I wanted to be Frantz de Galais. He was the real mystery – passionate, impulsive, exotic and, above all, mysterious, disappearing then reappearing in the distance, beside a hilltop church, along the road near the swamp, in the doorway of a house in the forest. Frantz would never be known, except in the imagination. Even then he would fade from people's minds, because he would never write his story. Other people would write his story. But I wanted to live like Frantz, *and* write my story too, though I didn't know if that was possible – until the day Byron appeared, and I found a place I could travel to that could become the *domaine perdu*.

He had always been on the list which told us of Keats's life – Shelley, Coleridge, Wordsworth. I didn't like it when teachers turned them into a gang called the 'romantics'. The label made them seem self-indulgent, as if their dreams and visions had no value in the 'real' world. Keats always said it best, the different worlds all carried together and transformed into one...*on the viewless wings of poesy*...while Byron lived as poem and poet and I hitch-hiked further than I had ever done before, out into the mist, beyond the road that I had taken east to Ely, and north into the Midlands.

The book I had devoured in a day – *Byron* by L.A.Marchand – had told me where it was I should leave the route near Mansfield, on reaching the grand gateway of Newstead Abbey. I could find this hero a day's journey away, not among the back allies of San Francisco or on the frozen fields of Minnesota. Keats had known him, and Keats was my friend. It was all easy now, the places and the people all close by, with me their legacy, young like them, dreaming, radical, because the British should be out of Ireland and the real enemy were the Tories. We were the same, believing the same things, our imaginations as real as the world around us – a world that our imaginations alone could transform and make beautiful. The castles were falling. People were no longer castles. Churchill and the Queen were not castles anymore. They were philistines. Byron's was the only life to lead, as he wrote by candlelight in a high room of the Palazzo Mocenigo that overlooked the Grand Canal, and rode in his carriage all the way across the plains of northern Italy in pursuit of a woman, before joining the ship that would take him to Messolonghi and death among the Greeks who would always remember him as their friend and hero.

*

The slow humming of the ship became a deep throb. Black smoke belched from the chimney, filling the soft evening air of the harbour at Haifa with the throat-gagging stench of burning oil.

'I hitched all over.'

'Where d'jer go? France?'

'England mostly, and Scotland too.'

'I've heard it's beautiful, Scotland.'

'Yeah, it is.'

'You got friends there I guess.'

'I went to work there, last summer.'

'Now, where were we in '81? Down in the US I guess.'

'Naa, last summer was the Caribbean.'

'Sure.'

I gotta go to Edinburgh. Is that how you say it? I heard it's beautiful.'

'Yes.'

'You went there?'

'No. I was in the Highlands. On a farm.'

'Beautiful. But weren't you at school? How old are you Mark?'

'Eighteen.'

'You travelled since you were young.'

'Yer family okay about that?'

'Sure.'

'You really oughta quite smoking.'

'Sorry. Yes.'

'But I wanna know, what's Scotland like.'

The Englishman who owned the farm he ran with his wife droned loud orders across the station car park at Inverness. The train had meandered the length of the country for almost ten hours, before squealing to a halt,

345

as a fine, clear evening spread out against the sky. We were herded into a van, under threat of being left to walk if we didn't move quickly enough.

I had never been so far away from home on my own. This should have been the evening before the rest of my life.

That summer – 1981 – school had come to an end. The kids from whose lives I had waited to disappear for so long were melting away, amid promises of addresses swapped and talk of reunions some time in the future. But I had had a first taste of failure. My exams had gone okay, but I knew I could do better and could get to a better university than the ones that had offered me places.

I could break further away. I had to, otherwise I would die.

So, as I stood in the station yard at Inverness and followed the orders of the farmer, the haunting feeling was of there being no tomorrow to look forward to. The sky and the hills were not the landscape of tomorrow. They seemed to be standing still, as at the end of the summer I would be in my room again, trying to learn, tomorrow remaining forever tomorrow.

We woke before sunrise, the blear of eyes emerging from our tents as bodies stooped into the dew and mist. We walked to the fields of ripe raspberries, the farmer yelling over a loudspeaker: 'Fill your punnets. You must fill your punnets.' We filled boxes with the soft sweet red fruit, our fingers dyed as blood, the farmer hurrying along the rows to ensure that the punnets were properly filled otherwise he would not be paying us for our labour.

We stopped when it rained hard. Not to keep dry, but because the fruit could damage if it was picked when it was too wet. Then, mud thick, the bushes shimmering with the fresh downpour, the land would steam as we edged along the rows again, occasionally standing from the picker's stoop to gaze out across the brown-grey-blue-red hues of the Beaulie Firth, which lured my mind's eye to a camp beside the water, where now there was an empty pitch and only the hint of a red sail gliding the ply of a bow across the salt-hint of a loch as it slid past the peering faces of the seals.

The farther shore was deserted.

There was no smoke rising from a hut in the silent darkness of the forest.

In the evenings we cooked on open fires. There were a few Scots, but mostly people from all over England – the daughters of a vicar from Suffolk, who earned extra money from cleaning the toilets the pickers used, travellers from the West Country, as well as a Welshman who worked the mines and made his way each year to the clean air, and Martin and Bernard from the Lake District, who had no tent and so lived in a hut the farmer rented to them. In the evenings, if it was raining, we sat in their hut and talked about music and politics and why Bernard's parents had decided to give him the middle name of 'Gladstone', after the prime minister. Bernard wore a sheepskin coat which he rarely took off. He had written a song, which he sang to us unaccompanied, about a girl who had left him for another boy who turned out to have been bad:

Who's crying now?
So who's crying now?
Who's crying now?
Yeah, who's crying now?

347

He sang the chorus with relish, because he still missed the girl, though only sang the song because his friend Martin encouraged him and told him it was good.

Martin laughed and smiled and wanted to leave the Lake District and live in cities and follow in the footsteps of his hero Julian Cope, the singer of the *Teardrop Explodes*. He dressed a bit like him, in a flying jacket and army surplus trousers.

On the weekend after we arrived there he told me about a place he wanted to go to on the coast.

'Findhorn. It's sort of experimental. People live an alternative life – growing their own food and stuff. We can make it in a day. Wanna go?'

We did not have to wait long before a bright orange VW Dormobile with the word 'Oceaneering' chugged to a halt just beyond where we were standing beside the road at the end of the track that led up to the farm. The driver nodded ponderously when we told him we wanted to go to the coast. We drove in silence for a while, Martin sitting beside him in the front.

'Where are you wanting to end up?' the driver asked in a slow, quiet voice. I guessed he was in his forties. His fair curly hair was long. He wore a faded pink tee-shirt and old jeans and was driving barefoot. He drove haphazardly, swerving across the road then edging back into the lane.

'We're going to Findhorn,' Martin told him.

'And why are you going there?' the driver asked, a strange tone in his voice that seemed both suspicious and inquisitive.

'Well, it's interesting what they do there. People live a different kind of life, growing their own food and the like.'

'Sounds like a place worth a visit. I'll come along. I'll go there with you,' said the driver. Martin glanced briefly at me. He was smiling, delighted that we had found a ride that would take us all the way. But by then my suspicion of the driver had grown. I shook my head, but Martin seemed not to have noticed. The man unnerved me. His erratic driving, and a manner that for me had passed from calm to strange, had begun to frighten me.

'That'd be alright?' the driver asked.

'Yeah. Sure,' Martin replied enthusiastically. 'That'd be great.'

The purple hills passed by, unable to help. I might have been able to run out and be quickly lost among the slopes. But the driver kept moving, swerving, sometimes nearly hitting oncoming cars.

'It's cool,' he said, grinding the gears. 'No worries.'

The land became more barren as we left the glens behind. Ahead, the sky shone with the glare of grey-blue eyes in ice water. The land was rock and moorland now. There would be nowhere to run to.

He stopped the engine. We waited in silence. He breathed in hard.

'So. Where shall we go from here?'

'Well. Findhorn is on the coast. Right on the coast,' Martin told him with a mixture of anxiety and irritation.

'Ah,' the driver replied.

'Let's go,' said Martin, aggravated by the driver's ponderous manner, not thinking then that there may be more to the driver than his attitude.

'To Findhorn?' said the driver.

'Yes.'

'Alright.'

He restarted the engine. An hour later we passed the sign for the grey stone town perched at the end of the land beneath a stark pale blue sky.

Martin and I got out of the van at the roadside.

'Maybe you should find a place to park,' Martin suggested.

'Wait for me here,' the driver told us.

He pulled away.

As he did so we ran. We kept running for a mile or more, out of the town, until all we could hear above the sound of our panicked footsteps were the occasional sounds of birds twittering over the moorland. It never occurred to us that because we were two we perhaps had nothing to fear from him. Perhaps we did not know our own strength. Martin was quite tall and broad. We would have been able to overpower him, though there was nothing about him that seemed violent. It was his silence, and the moment when he had turned off the engine and waited in silence, which had created the fear in us. We were at the end of the world with him, in a small grey town on the coast of Scotland. Nothing lay beyond, except the sea. That frightened us more – the realisation that the only road we could take to get away from there, was the road that he was bound to take. There would be no escape, and no one would be able to understand why it was we needed to escape from a man who had done nothing more than alarm us with his silence on a journey that had taken us well into the afternoon.

We stopped to catch our breath, eyes fixed on a slight turn in the road from which we were sure the orange sides of the van would approach us, stop beside us on the road, and the man demand that we get back inside.

And there it was, slowly edging along the road in our direction, just behind a car carrying an elderly couple. They stopped.

'Where can we take you?' asked a grey-haired, smiling, moustachioed man wearing a deerstalker hat.

'Towards Inverness,' I said.

'Sure. Jump in,' he replied, just as the orange van clattered by, the man inside not casting even the vaguest glance at us as we passed. After a few minutes we overtook him, neither Martin nor I giving any signs of recognition, as the afternoon glided towards evening and we wondered if we would reach the farm on the Beaulie Firth before nightfall.

*

The old couple took a long detour for us, saying that anyway they hadn't been along the Beaulie Firth for years and would love to see it again.

'You seem so young to be so far away from your homes. Particularly you, young man,' the woman told me, with a mix of motherly concern and teacherly scolding. 'But it is beautiful, the Firth. The farmer treats you well, I hope. He'll be paying you for your work, I take it.'

'Of course.'

'Not much, I'll be bound.'

'It's by the punnett.'

'Slave labour.'

'It's okay.'

'Well, as long as you're enjoying yourselves. Make sure that you're enjoying yourselves,' she said.

'We've been husband and wife for sixty years, and have enjoyed every day of it,' said the old man. I could see the smile on his face reflected in the rear-view mirror. We drove in silence beside the calm of the water.

'And you won't be taking any more rides from strangers,' said the woman. They had listened in silence as we had told them about the odd man who had driven us all the way to Findhorn.

'You mean people like us?' her husband said, laughing loudly.

'No. Not at all,' his wife responded indignantly. 'We're not strange at all.'

'No. You've been really kind to us,' Martin told them.

'Always try to be helpful. And expect the same of others,' the old man said with a vigorous nod, in a serious tone. 'Now, we must be close to your farm.'

A few minutes later he pulled up at the roadside. The safe, comforting lights of their car pulled away into the late evening, old lives moving ahead of us and then gone, while we stood still on the warm tarmac wondering if our lives could one day be like theirs.

We walked up the track to the field where the tents were pitched.

Close to mine a raging fire was flinging sparks into the night sky. There was shouting and singing from the drunken bikers who had turned the field into a track for their motorbikes, which stood gleaming on stands, chrome burning the reflected flames. Massive logs were thrown on to the pyre. My tent was too close, the sides warming in the heat I could feel as we drew closer. The bikers swigged whisky and shared spliffs. I wanted to move my tent, but couldn't without attracting their attention. I sat in the glare of the flames on the cold grass. Two of the gang started to brawl. A woman screamed as they rolled into the flames. They both fell back into the darkness and I dreamed of daylight and the silence and freedom of the open road.

On Sunday it rained all day. Martin, Bernard and I sat in their hut. They talked about life in the Lake District. Mum and Dad and my brothers and I had known it only as somewhere beautiful when we went there once and camped beside Ullswater.

'It's boring after a while,' Bernard said, though I envied them even so.

I told them about the bikers, how their fire had been so close to my tent I thought it would burn. They laughed, and I realised I had hidden my fear. They knew the bikers from the previous year, when they had come to the farm to pick fruit.

'They'll be back. They come most nights. They were away last week at some festival.'

The bikers came back a few days later, drunk again, and built another fire in the same place. They roared around the camp as the fruit pickers watched and the farmer and his wife were nowhere to be seen.

The embers were still glowing but the dew had cooled the air and the grass when I woke. The bikers lay asleep around the ashes. There was the silence I had waited for – nobody around, only the sound of the birds. I took down my tent, rolled it, and tied everything to my rucksack. Martin approached as I was walking across the field towards the track and the road.

'Where yer going like that? Sneaking away?'

'Just wanted to get away.'

'Bit sudden. There's a month of picking to go.'

'Wanna get away.'

'See yer then. Gimme yer phone number.' I wrote my number on a tear of paper. 'Right. See yer then.'

'Maybe.'

'I'll come and see yer in Harlow.'

'Yes. That'd be good.'

'Are yer hitching all the way today?'

'I'll try.'

'Not much traffic, being as it's a holiday.'

'Is it?'

'The royal wedding. Charles and Di an' all that.'

'Oh. Right. See yer then.'

'See yer.'

He had walked with me as we talked, then he turned back towards the farm.

The first ride took me a short distance inland, in among the hills. The morning was warm and sunny. The road was quiet. I was a figure cradled by the great rock arms of the land. I was left at a small café, one like the diners I would sit in one freezing winter years later along the road I drove from Washington DC all the way to Chicago and across America to Los Angeles. Big old lorries rested on the coal and gravel of the parking. Pines rose up dark behind the diner. The men inside sat alone, drinking from mugs. I watched them through the large windows, wondering which of them might emerge first and be ready to give me a ride.

'Where can I take yer then,' asked the first driver I approached.

'South.'

'I'm going to East Kilbride.'

'Is that south?'

'Aye. Near Glasgow.'

'Thanks.'

The engine roared. I watched the land from high up.

'So, you'll be celebrating, down in England. The wedding an' all,' the driver said.

'Yeah, I suppose they must be.'

'You're not a royalist then?'

'I…I don't really…know. Not sure that I have an opinion. I suppose I don't really care. They don't mean anything to me.'

'Nor to me,' he said, in a calm, soft tone. He was young, but had a wise face, his short black hair and checked shirt giving him the air of Kerouac. He was more of a listener than a talker. 'Still, not the best day to be hitching rides.'

'I wanted to get going.'

'Your folks are in London?'

'Near. They live in different places…since my parents divorced.'

'Oh, divorced are they. That must be difficult for you's.'

'Yes.'

'And who d'you stay with.'

'Neither really. I sort of move around. I travel, and I reckon I'll go to college next year. So I'll be off then. I'll take a few more exams. Then I'll move away.'

'Where'll you go?'

'A city. A big city. Maybe London. Or somewhere in the north. That's where I'm from.'

'You don't sound as if yer from the north.'

'I went south when I was young.'

'Oh, so you'll be going back to yer roots then.'

'I suppose, something like that.'

'And why a big city?'

'I wanna be in a place that's unknown...where there are places that are unknown...which I can discover. Not where everybody knows everybody.'

'You want to be lost in a place. That's what yer want, isn't it?'

'Yes. Yer right. It'd be good to be lost in a place.'

'And what d'yer do then? Wait to be found?'

'Make a home in somewhere that I never imagined.'

'Never imagined? Why that?'

'Well, I suppose I have imagined the place I mean.'

'What's it like?'

'A city street, with a milk float gliding through the early morning mist.'

'You're a poet, young man.'

'No.'

'Yer are, I tell yer.'

'It's how I imagine the city.'

'And what else'll be there?'

'Places under the railways. And warm pubs where people play folk songs.'

'And will yer have a job?'

'In a theatre. A travelling theatre.'

'Very nice. I like that.'

'Acting is what I like most.'

'I can tell. You'll write yer own plays, I take it.'

'Yes. And do some Shakespeare.'

'Oh, classy stuff too. And which part will you play?'

I thought of Lysander and the magic.

Then I thought of the Christmas before school had come to an end, when the main hall had been transformed into the battlefield near Agincourt. The story was all mine, because between each of the acts I stepped quietly onto the stage and authoritatively explained the events that had passed and what was about to happen, the words of the Chorus the most poetic ever heard on stage, as I calmly held a thousand eyes in the palm of my hand and politely asked the people of my town to…*entertain conjecture of a time when creeping murmur and the pouring dark fill the wide vessel of the universe*…and took them on a journey through the day, and into…*the crippled, tardy-gaited night, who, like a foul and ugly witch, doth limp so tediously away*…as the day of battle dawned.

A girl watching from the audience had fallen for the myth of the character I played. For a week or two around Christmastime we had lived among the images of each other, then winter bit and we drifted apart. I thought of her as the truck rolled south, and I told the driver I would play young lovers, and maybe some more serious parts, and we talked and fell silent as the hours passed.

'Well, I hope you make it, and you find the city you want to be in. I'll have to drop yer here. Nice to meet you Jack. I enjoyed talking with yer. Yer'll be able to get a train into Glasgow from here. That'll be the best way to get yer south. Goodbye now.'

I thanked him and jumped down from the cab. It was late afternoon. We had been driving for four hours, and now I was among the neat grass verges and modern homes of a new town just like my own. The hot evening sun glittered perfect molten lines out of the empty railway station. A chalkboard sign said 'Sunday service all day due to the royal wedding.'

The station was as far from the events of the day as it could have been. It was of no place. The only person

357

in the world who knew where I was was a lorry driver who had now disappeared, and who didn't even know my real name. The royal wedding had stopped the country. Everything had stopped, except me. I was nothing to do with the royal wedding. All I had was my rucksack, as I traced the gleam of the rail-track, which might some time hiss with the approach of a train, while people thronged behind barriers along The Mall in the shadow of the vast buildings that ruled us, and I wanted somebody to know that I was waiting for a train at East Kilbride station, where pasts and futures gathered with every tick of the clock, as the sun slipped lower and the big day ended on the platform amid the sounds of waiting.

Each compartment on the midnight train from Glasgow Central cradled a sleeping figure barely visible in the dim light. The carriage corridor disappeared into darkness, the roof lights of the station etching night with metal blue and sometimes silver. A short-haired man wearing round tortoise-shell glasses and a heavy dark suit shifted his feet off the opposite seat to let me pass as I slid open the compartment door. He grunted, arms still folded, then dipped his head back into sleep as I sat beside the window. A whistle cracked the hollow of the station and a city, now a name on my map, was left behind. I slipped from sleep to waking. Once I woke to see that the sleeping man had gone. I caught the names of stations I regretted simply passing through. Penrith, Oxenholme, Lancaster. I knew that just across the moors there was a place in which I might be remembered. I wanted the journey to end, and to see and hear the story in it. At dawn the train stopped at Derby. I saw the sign, dragged my rucksack off the rack and stepped out onto the platform just as the carriages began to move away.

I had not had the money for a ticket that would take me any further. Two hours later I was sitting in a walled garden telling the smiling, red-faced, grey-haired woman perched on the edge of a garden chair, all about the journey I thought I had had.

'From the Beaulie Firth. How lovely.'

She had sometimes reminded me of 'That Crazy Woman' Barbara Moore, the one who was what the 1960s might have become. This woman's name was also Barbara. She had lived along the valley from us when we had lived in Yorkshire, another family of southerners who had gone north to find another England. Her husband Mick and she seemed like radicals, a bit like my uncle and aunt in Hertford had appeared to be, before they went to live in Brussels to work for the Common Market. When Mick was dying, I sent him a poem I wrote about the house there in the Derbyshire village, where now I sat with Barbara, in her garden, on that warm July morning.

'I miss Mick terribly,' she said. I realised I did not know how to express the depth of sympathy I knew I felt. Mick had been as much fun as he lay dying, as he had always been when our family had been to see them. He had given the impression that we should think death was a bit of a laugh, if a bit of a bore. I wondered if that was how I should think of it, as Barbara spoke. Perhaps Mick had been pretending. Now it was Barbara who was alone. Mick was okay. 'And how are your mum and dad?'

'They're fine,' I said, adding, to fill the silence: 'But everything is still dominated by talk about the war.'

'The second war?'

'Yes.'

'Well, it had a big influence on all of our lives you know. Particularly your mum's.'

'Yes. Did it? Yes. I suppose so. But I suppose I don't know what to say when they all talk about the war.'

'All you can do is to listen. It made very difficult times for all of us.'

Then I felt stupid and ignorant and not at all like the worldly-wise traveller I hoped I might seem to her to have become. But she didn't seem to mind.

Next morning we took the bus into Matlock – she to work, me to the road.

'Bye bye. Safe journey,' she told me.

I hitched a ride to Nottingham, then another along the road to Mansfield, and by midday was walking up the long drive to Newstead Abbey. I ambled through the gardens, not really knowing what it was I was trying to find or feel there, and wished only that Byron had not written such a silly epitaph to his dog Boatswain, which stands in the grounds on a pedestal. A poem about a faithful dog was not the kind of imaginative feast I wanted. It made Newstead seem dead, and far from being the secret place I wanted it to be. After an hour or so I wandered back along the driveway through the woods to the road that would take me back to the deadness of approaching autumn.

After hours of waiting at junctions and exchanging words with strangers who by then should have seemed to me to be the normal people of my country, the stretch of road and lamps and history in rows and shapes, were a familiar face wrinkled in resigned recognition as I approached. So, you are back, my town was saying. But I had no answer.

I got a job near our house, serving drinks during dinner-dances at the Churchgate Hotel, where local people with a bit of money would dress in dinner jackets or long glittering dresses for formal evenings, where a band of old men played 'Tie A Yellow Ribbon' and 'Three Times A Lady' to a dance-floor which only filled after the dinner of roast beef and thin gravy had been served and eaten. People drank Blue Nun wine and treated each other to expensive liqueurs, some of them flaming in their glasses on the trays I carried across the dance-floor, where drunk women, dress straps slipping, cackled at the waiter and sometimes slipped pound notes deep into my trouser pocket as a tip and gave my prick a squeeze before taking their hands out with a laugh and a wink.

'Not just a waiter, eh love?'

I would grin, money in my pocket, all of it to be used one day for the escape I imagined would come, and which seemed to be just outside the kitchen door that gave on to the cold autumn night. Drunken couples were staggering to their Jaguars, and I wound through the streets to a party where people I knew from the pubs had spent the evening drinking late into the night. We danced and smoked and drank.

'Shall we go to bed?'

I was nothing and everything that night. I was the waiter at a hotel. The country roads I had travelled had taken me nowhere, only brought me back to this flat in a block beside the railway track at Harlow Mill. Byron and Jack were nowhere to be seen. Dylan could not be heard there. In the distance the one who told the story watched, as Frantz de Galais and the lover he almost died for when he had thought he had lost her, closed the door in the forest and left the world outside behind them.

'Yes.'

And we stepped inside a room that shook as the trains passed at the bottom of the embankment outside the window.

On a winter morning when we were children we had slid across the ice on the flooded meadow beside the river. Now, we undressed, and 'slowly slowly' she said, holding me in her arms, I gave her all that I had hoped might be my secret.

'First time?' she asked.

'Yes,' I murmured, wondering if I should have lied.

'Not bad.'

We slept, and in the morning she had me come again, and I washed and dressed and walked home wondering how I would explain my absence.

'Hello darling,' Mum said as I stepped into the kitchen. The morning was bright and sunny. 'Did you have a good party?'

'Yes. It was fine.'

But I could not be with the girl again. I could not pretend. There was no secret.

'Don't you want to walk with me?' she asked me some time later.

You don't know me. Remember that. You don't know me. I'm sorry if I tricked you into believing that you do.

But I said nothing. She had asked me to her room. She had had this virgin. I felt dishonest. We didn't lie together again, though to this day I think of her as the woman to whom I gave most, and as 1982 began I was able to look further than those streets, as I made my way to cities to be interviewed by professors at universities.

With most of them I had no idea what they wanted to hear. I had been through the same trial a year earlier, and had even tiptoed my way around some colleges in Cambridge, knowing that I must not tell the brilliant minds in those rooms filled with books, where coal burned in grates, that my heroes were poets and writers and singers and that I dreamed of travelling the world. They would not want to hear those things, because they were only the dreams of my town.

But at these later interviews I was asked about the history I had been studying. At York and Newcastle there was no sympathy for my enthusiasm. At Manchester I floated up the steps of the Faculty of Arts and was stepping on hallowed ground, because Mum and Dad had been there too, way back in a time I can remember now but which back then was a world away.

'Tell me about an essay you have written recently,' said Professor Terence O Ranger, smiling with expectation.

I told him all about Frederick the Great, about the enlightenment and about how he had been a king who was also a man of ideas who had known Voltaire. Frederick was inspirational, and was the kind of modern king Europe had needed, because he was not all about conquest. He seemed vulnerable, because he debated with philosophers and seemed less likely than other kings to punish dissent.

'Well, thank you for a very interesting discussion. I can see that the subject is one that has very much gripped your imagination, which is very refreshing,' Professor Ranger told me after an hour or so.

We said goodbye. I took a train out to the small town on the edge of the Pennines where I was staying with Mum and Dad's friends from their Manchester days, Roy and Jean. Next day Roy drove me to the motorway and I was soon on the way north. I would turn up at Peter's house in Newcastle, where he was now studying. I imagined his surprise. Many short rides took me into Lancashire, then across the entire country from west to east, over the moors that might once have been my home. At a junction somewhere in Yorkshire a police car stopped and two officers got out and approached me.

'Where are you going?'

'Newcastle,' I replied. 'To see a friend.'

'Empty your pockets please.'

I emptied them.

'Take off your coat please.'

I handed them my coat. They took it with them to their car and closed the doors. After a few minutes they emerged.

'We have found specimens in the pocket of your coat. Can you explain them?'

'Well…no…What kind of specimens?'

'It's your responsibility to explain what it is you have been carrying in the pocket of your coat.'

'Well, I had some biscuits in the pockets, which I ate earlier.'

'We could take the specimens for tests, and our laboratory would be able to establish whether there is any evidence of drugs, which would of course be very different.'

'Yes, of course it would be. But all that I have had in the pockets are biscuits.'

'I'd like to take details of your name and address.' I told them. They handed me my coat, and the cold of the junction diminished slightly as I put it back on. They got back in their car and drove away. I paused for a while, turned the coat pockets inside out, walked over to the A1 slip road and a few hours later, long after nightfall, was wandering along a dark lane on the edge of Newcastle having found that Peter no longer lived at the address he had given me.

I rang his parents, but they told me they didn't have a new address for him. I called the parents of a girl who had been a year ahead of me at school and who I knew was studying at Newcastle. They gave me her number, called Mum and Dad to tell them where I was, and at around midnight I was sitting in the girl's cold terraced house, where a bar heater glowed in the sitting room but threw out no heat.

The girl's housemate was dying pink streaks into her blond hair. They both cackled about nothing in particular. It was not how I remembered the girl when I had known her at school, where she had seemed confident and thoughtful. I felt out of place, because I was not the person she might think I was. I said I was tired and she said I could sleep in her room, assuming naïvely that she would sleep somewhere else. I had fallen into a deep sleep when I half woke to find her sitting astride me where I lay on my back.

'I always wanted to fuck you. I always wanted to fuck you,' she said, almost mad, with a hungry desperation that I had never known before. She screamed and moaned. 'It's been so long since anybody fucked me. Come on now. Fuck me. Don't you want to fuck me? Don't you find me attractive?' But she didn't want me to speak. Her orgasm made her shudder and she remained over me almost rigid. I came quickly. She eased her way off me, and we both fell silent and slept.

Early next morning her telephone rang. Peter had learned from his parents and mine that I was looking for him. An hour later he was at the girl's door. I closed it behind me, and we spent a day and a night wandering, talking, drinking in a pub at Whitley Bay, where he seemed keen for the locals who didn't like students to known that that was what he was.

I said goodbye to him early next morning as he lay reading in bed, and took a train to the city and a bus to the A1. I had forgotten about the professor at Manchester, about Frederick the Great, the police officers in Yorkshire who had been looking for drugs, about the dark lane I had walked along, and about the girl in the cold room. Those things had all happened to somebody else. There was no story to be told. Nothing had happened, because there was nobody to tell the story to when I got home that evening and hid in my room to study for the exams I had decided to take again.

As the days turned into weeks I began to loathe the books and the plays. I had hated *Othello*. It was a bad play, though I had no right to say so. There was no reason for all that happened. It was a failure, that play, because Iago's actions were never explained. But who was I to say so? I could sound as though I understood it, but I didn't. I didn't understand anything. I didn't know how to learn or know.

When winter came there was thick snow. I got a part in *The Boyfriend* at Harlow Playhouse, and acted and sang badly. After the last night party at the house of the director, I walked out into the snow, drunk on whisky, and fell to the ground in the snow along First Avenue, not knowing who I was or what I was for. I was seventeen years old, and I should have been in the dynamic, vibrant prime of my youth. Hours later a staggered up the gravel path of my home.

'Must speak. Must speak. Must talk,' I was muttering.

On the evening of the following day I went to the sitting room where Mum and Dad and Mike were drinking coffee. In an avalanche of tears and words they learned something of this story. At the end Dad and Mike walked out along our road, and when they came back Dad said I must take my exams quickly – in the spring – and not wait for the summer, and that I should get away from there as quickly as I could.

*

A big, hunched-shouldered, dark-haired man with a thick moustache, wearing a crumpled blue work-shirt and matching trousers, had met us at the airport at Tel Aviv.

'Geva,' he had called out a few times, towards the group I had become a part of during the flight from London. 'For Geva,' he had repeated, in a low, unobtrusive voice, his accent as heavy as his body.

We had followed him, his manner distant, sensing that we might not actually be welcome. He had driven us in a minibus, away from the coast, curtains that would not fully open partially blocking the land from view, the roar of air conditioning sending up the volume of the excited chatter among the soon-to-be students and others who were looking to see if the rest of their lives might begin there, on that day in early April 1982.

During the flight none of the group had quite ventured to predict that we would have a fine time together. The talk had been tentative. We didn't quite know why we were there, and didn't really know what it was we were travelling to. We might just skim across the surface of the place, passing through without making an impression. None of us knew much about Israel. If we had, we might never have gone there. In England, the country was a reminder of Hitler's cruelty as our new world was emerging. For us the torment was over, if you could cope with the memories of fear and loss. Now we should try to move on, if we could. New towns had been built on the old land. Men had landed on the moon. We had our own troubles, but things were changing for the better, and we could get on with our lives. It was dreadful what had happened to the Jews. But now it's over. So we can get on with our lives. The survivors have their own land, and we can get on with our lives. It was dreadful. But they have their country now, and the ones who can never forget are living a long way away, where they won't trouble us with their memory of the things that are too horrible for us to really think about. We couldn't have saved the ones who died, you know. There was nothing more we could have done.

I shared a room with two others – Clive, who was going to Durham to study geography and would then join the Royal Navy, and Andrew, who was going to go to Cambridge. At 6.30 each morning during the first weeks Matti, young, bearded, friendly, carried us on a trailer behind his tractor to the orchards where we picked grapefruit from luxuriant trees that rose up the gentle slope of the valley side.

Each day the heat rose a little earlier, and the morning sound of the tractor clattered the day into life at an ever-earlier hour, rousing us as the weeks passed until we were tiptoeing out into the pre-dawn darkness at 4.30, finishing our work by 9, when Matti would call through the trees:

'Breakfast. Breakfast.'

In the dining room where the *kibbutzniks* gathered, we would feast ravenously on cheese and fruit and vegetables, cool juice, yoghurt and flat bread heaped so high on our plates that people sometimes complained that we ate too much.

But usually it was quiet in there. The *kibbutzniks* were mostly old, which is why volunteers were recruited to work the fields and operate the machines in the small factory where rivets were made. Most of them were either of German or Polish descent, with a few Russians, all shifting from Hebrew to other tongues when they spoke. In the dining hall – the only place where I saw them – many sat alone, or sometimes in couples, silent but for occasional muttering. They didn't look to us outsiders for conversation. We were a different world. Sometimes I noticed them watching us, their stares seeming laden with disdain for our apparent frivolity. We were nothing to them. They told us nothing. The kibbutz told us nothing of its story, perhaps because the only way to tell it was for us to look at the story that was all around us. In the queue for fruit and yoghurt a wrinkled, sun-burned arm outstretched, big fingers taking bread to fill a plate, the loose cuff of a shirt would ride up an arm, exposing a number stamped deep into skin that would never wear so thin that the digits would fade and disappear. Then, the food chosen, the plate filled, the sleeve of the blue work-shirt would slip back over the ghost of a world nothing had prepared me to imagine.

I imagined the old men and women there might be wondering what my family had done during the war. Perhaps where I was from might assuage. I won't forget what you went through, I would have told them, if they had asked me to speak. But first I must understand what really happened to you – I have only seen photographs.

But there was nobody there to speak with or to learn from. I had to assume that they only wanted to forget, and that all that these young Europeans passing through their home for a few summer months served to do was remind them of the young Europeans they had once been, in Germany or Poland.

In response we made a small world of our own, in the row of chalets hidden behind bougainvillea. Our preconceptions about each other steadily fell away. The two cockney girls from Teviot Street became listeners, the prospective students from smart schools confiding their secrets. Relationships formed, men and women, women sleeping with women, the short ex-con who had fled Thetford before finding himself behind bars again, becoming the mate of the teenage loner from North London who later admitted that he had stolen money from my bag when the cash he earned from the sperm bank in Afula didn't bring enough to finance him through the rest of the summer. They hung around with the short, large, glitzy woman from Tunisia who had the presentational manner of a chat show host but who some of the longer-term volunteers said was really a prostitute.

Before he became boring, everybody laughed at the tall dark Jewish boy who changed his name three times while we were there, and was never clear about whether he came from Bethnal Green or Pinner.

There were people arriving all the time, friendships almost forming, but the landscape fluid. Just as people seemed to be opening up, they would be gone and never seen again, gone on journeys to Jerusalem and then on to Egypt, the border having been opened a few weeks before we had arrived in Israel.

I watched them leave, walking down the track to the road from where the bus would take them off into the morning haze. It was a change in me that I did not yet want to follow, and felt the need to stay a while despite knowing I could leave whenever I wanted. I wanted to be a part of the group there, accepted by them. The girls were not attractive, and I didn't want to be any more than friends, until one night after a drunken party I followed a woman much older than me back to her room. Afterwards, she would stare at me, wanting to assure herself that I felt guilty that we had had sex but that I had not committed to anything more.

She was the wrong person to have spent that hour with, and I began to hate the sight of her. She pretended she knew I was casual, but had no idea what I really felt. Then, for a while, I did want to run from there, and to take that road that two of the women who slept together had walked down with the two women from Teviot Street. But still I stayed, as the Royal Navy and the SAS were reported in the *Jerusalem Post* to be advancing across the Falkland Islands, and we began to hear convoys of lorries creeping each night along the road below the kibbutz that went north to Lebanon.

By mid-May we had learned our way around the small world we were part of. We hitched rides through

371

the country on the days when we weren't working. Sometimes there was the feeling that the whole world ought somewhere to come together on that land. This was where the religions and cultures and civilizations that were the foundation of everything, could all make sense to us. But our youth stopped us from seeing how that might happen. We were just bit-part players in modern Israel, not travellers in a place where our minds could settle. Out of place there, we were prevented from sensing the roots we might have. We were not a part of the history. The land had perhaps been stolen from us, just as some of us would learn much later about how it had been stolen from the Palestinians who we never saw while we were there. We drifted through that place as pure outsiders, picking fruit in the mornings, then hitching a ride to Armageddon in the afternoon, lighting a fire on the beach at Netanya and sleeping among the mosquitoes to the sound of the waves. Later, we wandered through the Damascus Gate and into the old city of Jerusalem, wondered what the Second Temple had been about, and paid to see what an orthodox priest took our money to point out was the place where Christ had been born. We left the Holy City sensing that civilization has no home, no building, no street. It is all in the mind. Its mystery and timelessness was an Uzi strapped across a shoulder at the Wailing Wall.

'Never played backgammon? Well, we'll soon change that. I'll teach you.'

It was evening, long after sunset, when the mood had shifted far along the path of wondering what we were all doing there.

The *kibbutzniks* sometimes gathered for hot chocolate in the *moadon*, a communal sitting room where there were books and armchairs. It was some time in late May. The girl sitting opposite me at the backgammon table had returned to Geva after a visit back to England. Her earlier stay had been for almost a year. She might have stayed there forever. She was a few years older than the others I had travelled there with. I liked her casual confidence. She was bronzed and thoughtful, aware of herself, not too much in need, slim and friendly, a woman not a girl.

'But you must promise not to beat me once I've taught you,' she said, as she explained the rules of the game.

Sometimes, in the days that followed, it was the signs of solitariness that drew me to her. She had returned from England on her own, whereas most of the women arrived at Geva in pairs. I learned that before she had left earlier in the year, she had been sharing a room with a Swiss man who had also returned home but would soon be coming back. She didn't talk about him, as we drank hot chocolate and felt the night gather around the amber light of the *moadon*.

'Cruel man, beating me so mercilessly,' she told me a few evenings later, as our games of backgammon evolved from being tentative and gentle to being rapid battles that saw her humiliation rise and me end each victory with a fresh challenge to her.

The weeks passed, and the Swiss man returned. He was agitated, uncertain of what he had returned to Israel for. The girl didn't want to be with him anymore. His English was not good, and she could not speak his Swiss-German. I spoke with him, but he was suspicious. I was not a threat. But he wanted to believe that I was. One evening he burst into a chalet room in which she and I were talking.

'I've been watching you. I know what you want. I know what you are doing,' he yelled at me, then stormed out.

'Oh, don't worry about him,' she tried to reassure me. 'He's like that because of the heroin. He doesn't take it anymore. It just does that to people.'

But her words made no difference. He became friends with the boy who admitted later to having stolen my money, and with his mate the ex-con from Thetford. The three of them together frightened me, reminding me of kids at school, and I told Clive – my roommate for all the months I was at Geva – that I wanted to leave, and suggested to him that we go to Egypt together.

The grapefruit harvest was long over by the time it came for us to leave. I had been working in the rivet factory. I missed the sun in the orchard, and the liquid used to cool the machine tools had covered my hands in small white spots, which turned sore and red. I was alone in the factory room where I worked, except when an English *kibbutznik* called Roger came to inspect my work, examining every rivet and criticising the quality when he could.

The days passed, until there were only a few left before we were due to go. The day before we left, the woman who had taken me to her bed after the drunken party back in April, was waiting outside the glass panelled wall of my factory room.

'Mark, can I speak with you for a moment,' she said, as I stepped outside. Her sanctimonious tone made her seem about to scold like a teacher, or to write a letter to my parents, and put a little note in my file. 'I wanted to tell you that there are people here who are glad that you are leaving.'

My mouth dried. She had had the effect she wanted. Somebody stronger than me would have responded by asking her why she had stripped so readily, and sat astride me on her bed. But I couldn't ask that.

'Fair enough,' was all I could tell her. Then I walked away, leaving her standing there. Perhaps she had wanted an argument. I had nothing to defend. I had done nothing bad. But all I wanted was to run.

Clive and I spent a few days travelling south towards Egypt, climbing the rock of Masada, spending a night near a camel market in Bersheba, then reaching the newly-painted border post at Rafah on the edge of the Gaza Strip. The Arab world from which we had been hidden, suddenly began to open up before us, becoming a story that I will tell another time, when I am older, and began to see the Middle East with different eyes. What mattered as we crossed into the Sinai desert was that our plan to end our journey through Egypt on a ship that would take us from Alexandria to Crete, did not happen.

We had planned to work on Crete, and wander home through Europe, arriving at our universities with tales to tell. But after travelling south to Luxor then north to the coast, we found there was no ship that would take us across the Mediterranean. I have a photograph of Clive sitting at the café outside the railway station at Alexandria, where I would take coffee on my visits there from Cairo years later when I was raising a family in Egypt. His look of despondency combined with his characteristic self-control, says much. We had begun to feel the difference between us by then; not to argue, just simply to realise that we did not have much further to travel together.

Twenty-five years later I saw a photograph of him in uniform, his naval captain's braid glittering on his shoulder as he posed in a cabin of HMS Bulwark, the ship of which he had taken command. The ship was on patrol in the Gulf, the waters I had flown over numerous times when I moved to the Middle East, which I would now look down on wondering whether he ever thought about what might have become of me.

Reluctantly, our plans for adventure seeming to have come to an end, we returned to Israel and walked back up the track to Geva.

Before we had made our plan to take a ship from Egypt, Clive had intended to fly home from Israel, while I planned to travel back across Europe by train. That evening, as we approached the homes on the hillside, I wondered how the girl and the Swiss man would respond to my arrival. I wanted to be with her. Most of the people I had arrived there with in April had left. Clive would be leaving in a few days. I had little money, and had a month to wait before I could use the rail pass I had bought in England.

The girl was happy when we stepped back among the familiar rows of chalets.

'Let's walk,' she said. We walked out among the orchards and followed a track that brought us to a cluster of empty rooms that had been built by the first settlers. 'This one is open,' she said. We went inside, locked the door, and made love in the still, warm air.

Long after dark we walked separately back to where our remaining friends among the volunteers were gathered on a veranda.

'You're in real danger,' the boy who had stolen my money whispered in my ear. He had been talking with the

376

others there. The Swiss had been looking for the girl and me.

'Come with us to the kibbutz we are staying at across the valley,' said Alan, who had travelled there from England on a motorbike. 'We have a tractor. We're leaving now.'

'Okay. I'll come with you.'

'He'll know you're there,' said the thief. 'Watch out,' he called out, as the tractor clattered, and the trailer we were clinging to lurched onto the track and sped down towards the road in the valley, where huge trucks carrying tanks were edging their way northwards to the war that was raging in Lebanon.

*

From: Mark P <█@gmail.com>
Date: Tue, 30 Apr 2013 21:22:35 +0100
To: Mark Huband <█>
Subject: From Mark...

Dear Mark,

I loved part four of your memoirs. Wow! It's hard to say how enjoyable it was to read, without using the usual list of cliché superlatives. So having said that; brilliant, superb, excellent, many more spring to mind. So many adventures at such a young age and, as yet, you haven't even become a journalist. It is so easy to visualize you, the person I know, within each given scene that you always describe so beautifully. You really are your own person. As you know, at our age, we all have deal with our so-called midlife crises', us men especially, or so they say, but I have to say that reading your story made me want to be young again and go travelling. As you know, I have done a fair bit of travelling, but very rarely alone. There are so many things within the story that I'd like to discuss when we next meet, though I daren't mention any details now because I'll end up writing a hundred pages. One thing I must say though and that is how sad and surprised I was to hear that your Mother & Father were divorced. That really shocked me because your family seemed to me to be ideal, your way of life in that lovely house as perfect as things could be. But what does an eleven year old kid know about these things?

The poem is beautiful, though I have to admit, I have less capacity to judge poetry, but I liked it very much. I have written a few poems but haven't the facility to tell if they are a pile of worthless trash or works of pure genius. Yours, by the way, edges elegantly towards the latter.

I enjoyed our last meeting very much. Thanks again for the meal.

Things are looking up regarding attending you birthday party. It looks as though we may be celebrating T's grandmother's ninetieth at lunchtime, so we wouldn't be able to get to yours until the evening and we have to work out how long the journey takes and hotels etc, but it's looking promising.

I won't keep you much longer, but have to tell you a few more things: I have just purchased copies of A Farewell to Arms, For Whom the Bell Tolls and The Old Man and the Sea, so I should have tucked well into those before we next meet.

The Bowie exhibition at the V&A is mind-blowing. I won't go into details and shall avoid the list of superlatives again, just to say that I really can't recommend it enough. I've heard that it is the most commercially successful show that the V&A have ever put on, which is crazy when you think about it, considering how old it is. All bookable tickets were sold instantly so we did have to queue for almost an hour but it was well worth it.

I must quickly apologize for taking this long to read you story and get back to you. The only excuse I have is that I had just started Cormac McCarthy's Suttree, which was brilliant but happens to be a five hundred and eighty-odd page bugger.

Anyway Mark, I've kept you long enough. I hope you and your family are well and I will see you soon. Mark.

Ps – I quit smoking a fortnight ago. Hoorah!

...where pasts and futures gathered with every tick of the clock...

On 1 May 2013 07:50, Mark Huband< > wrote:
Dear Mark

Wonderful to hear from you.

One thing to say - and it's been troubling me all night - is that the conversation I had with the lorry driver when I was winding through Scotland in a truck, was me seeing how far I could go in creating a persona in the eyes of a stranger; the conversation happened over the hours of that journey, and I wanted to see how much could sound true about me that was not.

It's the only time I ever did it, and is the only point in the book where I relate an untruth - a deliberate one, by a lost boy alone in the world - because I very quickly - when I was 16 or 17 - became obsessed with truth and knowledge and reality; truth really is stranger than fiction, though the phrase is a tarnished one.

The book you have been so encouraging about, is viscerally real, with not a grain of fiction in it. But at that moment in Scotland, part of the fiction I realised I could try and create on that journey in the eyes of a stranger, was that I had "no direction home", that I had no home, no parents, no family, nothing but myself. So I told the driver my parents were divorced - to see how it sounded, to see how it might change how I seemed to him and to me. I felt alone, and wanted that kindly lorry driver to really know just how alone I felt; it wasn't enough just to tell him I was alone - at that moment I needed to show him proof that I had nothing in the world, and that my parents' being divorced was part of that.

But the fiction was for that stranger, not for the reader of the book (I am glad you mention it, as I shall have to make it clearer in the narrative that I was deliberately fantasising about my background). My parents are not divorced - sorry to have shaken you up by relating how I said they were - and had their 50th wedding anniversary in 2011, which was great! And our home in Harlow really was the place you remember it as having been, and the bonds between me and my family, and their bonds with each other, are really as strong as you remember them being. It's just that at that moment - on a road winding through the Highlands, talking to a stranger - I wanted to see how the tale of a fictional life could sound if it was told out loud.

I really appreciate your and T's plans for 15 June; arriving late afternoon/early evening will be fantastic. It's 90 minutes by train - Paddington to Stroud - and we can meet you at the station; driving is about two hours. We have a room for you in our house, so no need to book anywhere.

I just can't wait to meet again. We can chat all night of the party, and then all resume on the Sunday. Am half way through 'No Country for Old Men', and am mesmerised, as I hope you will be Hemingway.

Glad you kicked the habit; I'm wishing I could take it up!

That skinny white kid (wife says I must lose some weight)

M

From: Mark P <█@gmail.com>
Date: Thu, 9 May 2013 13:06:01 +0100
To: Mark Huband<█>
Subject: Re: From Mark...
Dear Mark,

firstly, I must apologise for taking a week to reply to your email. I was away for part of the weekend and we have had a friend stay for a couple of days and it's a fight to get on our computer in the evenings (I work on my lap-top in the basement, but it is not hooked up to the Internet). Having said all that, I must admit that I am a bit of a dinosaur when it comes to technology. Friends are constantly complaining that I never bother to take out, or even charge, my mobile phone and, I have to say, I would be utterly useless on facebook or twitter. So, sorry about that.

I'm a bit embarrassed to have not realised that you were blagging the lorry driver in Scotland but am relieved that your parents didn't get a divorce. I was so shocked because it would have meant that it would have had to have happened so quickly after I'd known you all.

381

Anyway - I feel like bit of a plonker, but am glad I got it wrong.

Yes - looking forward to your party. It's great that you can let us stay as this will save time. You don't have to pick us up from the station Mark - Wouldn't you like to have a few drinks in the afternoon? I would hate to think that we'd keep you off the booze at you own party. We would be happy to get a cab from the station to your house.

'No Country for Old Men' is a great book. Crazy-as-Hell and extremely violent. Not my usual kind of book when you think about it in those terms, but it is so well written that he take such stuff into the lofty realms of art. In fact, I heard somewhere that he was nicknamed 'the poet of violence' by some well respected critic.

I'm about halfway through 'A Farewell to Arms' and am enjoying it immensely.

Lots to talk about. Let me know when you are next in London. It would be great to hook up one more time before your party.

Kind regards - Mark.

On 29 May 2013 08:54, Mark Huband<█> wrote:
Dear Mark

Thanks for your email, and sorry not to have responded earlier.

This week has taken a couple of unexpected - albeit pleasant - turns, and Friday has become a bit complicated. Can we meet next Friday? That would be great.

Best

Mark

On 21 May 2013 22:53, <█> wrote:

Dear Mark

Great to hear from you. A Farewell to Arms has such an atmosphere to it - I think always of dusk when I remember it, a purple sky somewhere in Europe.

Yes, let's meet before the party. How is next week looking for you?

M

From: Mark P <█@gmail.com>
Date: Sun, 26 May 2013 14:39:38 +0100
To: <█>
Subject: Re: From Mark...

Hi Mark,

This week would be good, except that I have to look after my daughter until three in the afternoon, which means we wouldn't be able to have lunch. So, what would you prefere - Meeting this Friday for a late afternoon beer, say four o'clock, without lunch, or meeting next Friday, for lunch? - Which is my shout this time, don't forget. Let me know. I'm happy either way. Mark.

From: Mark P <█@gmail.com>
Date: Thu, 30 May 2013 20:07:05 +0100
To: <█>
Subject: Re: From Mark...

Hi Mark,

Not this week then, but next. That's fine with me. I'll email you next week to arrange.
Cheers
Mark

On 4 June 2013 20:50, Mark Huband< ▮ > wrote:

Hi Mark

Really looking forward to meeeting Friday. Shall we say 1pm same place?

Best

Mark

From: Mark P < ▮@gmail.com>

Date: Wed, 5 Jun 2013 20:37:04 +0100

To: < ▮ >

Subject: Re: From Mark...

Hi Mark,

Yes Mark, I think we can start to call it the 'usual' time at the 'usual' place. Looking forward to it - See you then.

Mark.

On 5 June 2013 21:30, Mark Huband< ▮ > wrote:

Great. The usual it is! M

*

The ship was floating in silver by the time my voice fell silent. The Canadians had listened, but did not fill the hum of the engine and the faint wash of the bow. Night was like an evening running home beneath the silver-blue-black moonlight of a cut-glass sky. Same moon, watching. Same moon. The moon alone was the same. All that remained.

The Canadians laid out their packs, made a bed of sleeping bags on the deck, lay down together and slept. I envied them, their friendship. They had everything. I had told them my story. They had listened in silence, nodding, then remaining silent, and now they were sleeping in the moonlight, their journey all going according to plan. I hadn't asked them to tell me their story. I wanted my story to be like theirs. They might once have had suitcases emblazoned with their initials. They would have known what to do at airports. We were the same – the three of us. I regretted telling them my story. Everything I had said made us different, when all I wanted was to have what they had, to be sleeping there comfortably, in the moonlight. We were clinging to the surface of the world, somewhere along the faint line – perhaps a trick of the eye – where night sky met black water, where the names of the stars tangled with the surf. The unreachable horizon was what made us the same. They slept into the night, while I watched the stars and the moon I had once chased – all the same, looking for purpose, with time our discipline: must reach the destination by then. But there was no destination. There were only places on the way.

Next day the ship edged into a port. Somebody said this was Cyprus, where the two women from Teviot Street had gone when they left Geva. Perhaps here, perhaps this was where I should step ashore, and wander through somewhere unknown. But I stayed on board, feeling that I might never earn enough money to be able to leave the island if I left the ship.

After a few hours, port sounds, ship horns thundering among the harbour houses, Cyprus left us behind and we remained out of sight of land for more than a day and a night, until we woke on a warm morning

385

to find we were edging between jewels of islands that rose from the turquoise sheen of the southern Aegean.

Islands specked the sea like a treasure cast from the long-sunk wreck of a ship, islands I knew from Odysseus' travels, whose frayed pages buried in my pack sang of this place to which my imagination had now brought me. The place was like every poem I had ever read, like every beautiful line ever written. No dream – a white ship ploughing through the white and the blue, between islands.

'Good luck with your journey,' the Canadians called down, from where they stood leaning against the white railing of the ship, whose sides nudged the quayside at Heraklion.

'Thanks. You too,' I called back. We waved. They watched, I could feel. But I didn't turn again. To have turned and waved again would have been a sign that perhaps I regretted not continuing with them to Piraeus and Athens. Then I would have seemed to have been running from my story.

'Good-bye,' I heard them call. But I pretended I was out of earshot, that my mind was set on finding a place to stay for the night, on getting a job beyond the Cretan hills that loomed out of the pale blue haze, in one of the ports along the southern coast.

At Geva I had been told by people who said they knew Crete, that I should make for Matala, get a job in a bar and sleep on the beach in the tent I had been carrying with me since leaving England.

The bus to the southern coast clattered out of Heraklion, filled by agèd women in black and a group of priests in long robes and tall hats. I had spent the night on a park bench beneath a lemon tree, was tired but exhilarated, as the bus chugged through villages, heat pulsing, hill roads twisting among olive groves, music rising and falling from the driver's radio, always the promise of the sea just beyond the next brow.

The day was old and dusty by the time the engine rattled to a halt beside the quay at Matala. The air hummed. Water lapped the stone jetty. The light was as soft as the sound of the voices I wandered past on my way to the bay between tall cliffs gouged with small caves, and stepped onto the beach where a few tents had been pitched among blackened scars left by fires hollowed into the sand.

But as the tranquillity of the place lulled my senses, my body ached.

I lay on the hot sand in a sweat. The sun blinded. The faint sound of voices boomed in my ears. My legs would have given way beneath me if I had not been lying on the hot sand, my head resting on my rucksack, my stomach tightened into knots. I could barely see through the blinding ache inside my head.

People walked past, oblivious. I lay still, slowly turning from side to back to side. The soft ripple of the waves scratched like steel. I breathed in hard, and the heat left my dry throat gagging. I saw black-clad priests walking barefoot into the sea, their robes hitched above their knees. Priests don't do that, I heard myself say, perhaps out loud. But in the blur of light and water they looked like priests. I could go to them and ask for help. I could go to them and ask for help – the last words I heard before my eyes closed, a sound like the pouring of sand filling my ears, as I slipped out of sight of land.

It was night when I woke. The beach was empty, the tents at the far end closed. Some people were moving in the caves cut into the cliff at the far end. There were coloured lights strung from poles along the quay. Moonlight caught the white crests of the wave ripples. There was a faint sound of music.

I lay unable to move, not enough strength to even look at the time on my wristwatch. The moon was vast, its glittering silver trail the illusion of a path across the black sea and up, up into the night sky. I was stone, bound to the earth, my gaze fixed on the light that had followed me, which was peering down from the cut glass of night clouds still drifting over my hometown.

It span – the world – that night. I could feel it beneath me, beneath the sand. The cliffs whirled. The ink sky of stars, the black water iced by silver, were all spinning, turning, with me at their centre, spinning, turning on the still-warm sand that was hollowed by the body lying there.

I woke again, and it was morning.

Swimmers played in the sea. People lay on towels, eating bread, swigging from bottles. I had been cold, I could feel it. But now the sun warmed the clothes I had been wearing for the days and nights since I had walked down into the valley and stood on a road that went north to Lebanon and south to Afula and the coast.

The journey that had been without mishap, without incident, now seemed like a journey along which every step had been a further fall into the unknown. There was no reason for it, but I was afraid.

I could see from the sun that the morning was rising towards midday. Families on the beach were unpacking lunch, laying food on cloths they spread out on the sand. None knew I had been lying there for a day and a night, that I had not moved – for fear, of what? Of rising from the earth, perhaps – on a cold November night I had gripped the earth, hoping it would protect me, soak me up, as bright lights sped towards me across damp grass. But then the earth was hard. The warm sand moulded then slipped away from the brows and furrows my body made. Now the sun was at its height. Mosquitoes had savaged my neck and arms during the night. My clothes were thick with sweat and oil. Only then did I begin to wonder if I was sick. I had neither eaten nor drunk anything since waking beneath a lemon tree in Heraklion. But the fear of making a decision kept me bound to that hollow sand. Better to remain still – as still as the horizon. My ship had sailed from the east, across the horizon. Now I am too frightened to move on. I have been lying unnoticed on a beach since yesterday. People are all around, doing normal things. The knotted pain inside is a dull ache now. The sea is soothing, but I am in the wrong place. The mosquito bites are itching. Some children run close, kick up sand, and stare at me for a while before running away when I stare back. I need to run from there before the moon rises again. I don't want the same moon to watch me for a second night, as then I would be trapped, the cliffs as walls. Must move, I thought, or perhaps mumbled. I had heard that before, though could not remember when.

Must move.

So I waited for the beach crowd to thin, not wanting to be noticed, and sat up for a while, smoked a cigarette, then slowly stood, as if for the first time in an age.

I looked at nobody, not wanting anybody to ask after me. I wondered what I looked like – probably entirely normal. All was normal – the lapping of the ripples, the sound of a voice. People ambled across the sand and along the quayside. And I was running away, too afraid to become a part of that pleasant, tranquil place. I must run from the moon that will rise, must reach the next lamppost, before the car approaching from behind catches me up and passes me by.

But all that lay behind was the emptiness of the sea. I had not been born to look out over an emptiness in which I was invisible.

The fear came from wanting to be unseen, while knowing I could not survive alone. I could never explain to the girl back at Geva what it was had driven me to disappear at dawn from that room across the valley. She would think I wanted to be like that. She would judge me. But it was not what I wanted. I needed to be with her, or somebody, while everything I did made it appear that I was only ever wanting to be alone. I wanted both – to be alone with her on the beach that was at my back, in the place that I was running from.

The fear came from knowing it would never be like that. I didn't even know if she wanted to be with me. I was tired and dirty. Was I sick, or just afraid, too far from what I knew, to feel that I was in a place I was meant to have reached? Somebody had said I should take a bus to Matala, and take a job in a bar. But there were no jobs there. There was only a small café run by an old man and his wife. There was no life there for me, and the fear was of having the same feeling wherever I went.

My shoes filled with sand as I walked up the beach to the quayside and the street where the bus had stopped. Every step was like moving as stone. Nausea oozed inside. Nobody could see me as I ambled, the bright sun gleaming blind on the quaint buildings. Then would have been the moment for somebody to approach me, saying: 'Are you alright?'

But everybody was drifting, just like me, shuffling to the beach, sipping golden tea from glasses.

In the shadow along the street that led out of the village and up into the hills I sat leaning against the wall of a house in which a group of women – young and old – were cackling and screeching then laughing and laughing. The bus will be along in the afternoon, I was told. When it turned a corner and came into view I knew I was saved. It would take me away from there, that place where I had come looking for something that was not there – a role; somewhere to stay for a while. But I knew I must run again, even before anybody noticed I had been there at all.

Five days later I was on a street in Athens, the engine of a coach roaring with an irregular beat as luggage was stowed in the darkness beneath, and the sweating driver downed a final glass of ouzo, cigarette in hand, the straps of his sandals crushed beneath the cracked heels of feet that for the next three days powered us through northern Greece, the Balkans, across Germany and into France. Police stopped us on the way, demanding papers, passports, and information from the driver about how many hours he had driven without a rest. He drove for days and nights without more than an hour's stop. Somewhere in West Germany two green-uniformed *polizei* threatened to stop us for an entire day, until one of the passengers – a grey old man in his seventies – lifted up his shirt to reveal a huge scar across his chest.

'But I have to get to England, to the doctor,' he told the officers. They let us go, the old man laughing at how easily they had been duped. 'It's an old scar. I'm in good health. And I'm not even going to England,' he told us all, and everybody on the coach laughed.

People got off along the way, at service stations and isolated crossroads and junctions. By the time we reached Calais only a few of us remained. Our driver almost said goodbye, with a slight nod of his head. There was another coach waiting in Dover, and he was going back to Athens. Back there, to from where I had run. Running away was all I seemed to have done, as I pretended to myself that I had really been on a long journey, and that now was the moment at which it could end.

But really it was not like that.

That day my train edged through the London suburbs, and I still felt I had no story to tell to the people around me. Things had happened. But there was no story. I didn't know what had happened. I thought of the two Canadians and the ship from which they had called out their last goodbyes. I wondered if they thought there was a story, about somebody they met on a ship that was sailing from the Middle East, who was running away from a tangled tale of sex and threats and anger.

Back home, that story could never fit into the life of the boy who had gone away in early April. Among the faces at the bar of the Queen's Head I would never be able to explain why it was I was different now.

'I heard you were back,' was all that Peter said, when I went there one evening, a few days after my return. I knew then that I must go away again, but had no idea to where or with whom, until the girl from Geva telephoned a week later to say that she was back in England.

*

The evening was warm and quiet when she stepped off the train at Harlow Mill. We were not the same, there, in my home town. The story seemed to be going in reverse. I didn't want her to think I was bringing her into my life. I wanted her to think that my life was in the place where we had first met, or on the roads and islands and cities in between.

We walked through the evening, wondering if we were lovers.

'I hope you won't be making a habit of disappearing,' she said with a smile, the slight hint of a scold in her Manchester voice.

The months in the Middle East had tanned her deeply. Her hair was blonde, her white shirt crisp, buttoned low so her small breasts were almost visible. She wore shorts, and her tanned legs were long and thin. I wondered if she was looking at me.

We walked past a small flat where the trains rattled past at the bottom of an embankment below the window. The flat was empty now.

Old Road was dry and warm, always long and winding, a road that long ago had led through cold mist to the fields and a river that one day we would discover. On wet summer evenings the pavement oozed with snails that would crawl out of the hedges and be crushed underfoot, unseen in the dusk light.

I wondered what I would say if we passed somebody I knew. I hoped it would not happen. I didn't want to have to explain who she was, this blonde girl with tanned skin who was walking beside me down Old Road towards my house. People would think that I had brought her there because I had failed with the girls from my town. They would mock, seeing this girl who they knew was unlike any of the girls that had been part of my world until then. Then I would have to tell them I was different because I had been away, when really I was just the same as before, but that they had never known me in the first place. Then she said she wanted to meet my friends, and I told her people were away, that there was nobody around because it was summer.

'Are you embarrassed by me?' she asked. I told her no. But I suppose I was embarrassed. I would not be able to explain why I was with her, if somebody asked. I couldn't tell anybody that we were together just for sex. But that was the reason. The people I knew, who had seen me at the pub bar, who had passed their spliffs around on cold nights on Mill Lane, they would know, and would leer and would look at the place where her shirt was open. They would see that I had become somebody else, while I didn't want them to know anything about me except what I told them.

Our house was empty, Mum and Dad having gone on holiday, Michael away. Paul came home from work and met the girl, and was polite and welcoming, and I knew that I would one day have to tell the story of why she was there, setting her bag down on the floor of my childhood bedroom. I wondered if she would ask if she was the first woman who would sleep in my bed. But we stepped out into the evening before she could ask about our house and what had happened in it.

The streets were near-deserted as we walked. We sat on a bench outside the pub. There were only a few people there, nobody I knew well. She might wonder if I knew anybody. My friends were away on holiday, I explained, as night fell and we wandered back home.

An early morning train pulled out of Harlow Mill. London was going to work when we arrived in the echo of Liverpool Street. We crossed the city to Victoria, where the civil servants strode along the platform and out among the powerful buildings of Westminster. The train to the coast snaked among the suburban homes. Somewhere, there were children laughing, staring from the carriage windows into the tangled gardens that led up to sitting rooms from where people sat watching over shrubberies that were a trouble. They were the passing scenes that were caught in the eyes of the travellers, staying deep and long in the mind for no particular reason, as the light changed and the train edged closer to the bright luminescence in the sky that promised beyond the next brow would be the sea.

We had only a vague conversation about where we were going.

As trains took us south, I gouged a journey out of the landscape. Only my heroes could know what I was doing – the boy with a blonde girl following him a few paces behind, down into the Metro at Gard du Nord and up into the light of Paris, where I could have been walking to cafés with cousins who would ask me about my journey, as we sat in the breeze shift of plane trees that traced the boulevards and all the roads south. She would not be there then, the girl. She might have passed by on the street with somebody, before I turned back to my cousins and friends and we made plans to travel to the Sologne for the weekend.

'My brother Frantz can't wait to meet you. He wants to hear all about your journeys. You're so similar.

It's almost impossible to imagine that you are not brothers.'

'He's done so much more than me.'

'No. And he has been waiting all summer for you to come and stay with us.'

'I have heard so much about him. He'll find me boring, I'm sure of it.'

'Not at all. And you'll meet as if you have known each other for years.'

'I feel that I have.'

'That's because I have talked so much about you both.'

'But everything he has done – his romance – I'm not like that.'

'Oh but you are. Your dreams. All your travels. He envies you your travels.'

'But I've not been far. Not really.'

'But you've wandered. Frantz married too young. That's why he wants to hear your stories. He fell in love, and he never went to the places he had dreamed of as a boy.'

'Which places?'

'He dreamed of the Caribbean, of growing sugar in the Indies, and of Africa. Our great uncle fought in Algeria, and we had a second cousin who died in Gabon, or was it the Congo? It hardly matters.'

'But I have never been to those places.'

'No. But you will. I know you will. And when you come back, we will all sit and listen to your stories.'

Then we took a train south from Paris, reaching Milan the next morning. Already, I wanted either to be away from her or to be obsessed by her. I watched her sometimes, as she walked beside me or a little ahead, and wanted then to be the happiest man in the world, travelling south with endless weeks ahead of us, no one but each other to think about, as we gazed at the names of cities on towering lists of destinations we could reach down the track that wound out of Milan's vast station and out across the plains and mountains of Europe.

Her mood would become subdued as my silence left her lost. I could not explain my journey to her. I strode along the carriages, which in those days had long narrow corridors opening through sliding doors into small compartments that always seemed to be full. People crammed into the space above where the carriage couplings clattered and screeched, and light glittered through the torn plastic concertina drawn across the void above the steel tracks that led Europe on its journeys to mountains, journeys of escape... *I will take that train tonight, I've nothing to lose and nothing to gain, I'll kiss you in the rain, Kiss you in the rain*. But for us it was the sun... *The sun poured down like honey...* and humming somewhere was a melody that had been written only for this journey, as the lush plains gave way to the parched lands of the south and we thundered into the summer night.

The following afternoon the train halted at Brindisi, and we wandered through the town to the port to be told by a harassed man in a uniform that all the ships to Piraeus were full for the next two days.

A big white ship was edging away from the quayside and out into the Adriatic. It would reach Corfu and pass Messolonghi and moor at Patras then glide along the Gulf of Corinth and reach Piraeus after days and nights under the sun and stars. I couldn't bear to be still, waiting there on the quayside, waiting in the dusk light as we ambled inland to find somewhere to sleep.

There was an old church with a cloister, its iron gate open, and we hid in the shadow of the pillars until we heard the gate creak shut, a key turn in a lock, and the place become ours, where we lay warm together in the spying light of the stars, until dawn and a voice called to another and we slipped out into the street again. The afternoon ship was roped in the fresh morning light of the quay. Yesterday's heat had gone. The day was cool, smelled of coffee, morning sounds, the sea our route, deep blue to be drunk as we moved. The same uniformed man was there, checking tickets. The planned days of waiting had disappeared.

'You go on this one,' he told us in English, with a smile of relief on his face, happy for us. And we were gone from there, the warm day unfolding before us across the morning light of the sea.

Now it was clear where we must go. Vaguely, I told her about some family friends who were staying on Kos, an island at the furthest edge of the Aegean. We must go there. We must see them there. They must see us – her and me – together. Then they would see that something had happened after I had gone away, that something had happened since a January morning deep in snow, when we had walked out across to the ice field during the first days of a new decade with Philip and his daughter, walked out of their dark house which was one of the poles around which our world had revolved.

We perched on a low wall that ran along the top of the beach. Our ship from Piraeus had docked at Kos early in the morning. It was impossible to know how many days we had been travelling, to a place far away in the sun, where we might see people from the past. They would see her, the girl from Geva, her beautiful body emerging from the sea, and would see the change in me, as I watched trains from the distance of the ice fields and staggered through the flooded meadow to the white bridge beside the river.

Philip walked past me on the way to the beach, his familiar gait stepping off the river path. He smiled and laughed and I hoped he was happy I was there. He would not ask why we had come all that way, to this distant island. Perhaps I had passed it aboard the ship I had travelled on from Haifa. I was resuming the journey, as if the frightened hours on the beach at Matala had been the experience of some other. There, sipping coffee beneath the straw canopy of a beachside bar, the story was being told in different voices. We had gathered, and all our stories mingled, and in the end little was said and we were all left to assume that Kos was where a part of the past came to an end, because Philip who had watched me since a first time when he had cycled with one of his daughters to the Harlow house into which Paul and I had fled from the 'Station Dog' and its owner, now sat with me and Carla as the girl from Geva strode wet and tanned out of the warm blue sea and towards us on the beach.

'Beautiful. She's beautiful,' Carla said, and all her enthusiasm which in the past had seemed eccentric because only the adults of our world could be a part of it, was now mine to feel, because now I was a part of their adult world and they could imagine me with the girl, no longer a child.

For five days we met on the beach when the sun was high, and then took bicycles and glided along the gentle slopes inland among the olive groves. *The sun poured down like honey...* and we would stop on the roadside to ease the red flesh from figs and suck at the small sweet seeds and become part of a land whose fruits could sustain us as we journeyed across it like travellers.

But she had nothing to say to Philip. It was only Philip who travelled inland with us. Carla had been ill for a while, and would stay in their small hotel or in the shade near the beach, while we left the silver blue of the water at our backs, and breathed the inland heat where the breeze rarely reached. It was when we stopped to eat salads and drain the rich tang of retzina that the bodies and minds tangled rather than flowed, as I had dreamed they could, or must.

'So, what were you doing in England, before you went on your travels?' Philip asked the girl from Geva.

'I was a dressmaker.'

'In a shop?'

'Yes.'

'And that was in Manchester, was it?'

'Well, just outside. In the suburbs I suppose. In a place called Wythenshawe.'

'Yes, I think I have heard of it. I don't know Manchester well.' Then he would say something interesting and observant about somebody he had known at Cambridge University in the 1950s, who was a Mancunian or had had an experience there. Philip often had an anecdote to relate about people he had known, always told in an interested tone, sometimes with a wry smile. That was how he asked the girl what she had done, where she had been. He wanted to bring her story out of her. But she had little to say. She didn't think she had a story to tell.

'She is very pretty. But she doesn't give much away,' he told me some days later. As with all things he ever said to me, I was thrown into confusion, and

400

wondered how I could defend, and wondered what there was to defend. I didn't realise that his comments weren't criticism. But in my school, among the people I knew in my town, in the whole world, if something said was not favourable, then it must be an attack. That was how it was. I must defend her. But I knew couldn't.

'Well, she...I think she...'

'But you're lucky to be with her. I can see you're having a nice time together.'

'I expect only for the summer.'

'It'll be a summer you'll remember.'

'I've not started remembering it yet.'

'No. Still in the middle of it all. Where will you go from here?'

'Athens. Sounien. I want to go to Messolonghi.'

'What's there?'

'It's where Byron died.'

'Aha,' and he laughed a little. 'The wicked lord.'

'That was his uncle.'

'You've been doing some homework. Do you like his poems?'

'I think I prefer the stories about his life.'

'Well, I admire your frankness.'

'I prefer Keats.'

'Yes, I think I do too. But Byron was more of an adventurer. Keats seemed rather fey.'

'Yes, I know what you mean.'

'But perhaps that's what you like about him.'

'Yes,' I replied, wondering what he meant, as the girl sat down at our table and we ordered pastries and listened to the *crickets talking back and forth in rhyme.*

The decks of the evening ferry were traced by bright white lights, which rippled as we slipped out of the harbour. A wave from the quayside and we were gone, and we would wait forever to know where the days we had passed there together might one day fit into the years.

Tentatively then, I tried to give a voice to the momentum. She could not hear. Greek families were grouped among bags and suitcases in the dim light of the ship's saloon. We sat at a table on the edge of a large silent group.

'Did you like Philip and Carla?' I asked her.

'Yes, they were alright.'

'I hope they liked us being there.'

'We spent too much time with them – we imposed a bit on their holiday.'

'No. Well, I hope not. Perhaps we did. I hope not. I think they liked us being there.'

'I'm not so sure. They probably wanted to be on their own a bit.'

'Yes. But they were alone quite a lot. I don't know.'

'Well, it seems obvious. I would have wanted to have my holiday to myself if I had been them.'

'Yes. I hope they didn't mind. I think they would have said if they had.'

'They were probably too polite.'

I didn't want to believe her. She had turned the days sour. I wished that Philip had been there to tell her that he had been happy that we had met them on the island. He had seen me differently. I wanted to tell her that he had seen me differently, after all these years. He wouldn't have had to tell her anything else – just that things were different now.

'I felt a bit embarrassed,' she went on. 'They never let us pay for any of those meals.'

'They didn't want us to.'

'Well, we should – you should – have said no sometimes.'

'We were only there for a few days.'

'All the same, it was a bit embarrassing.'

'I don't think it was embarrassing. We offered to pay.'

'But he never let us. Actually, I think they are a bit desperate.'

'No. No, they're not like that.'

'They never seemed to want to be together.'

'Well, they like to do things on their own. They've always been like that.'

'Seems a bit strange to me.'

'Perhaps.'

Then there was silence between us, her face fixed with the hint of a smile, my gaze transfixed by a moment of the past where there was nobody in my world but me.

Night fell, and the saloon faded into the deep light of sleepy faces. The long hum of the engine was as if silent. The ship was anywhere in the humming world. The scars and folds of faces trembled in dreams flung back on the headrests of easy chairs. Night stars sprinkled with spray on the salt windows. We were silent, she and I, aware for the first time that we were as much strangers to each other as we were to all the sleeping, watching, silent faces there. We had gone looking, back in the spring and into summer. We were trying to share something that made us different from all the people there. But she and I were on different journeys. I wanted her to see inside me. I had shown her to Philip and Carla. Now I wanted to take her to the places where Lord Byron had stood. I might have told her about an old abbey off the road near

Mansfield, where perhaps we could go, after we had stood on the promontory in the shadow of Sounien temple and run our fingers across the signature carved into the marble that I had seen in a photograph, and which would now be worn almost smooth. In Venice I would tell her of the times when, during the last winter I had passed, I had heard a sound during a dream night after night, when I had been on a ship with sails that had taken me on and on through white surf to a shore, and the sound had carried me to the springtime when I had seen vast plains that led to mountains that I would cross on my travels. And I looked at her and hoped she saw the stories in my eyes. But she was staring beyond me, at the sea night outside the window, and I took out my notebook filled with scribbled lines from the previous months, and scratched words about the Athens I was dreaming lay ahead of us.

'You are writing poem? A poem?' asked an ancient man watching from the far side of the table we were sitting at.

'Yes. Trying to. Trying...to,' and I bowed my head deeper towards the page and wondered whether I would one day look back at that time, look back and write about the words I had written then, as the old man watched, and she watched, and the ship hummed across the sea of my dreams between the islands Odysseus had voyaged among. Then I wanted to be looking back, and to be able to place myself there, somewhere among islands and friends and legends. Somewhere in time. With a lover. But I looked at her and could not hear her telling me what would happen next.

In Athens she said she wanted to wander around the city rather than take the train with me along the Gulf of Corinth to Messolonghi. I misjudged the distance and never made it there. The train ambled along the coast of the northern Peloponnese. I met her in the room of the Athens hostel that smelled of old wood, where we had spent the last of our drachmas to pay in advance for two nights stay. She had bought a brightly coloured dress with some of the money we were keeping for our days in Venice. She asked me if I liked it, and all I could say was that it looked expensive.

Next day a bus took me south.

Somebody told me recently that Sounien is now a suburb of Athens. Then, it was hours away, across empty hills that sloped down to the sea. I walked quickly up the gravel and stones to the towering perfect timeless pillars that were a voice of white marble speaking to the blue of the sea that listened way below. I could not be seen to be looking, nor even think of asking, and so wandered around for a while examining the pillars until I saw the word 'Byron' that he had cut in elegant swirling letters into the marble, and ran my fingers across it like many others who had worn the stone smooth and turned the white to brown. I felt a part of a secret, there, from where a poet had looked out over the same sea. Byron was no more a myth. He had been there. Here was the proof. Me. Him. In the same place, listening to the temple speaking with the sea, looking back, forwards, spirits between ages that were all we wanted to imagine. There, there was no limit to the truth of the imagination. I was there and I was not, just as he had been, imagining the same things as me.

Our train pulled out of Athens late the following morning. I wished that I was alone, and then shuddered at the memory of when I had been alone on that same journey by coach less than a month earlier. Only I knew that I had a second chance, to retrace the steps in another guise and to see which version I preferred. She would never know how it was I had felt that first time round. Sometimes I wanted to tell her about it – I would have liked to have told her that this time it was better. But really I didn't know, didn't know which of the stories was real.

'So, have you stopped chasing after poets at last,' she asked, as the train glided into the rugged lands on the route north to Thessalonica.

The train was of nowhere, like us. Orders and warning signs and German and Greek and languages that could have been Russian or Serbo-Croat or Hungarian, were stuck peeling to smeared windows and the gashed wood of once-polished doors. The ticket collectors and waiters in the dining car were of no place, no country. They meandered across the borderlines of the Cold War, as the train rattled into the night. Sometime we would reach Zagreb. The world there would remain hidden beyond gates and guards, who watched us where we sat on long, deep-sprung bench seats crammed with ageing strangers whose journeys might never have crossed our paths. The carriages lurched then clattered across black plains where there were voices without light, as she slept peacefully beside me and I wanted to hold her but knew I should stay awake to deter the pickpockets we had been warned stalked the night trains as they slipped through the early hours.

At first light I was awake. Venice echoed beyond the shutters. I could feel the water in the rippled glimmer that carried the light.

The light was harsh in the white room at Ca' Rezzonico. At the height of the summer we should never have been able to find such a place, where lovers lie together among the shards of golden sun that pierce the shutters, lovers lost in dreaming, lost and drifting and perfect, coming together in their own perfect timeless moment.

She slept naked, wrapped in the white sheets. The keeper of the *pensione* spoke out on the landing. The day was rising. Her first words would end the day as it had begun:

'Walk with me. Let's walk,' I wanted her to say. 'Let's walk, and discover, before the sun is high and the streets too full for us to walk.'

But we passed the days in near-silence, early one morning leaving our room at sunrise just so as we could walk across the deserted Piazza San Marco. I have a photograph of the square, the first rays of the sun caught gliding over the domes of the Saint Mark's basilica, and another photograph, of her resting on a bridge, no people around, as we walked to breakfast somewhere near the Palazzo Mocenigo.

'Byron lived there,' I told her.

'Not him again,' she replied, smiling, offended by the imposition of others into the world the two of us together might have made.

'And one night he swam all the way down the canal to reach the house of a woman who had become his obsession.'

'Silly man. The water's filthy. Bet it was even worse then.'

'Yes...but it was late, and all the gondoliers had gone home.'

Then we were silent again, like the cool shade of the alleys where the shadows ahead sometimes unnerved us, turned us back to where there was noise, where the confusion of the maze opened onto space and we were two in the crowd again, strolling back to our soft bed behind the shutters above the water at Ca' Rezzonico.

Two days later, when our train pulled out onto the long causeway that crosses the lagoon, it seemed we were leaving a room that would be the only one in the world that would ever have been ours. Whatever we would be together, had happened there. We would never become more than that. For a few days, a room had almost been our home. We had tasted each other there. Now we were moving away.

North had always seemed homeward, until I went to live in Africa seven years later, when north became a journey into the deepest unknown. But as the summer of 1982 showed the first signs of becoming autumn, north marked the end again, a journey to a place where the days were shorter. Now I could tell her of the new home I would have in a new city. I would not be far from her. We could meet in cafés sometimes. Manchester might be the place where there would be music and poets. As our train sped across the plains of northern Italy towards Switzerland and Austria, I was more exhilarated than I had been since watching a distant shore from our boat, its red sails full, laughing smiling with my dad, as we captured the wind and skimmed the water, and nothing had been there to stop us. North was taking me back to my homeland. But everything would be different. I would be a student at Manchester University, and might tell people that I had spent my summer travelling. I could tell people that story. No need to tell them of the winter before the spring, nor why I had crossed Europe three times, from the islands of gold and blue to the land in the north. I would tell people I was going north, to Manchester. I would tell the truck driver who had heard my dream of a city as we rattled through the Highlands towards East Kilbride on a day when the country had closed for a royal wedding. In Manchester I would read about the Crusades and Venice and the ancient Greeks. I would be with new people there, in a place where nobody would know anything about me, except for what I wanted to tell them.

'So, following in David and Ann's footsteps. How lovely.'

Uncle Jimmy sat beneath a tree in the garden of his large villa on the edge of a hillside village in the heart of the Luxembourg countryside. This was where the young idealists of the 1950s had reached, a nephew travelling with a girl calling from the railway station to say they were passing through and could they stay a day or two, and of course, you'd be very welcome.

And hours later we were drinking Campari beneath the tree, the journey there having been so much longer than could ever be explained. Nothing could ever be explained. Perhaps we were simply passing through the country they had found their way to after leaving their home in Hertford, where the talk had been of the big issues of the day, in a room where the bookshelves were filled with the works of Jean-Paul Sartre and Lawrence Durrell.

The books were almost hidden, in a corner behind a door in their home in Luxembourg. My uncle worked among the European institutions that were housed along neat streets. I wondered if his role was part of the plan he had had, and if it had resulted from all the discussions over dinner in Hertford, at the address to which letters were sent from all over the new world that was emerging out of empires. I wondered if he was still a part of that new world, but then saw that it was only me who had ever thought he might be a part of it.

'Jimmy sees books all day. He doesn't want to see more when he comes home,' my aunt told me, when I mentioned that I always thought of their house as being one that was full of books that were different from those we had in our house.

For two days I asked them questions. At some point my aunt's memory would be jogged, and she would mention the time when I had been sick in their house. I needed to know if she remembered, and what she remembered, as I edged them back to the times in which I needed them to see me, so they could see now that I was no longer that boy. I was there with a girl. We shared a room. I was sick in your house when I had been a boy, because I hadn't wanted to be with you. Now, it doesn't matter if I want to be with you. All I want is for you to see that I am not the one I was. Say what you like. I am different now, and I need you to see the difference. I am a man now.

'You didn't always like my food,' said my aunt, as we sat at their table for dinner. She spoke with a mixture of slight embarrassment and a hint of condescension. 'I remember when you came to stay with us in Hertford and you were very sick. And I thought it was my food. But I think perhaps it was more than that.'

'I don't remember that,' I said, knowing that whatever I told of myself, whoever I arrived with by train years later, I would never escape from how things had once been. I made it so. I had taken them back with me, to that time I wanted to have seen and remembered for

410

what I later became. But nothing was changed – not the present, nor the past.

'I'm quite bored actually,' the girl from Geva told me when I asked her how she was finding it, being there. I knew then we must leave, and our train pounded relentlessly across France to the coast, Calais, the ship to Dover, on to London, and she was gone and I went back to Harlow for the last time.

*

On 22 Jan 2015, at 21:05, Mark P██████████
<██████████████████> wrote:
Hi Mark,

as is so often the case, I start this email with an apology, this time for wishing you a happy new year so late. So Happy New Year and, sorry it's a bit late. I hope you had an enjoyable holiday and that your family are well. We had a nice time, busy as hell, lots of running around, but good fun. I also wanted to say what a great time I had the last time we met. And a jolly decent session it was to, sir. We must do it again soon.
Speak soon ...
Mark

On 4 February 2015 at 20:57, Mark Huband <██> wrote:
Mark

Gaaaad, another year. Pass me the whisky. This year I will do a multiple portrait of the wife and kids, will finish an epic poem about a war in a city I once knew, lose some weight, and learn how to cook perfect pigeon pie; oh, and maybe we'll find Chris McW...how about you?

411

On 18 Feb 2015 at 20:51, Mark P <██@gmail.com>
wrote:

Hi Mark,

I've been thinking long and hard about your question. (Pass me that whisky when you're finished). I will fight my way into our garden with a razor-sharp machete and tame the beast. I will finish my award-winning children's book and learn how to play the blues on the harmonica and I will track down the elusive Chris McW... with my intrepid friend Mark (Hubie) Huband. I will try my best to get a little fitter and drink a little less. Though, having said that, where's that blasted whisky?

*

A few days later I was driving north with Mum and Dad, along the vast and furious motorway that had brought us south when we, my brothers and I, had been the new world.

We pulled up by the roadside in Fallowfield, a mile or two from the centre of the city that would become my new world. But as the weeks passed, and the people I would come to know in the years that followed, flowed in and out of those first, shapeless days and nights, and the girl from Geva didn't come back again, the story hung in the air with only me to hear its end being told, until I woke to the November cold and was soon on the train that might be the last on that journey.

Then I was walking high onto the moors above Low Bentham, a dog yapping as it trotted back towards the dark low roofs that hunched in the dusk light against the open moorland. And every step was perfect. Holy. Everything that I and my family seemed ever to have been, was there in the light and the sound and the memory – there, at the beginning, where our imaginations started, in the dim light of the porch bulb, where a small woman with hooded eyelids and curly permed hair, who hobbled because of a bad hip, could tell me with a few words whether I was a part of that place.

Joyce Cornthwaite stared. From inside, a voice called out: 'Somebody there then?'

She looked at me harder in the dusk light.

'Aye Thos, there certainly is. Now. Which one are you?'

I had said nothing. She paused. Then: 'Let me think on't. I'd say you must be Mark.'

I slept the night there, in a room with a small window that gave a view out across the moors. I could not think of what might have been. After a big breakfast Thos and I trudged in boots to the chicken shed. It was warm inside, an endless row of feathers and beaks and startled tiny eyes. Thos grabbed at the squawking, frantic birds, and with a tiny movement plucked the life out of them.

'I'll set yer to work,' he told me with a grin, his big red face lighting up.

We spent the hours plucking chickens, sometimes talking, sometimes silent, my words too carefully chosen, as I tried to avoid speaking as if I knew where it was I had reached. They could know nothing of me but what they saw. A very young child had become a man. Perhaps there was nothing more to say, and we could let the landscape tell the story of how we had lived.

In the afternoon they both drove me down to Low Bentham station.

'Come again,' said Thos.

'Tell yer mum and dad to come and see us,' said Joyce. I said I would.

It was late, approaching midnight, before I reached Manchester Victoria station. I walked up through the deserted streets. Winter gripped the air and sky. A mesmerising squeaking sound filled the night, like an unoiled wheel slowly rotating. I walked on, wondering if I was being followed. But there was nobody behind me.

The city had put its Christmas decorations up early and large boards with smiling cartoon figures were suspended from the lampposts. Each figure had a moving part – an arm, a leg, a head – which squeaked as it moved. Hundreds of small squeaks were nodding or waving or striding above the empty street, where a single passer-by was walking home from the station, returning from a journey he had just made.

Where he was heading there might be somebody to whom he could tell his story. But it would be late before he reached his room, and anyway it was always difficult to know where to begin with stories, so maybe he would keep it to himself.

Epilogue

From: T P [mailto:█@gmail.com]
Sent: 18 July 2015 21:02
To: Mark Huband
Subject: Dear Mark, from T
Dear Mark,

This is a really hard email to write to you. I have to tell you Mark suffered a terrible stroke on Wednesday morning and passed away this afternoon, he hasn't been too well recently but did not expect this to happen. I am absolutely devastated, and I know Marks friends are letting everyone know but I know they haven't got your email address, so this is so hard for me to write to you. I have just had to tell L, and it's been the hardest thing for me to do.

I am so sorry for such sad news,

T x

Postscript

Brimscombe, Gloucestershire

20 August 2015

Dear T

The struggle to come to terms with an absence which had only so recently come to an end when Mark again became a part in my life, has been such a shock that it has been getting the better of my anyway rather brooding character. Perhaps it was because I did not know that Mark had been unwell, that the vision I had had of more great times being spent together has been so violently smashed. I admire him all the more, his sanguine approach to among other things the slow debilitation of MS; that we talked mostly of good, funny, positive things is what still rings in my ears. Curiosity, stories, reflections on past and present, were the heart of our long and magical conversations.

But the struggle now is profound. Perhaps he mentioned something similar to you, but for me our meeting again after all these years was life-changing. It was not simply that we met again after nearly 40 years – a feat in itself, in some ways. More, that he shared insights and observations about the past which have since changed how I now see much that followed. When I left the same town in which he stayed, I felt rootless. His insights showed that I needn't have felt that way, because he connected what he remembered of me aged 10 or 11, with what I did next. Nobody had ever done that before – there was nobody to do it, expect my parents. I felt as though a completeness to experience had been crafted by him, which I could never have done on my own. At last, there was somebody with whom to share stories, who knew the 'before' and who wanted to know about the 'after'.

That kind of magic is rare – it never happens, really. But it did for me, and so for me – and, I had hoped, for him – life will never be the same again. I tend to remember things – probably far too much than is good for me – and carry things along in my head which saner people would forget or push to one side; but for me, memory of the paths followed, the friendships made, the places lived in, form landscapes which for long had seemed to be endlessly forming without taking me towards any kind of 'destination'. I had this need to reach a point where I could stop, share, communicate, and trust. Talking with Mark, hearing all about him, his recollections, his meeting you, his life in our hometown from which I felt alienated but which for him was a vibrant and creative place – all these things brought me to a place I had only dreamed of one day reaching: somewhere I found to my wonderment I had long-been looking for.

It was a place where I never expected I would ever be – sitting in a pub with Mark, casting our minds and talk over situations, eras, misunderstandings, arrivals, departures, adventures, dangers. There was a language to our talk which I had forgotten that I had inside me – a language he brought out of me, and which had lain dormant because in the end the only people who know you are those you grow up with. It was only three years ago I heard it again. But it was deliverance – pure, though far from simple.

Because of how far back our lives go, there is nobody but Mark who could ever have opened up in the way that he did, all that has gone on since then. And because of all these years lying behind us, there is no one who could have brought a seemingly endless, linear life to a point where I could at last take a deep breath and reflect honestly, with trust and openness and not a hint of anything other than deep humanity, on what on earth all this struggle and travel and endeavour has been for.

So, it's been a magical time, these past few years. It has been marvellous seeing you and Mark and L together. I hope that the times we shared are as memorable for you as they are for me. Sometimes I can be a little too full of expectations: cool doesn't come naturally to me – too much to do, too much to hope for, too much going on for me to calm down. I hope I didn't seem to have tried too hard. But seeing the three of you together, I watched in awe and admiration: artists together – wonderful, making a life, bringing up a gorgeous daughter. I see them dancing on the sand of the circus ring. The circus is back on the Common this week – my daughter Z got a job there. But I can't go and watch it again – just too sad.

My family are grieving with you. My parents, M, and our kids O and Z all send you much love. They all think of you, L and Mark very often, and always will.

Brimscombe, Gloucestershire

14 May 2017

Dear T

When Mark died, a vast, beautiful, ecstatic part of me disappeared. I have spent the past two years trying to find it again. I have failed, and have instead been mourning. It has stayed with me night and day, the grief, and I have not wanted to share it with you, because it would only have made your own grief worse. So, this is why I have been silent. I have not been a good friend to you these past two years – because I couldn't be. You and Mark have been living in my imagination, my senses, on my landscape, and in the tone of my reflections, every day since that dreadful day.

For something that ought to have seemed so normal – meeting a friend again, after many years – to have marked me so deeply, and for it to have been so evident from that very first time we met again, that that point in both our lives was so rare, precious and profound, has been one of the causes of the grief which today sits inside me like a stone. When we met again, Past, Present and Future all changed. There was magic.

There were many causes of this, but I have to tell you of one which I think will always be the most powerful.

It is important to me that you know – and Mark may have told you this – that when we met, he and I did not talk of the Past in a nostalgic way; we talked of Life. We talked of Life, and plucked experience from our shared Past – childhood – and told each other of 'what happened next' – what we did afterwards, after we had spent all those hot summer days and snowy winter mornings and wet spring evenings together; he remembered, I remembered. But we were not dwelling on the Past as a 'golden time'; we reflected.

But more than that – and this is the point I want to make – much more than that, we realised that we had both had witnesses to our childhoods, who – nearly forty years after we had last swaggered together through the streets of Harlow – could see the child in the adults we had become, and could see the makings of the adult in the children we had both been.

I had no knowledge – all those years ago – that Mark had been watching me as closely as he did. He told me about myself as a child. He was confident in telling me about what I had seemed like, all those years ago. His confidence was – when we met again – exactly the same as the confidence which had drawn me to him as a 10, 11, 12 13-year old. It was a confidence I didn't have as a child, and which I adored in him, almost envied – though of course I kept both to myself, like I did most things at that time. But it was also a confidence – and a power of observation – which distinguished me from him when we met again. I realised then – and only then, because nobody else I had ever known has been the same – what it meant to grow, what it meant to have Past, Present and Future. Mark showed me that I had not been alone as a child, when all the time – all the time – I thought I had been alone, even with him as a friend.

When we talked all those years later, I realised that I had had a witness to my childhood; the witness could – forty years later – tell me who it was I had become, because he had seen that child, had known that child, had seen that child take the risks he took, and do the things he did. Mark made sense of my life, by first showing me that he had been there watching when the boy was a boy, and then telling me my story – the story of what I had become.

There were so many times when we talked, that by piecing together the fractured and wild actions of a child, he told me who it was I had become. He had been there at the beginning – when I was setting out into the world and finding friends who excited and challenged me, friends who sometimes frightened me, friends whose lives seemed fuller than my own; but then – those years later – he was there to place that child into the body of an adult, and say – as he actually did: "I always knew that you would do what you eventually did. I could tell: you could have played with the posh kids on your street. But you wanted to be with us lot from Chippingfield instead. That took courage. You could have been safe. But you didn't want to be safe. So when I learned you went to Africa, I knew why. You were the same as the one who didn't want to be safe playing with the kids on your street. Same kid."

He said this. I wrote it down. It brought my life together as a vast universe. Mark did that. Nobody else in the world could have done that. Only Mark.

But how did he do this? When Mark first wrote back to me – after I had written to you – a whole new world opened up in front of me. When we were kids, we had a language. Or, rather, he and Mick and Steve and Paul and Bennie and Deena and Stewart and everybody else, had a language. I had to learn that language. I learned it well. Sometimes I would use the wrong words – 'posh' words, I guess – and I would remember not to use them again, because Mark would say – as he once did – things like: "Squabble? What's a squabble? It's not a 'squabble'. It's a 'row'. A 'row' – not a squabble." So, squabbles became rows, and old words became new words, and so I learned to speak like my friends, like the gang we were, like the kids – the 'Skinny White Kids' – that we were for those long summers of the 1970s. I learned a new language, I learned how to walk in a gang, I learned to pretend I might not be a virgin – and I learned that I had to fight without crying. That was hard, because I was fragile.

But it was the words that I learned from Mark. There were words, and there was silence, and there was the unspoken. All were part of the dialogue – particularly the unspoken. So, imagine what it was like when Mark responded to my email to you, using a whole new language – the language I had 'unlearned' all those years ago, a language which was in itself the passing of time, the making of lives, the forming of reality. His being a witness to my childhood – the only witness – was made real to me because when we then met, he talked to me – he told me about myself and about himself – in a language which showed experience, life, and time, to have really happened. It could only really happen between two people who had known the Past, lived the Present, and would now imagine the Future. Without Mark having been able to – first – remember, and – second – recall – in the ways that he did, I would have had no Past other than what I remembered myself. He made my life into a vast and complete universe, by bringing all the times together.

So, now, I am alone again with my Past. I am not self-pitying, but the loneliness is unbearable. So many times over the past near-two years, I have said to myself: I will talk to Mark about this or that idea or memory or thought – Mark will have something to say; he'll listen hard, with those hooded eyelids peering hard, his head slightly bowed, accentuating that attentive stare creating that sometimes unnerving mix of scepticism, empathy and hunger for new experience; he will share and listen some more, and maybe say something and maybe not…and whatever he says will be fine.

And then there is just silence.

And I suppose the silence has created the book I am sending you. Mark's Book. I wanted to bring together poems which are both for us – you, me, his friends, L – and for him. There are many I didn't include, which may come to light later. I wanted a book which he would have read, something intimate, published and printed just down the road from where I now live, where we all shared the loveliest weekend I can remember. The title is one he heard me use – the same as a memoir I showed him parts of; so, we can hear him say it. The title is something of the story of us; he liked the parts of the memoir of the same name which I showed him – like me, he saw there had been a witness to his childhood, though I think he placed it in a different way from me. A part of me doesn't want to be thinking: what would Mark have thought of this poem or that poem; but a part of me can do nothing more than dwell on what might have been.

These poems for Mark have taken me some way down the road towards creating a life knowing that this friendship, rapport, empathy and witness I shared with him can never happen again. I so treasure the magic of what we shared, but so mourn that we are all so alone in knowing that it is gone. Poetry is my voice. I can't help but feel huge regret that I had not seen him during the months before he died. I worry still that he may have felt that the renewal we had created, had passed, lost its lustre. It was just the opposite. I loved to imagine the two of us aged 100 years, glugging beer in a pub, having realised that giving up smoking was a stupid idea, as we wobbled through the woods having drunk a little too much. That was the Future.

I hope you like the poems. I am not good company, but it would be lovely to meet. And, this summer, please do come and stay in our house, if you and L would like to. We will be away in August – would then be a good time for you to have a holiday here? We could overlap by a day or two, so we can show you around, before we go away. Do let me know if that appeals to you.

Printed in Great Britain
by Amazon